Web Development with Go

Building Scalable Web Apps and RESTful Services

Shiju Varghese

Apress®

Web Development with Go

ISBN-13 (pbk): 978-1-4842-1053-6

ISBN-13 (electronic): 978-1-4842-1052-9

Managing Director: Welmoed Spahr
Lead Editor: Celestin John Suresh
Technical Reviewer: Prateek Baheti
Editorial Board: Steve Anglin, Louise Corrigan, Jim DeWolf, Jonathan Gennick, Robert Hutchinson,
    Michelle Lowman, James Markham, Susan McDermott, Matthew Moodie, Jeffrey Pepper,
    Douglas Pundick, Ben Renow-Clarke, Gwenan Spearing
Coordinating Editor: Jill Balzano
Copy Editor: Nancy Sixsmith
Compositor: SPi Global
Indexer: SPi Global
Artist: SPi Global

Distributed to the book trade worldwide by Springer Science+Business Media New York, 233 Spring Street, 6th Floor, New York, NY 10013. Phone 1-800-SPRINGER, fax (201) 348-4505, e-mail orders-ny@springer-sbm.com, or visit www.springer.com. Apress Media, LLC is a California LLC and the sole member (owner) is Springer Science + Business Media Finance Inc (SSBM Finance Inc). SSBM Finance Inc is a Delaware corporation.

For information on translations, please e-mail rights@apress.com, or visit www.apress.com.

Apress and friends of ED books may be purchased in bulk for academic, corporate, or promotional use. eBook versions and licenses are also available for most titles. For more information, reference our Special Bulk Sales–eBook Licensing web page at www.apress.com/bulk-sales.

source code or other supplementary material referenced by the author in this text is available to readers at www.apress.com. For detailed information about how to locate your book's source code, go to www.apress.com/source-code/.

I would like to dedicate this book to my parents, the late C.S. Varghese and Rosy Varghese. I would like to thank them for their unconditional love and life struggles for the betterment of our lives.

I would like to dedicate this book to my lovely wife Rosmi and beautiful daughter Irene Rose. Without their love and support, this book would not have been possible.

Finally, I would like to dedicate this book to my elder sister Shaijy and younger brother Shinto.

—Shiju Varghese

Contents at a Glance

Contents

About the Author

Shiju Varghese is a solutions architect focused on building highly scalable Cloud native applications with a special interest in APIs, Microservices, containerized applications, and distributed systems. He currently specializes in Go, Google Cloud, and Docker. Shiju is passionate about building scalable back-end systems and Microservices in Go. He is a pragmatic minimalist who focuses on real-world practices for architecting solutions. Shiju worked extensively in C# and Node.js before adopting Go as the primary technology stack. As a consulting solutions architect, he provides guidance and solutions for the successful adoption of Go in enterprises and startups.

About the Technical Reviewer

Prateek Baheti is a senior application developer at Thoughtworks, a global software company. He has worked in the test automation space for the past 3 years and has been a major contributor to the open source test-automation tool, Gauge (which is primarily written in Golang). A practitioner of agile software development, Prateek has experience with building tools and services in Java and Ruby on Rails. He is a polyglot programmer and a tech enthusiast. Prateek loves traveling, going on long drives, and spending quality time at home with his family. You can find him at tech conferences, watching movies, or exploring new restaurants and breweries.

Introduction

Go, often referred to as Golang, is a general-purpose programming language that was developed at Google in November 2009.

Several programming languages are available for writing different kinds of software systems, and some languages have existed for decades. Some mainstream programming languages are evolving by adding new features in their newer versions, which are released with many new features in each version. Both C# and Java provide too many features in their language specification.

At the same time, lots of innovations and evolutions are happening for the computer hardware and IT infrastructure. Software systems are written with feature-rich programming languages, but we can't leverage the power of modern computers and IT infrastructures by using them. We are using programming languages that were created in the era of single-core machines, and now we write applications for multicore machines using these languages.

Just like everything else, computer programming languages are evolving. Go is an evolutionary language for writing software systems for modern computers and IT infrastructures using a simple and pragmatic programming language. On the Go web site at `https://golang.org/`, Go is defined as follows: "Go is an open source programming language that makes it easy to build simple, reliable, and efficient software."

Go is designed for solving real-world problems instead of academic theories and intellectual thoughts. Go is a pragmatic programming language that ignores the programming language theory (PLT) that has evolved in the last three decades; it provides a simple programming model for building efficient software systems with first-class support for concurrency. Go's built-in Concurrency feature gives you an exciting programming experience for writing highly efficient software systems by leveraging concurrency. For every programming language, there is a design goal. Go is designed to be a simple programming language, and it excels as a simple and pragmatic language.

Go is the language of choice for building many innovative software systems, including Docker, Kubernetes, and others. Like Parse MBaaS by Facebook, many existing systems are re-engineering to Go. I have assisted several organizations to successfully adopt Go, and the adoption process was extremely easy thanks to Go's simplicity and pragmatism. I am sure that you will be excited about Go when you develop real-world software systems.

Go is a general-purpose programming language that can be used to build a variety of software systems, including networked servers, system-level applications, infrastructure tools, DevOps, native mobile applications, graphics, the Internet of Things (IoT), and machine learning. Go can be used for building native mobile applications, and I predict that Go will be a great choice for building native Android applications in the near future.

Go is a great choice of language for building web applications and back-end APIs. I highly recommend Go for building massively scalable back-end RESTful APIs. I predict that Go will be the language of choice in the enterprises for building back-end RESTful APIs, the backbone for building modern business applications in this mobility era.

In this book, I assume that you have knowledge of at least one programming language and have some experience in web programming. If you have prior knowledge of Go, it will help you follow along in this book. If you are completely new to Go, I recommend the following tutorial before you start reading the book: `http://tour.golang.org/welcome/1`.

When you go through the language fundamentals, I recommend accessing the following section of the Go documentation: `https://golang.org/doc/effective_go.html`.

The primary focus of this book is web development using the Go programming language. Before diving into web development, the book quickly goes through language fundamentals and concurrency, but doesn't delve too deeply, especially regarding concurrency. You should spend some time exploring concurrency if you want to effectively leverage it for your real-world applications. I recommend the following resource for learning more about concurrency and parallelism: `http://blog.golang.org/concurrency-is-not-parallelism`.

This book explores various aspects of Go web programming, with a focus on providing practical code. Chapter 9, "Building RESTful Services," can help you to start developing real-world APIs in Go.

I have created a GitHub repository for this book at `https://github.com/shijuvar/go-web`. The repository provides example code for the book and a few example applications in the near future to help you build real-world web applications.

CHAPTER 1

■ ■ ■

Getting Started with Go

Everything in this world is evolving, including computers and computer programming languages. Ideas and approaches for building applications are also evolving, based on past experience. Although highly evolved modern computers now have many CPU cores (32, 64, 128 and many more), we still cannot leverage the full power of modern computer hardware by using most of our existing programming languages and tools. Our programs still run slowly, even in high-powered servers with many CPU cores.

For the last decade, many existing programming languages have been evolving with many new features. Language authors have been adding these features based on programming language theory (PLT) and other intellectual thoughts, which make the languages more complex. In today's computing, many people prefer a minimalistic and pragmatic approach for writing applications.

Programming languages are used that excel in specific areas. Some programming languages are great for rapid application development, but would not work well for writing high-performance applications. Other programming languages are very efficient for writing these high-performance applications, but would be difficult for writing applications in a productive manner. It would be great if there were a general-purpose language for developing a variety of applications with a greater level of efficiency, performance, productivity, and faster compilation time. The Go language meets these criteria.

This chapter shows you why Go is a great programming language for solving modern programming challenges. You will learn use cases for adopting Go for your next application.

Introducing Go

Go, also referred to as *Golang*, is a general-purpose programming language, developed by a team at Google and many contributors from the open source community (http://golang.org/contributors). The language was announced in November 2009, and the first version was released in December 2012. Go is an open source project that is distributed under a BSD-style license. The official web site of the Go project is available at http://golang.org/. It is a statically typed, natively compiled, garbage-collected, concurrent programming language that mostly belongs to the C family of languages in terms of basic syntax. Let's look at some of the features of Go to understand its design principles.

Minimalistic Language with Pragmatic Design

The Go programming language can be simply described in three words: simple, minimal, and pragmatic. If you look deeply into the language design of Go, you see its simple and minimalistic approach, coupled with a pragmatic design. You can observe this simplicity with all the Go language features, including the type system. Today, many programming languages provide too many features that make applications more complex for developers. The design goal of Go is to be a simple and minimal language that provides all the necessary features for developing efficient software systems.

Although Go has fewer language features, productivity is not affected by its pragmatic design. A new Go programmer can quickly learn the language and can easily start to develop production-quality applications. Go has simply ignored many language features from the last three decades and focuses on real-world practices instead of academics and programming language theory (PLT).

From a practical perspective, you might say that Go is an object-oriented programming (OOP) language. But Go's object-oriented approach is different from programming languages such as C++, Java, and C#. Go is not a full-fledged OOP language from an academic perspective. Unlike many existing OOP languages, Go does not support inheritance and does not even have a `class` keyword. It uses composition over inheritance through its simple type system. Go's interface type design shows its uniqueness when compared with other object-oriented programming languages.

Is Go an OOP language? The answer is both yes and no. Go language includes all batteries required for writing applications with an object-oriented approach, but it is not a complete OOP language because it lacks some traditional OOP features.

■ **Note**   Programming language theory (PLT) is a branch of computer science that deals with the design, implementation, analysis, characterization, and classification of programming languages and their individual features.

A Static Type Language with High Productivity

Go is a statically typed programming language, with its syntax loosely derived from the C language. Like C and C++, it compiles natively to machine code, so Just-In-Time (JIT) compilation is not needed to run its programs. (Programming languages such as Java and C# use JIT compilation to run applications.)

For writing applications, a dynamically typed language provides lots of productivity and expressiveness because you don't have to worry about the data types of the variables you use. In dynamically typed languages, the type of expression is known only at runtime, which provides a greater level of productivity and expressiveness in the syntax to quickly build applications, especially web applications. But when working with a dynamic type language, the performance and maintainability of the applications are affected. Sometimes the debugging experience of an application written in a dynamic type language can be very difficult due to its lack of type safety. Even today, developers use static type languages to generate code for their dynamic type languages. For example, JavaScript developers use statically typed languages such as Microsoft TypeScript for type safety, which finally compiles to JavaScript code.

Although static type languages can provide type safety and performance, working with them can affect the productivity of application development, and compiling larger programs can take a long time. It would be great to have a language that provides the power of both static type and dynamic type language to blend the performance and type safety of a static type language with the productivity of a dynamic type language.

Go is that perfect blend of the power of static type languages and the productivity of dynamic type languages. Go can be called a modern C language that provides faster compilation than C, coupled with the productivity of a dynamic type language.

Concurrency Is a Built-In Feature at the Language Level

Computer hardware has evolved to have many CPU cores and more power, but the power of modern computers cannot be leveraged by using the current programming languages and tools. When production applications are run on high-powered servers, there are performance problems, even though CPU utilization is very low. In some programming environments, concurrency and parallelism are available for better efficiency and performance, but these features are available as a separate library and framework, not as a built-in feature at the language level, which adds more complexity when you write concurrent applications.

In Go, concurrency is built into the language and is designed for writing high-performance concurrent applications for modern computers. Concurrency is one of the unique features of the Go language and it is considered a major selling point. Go's concurrency is implemented using two unique features: goroutines and channels. A *goroutine* is a function that can run concurrently with other goroutines. It is a lightweight thread of execution in which many goroutines execute in a single thread that enables more program performance and efficiency. The most important feature of goroutine is that it is managed and executed by Go runtime. Many programming languages provide support for writing concurrent programs, but they are limited only to communication and synchronization among the threads being executed. And most of the existing languages provide support for concurrency through a framework, but not a built-in feature in the language, so it makes restrictions when concurrency is implemented with these languages.

Go provides *channels* that enable communication between goroutines and the synchronization of their executions. With channels, you can send data from one goroutine to another. Channels also provide a greater level of synchronization between goroutines and ensure that two goroutines are running in a known state. Concurrency is a major reason for adopting Go as the language for building highly efficient software systems with greater levels of performance.

Go Compiles Programs Quickly

One of the challenges of writing C and C++ applications is the time needed for compiling programs, which is very painful for developers when they work on larger C and C++ applications. Go is a language designed for solving the programming challenges of existing programming environments. Its compiler is very efficient for compiling programs quickly; a large Go application can be compiled in few seconds, which is attractive to many C and C++ developers who switch to the Go programming environment.

Go as a General-Purpose Language

Different programming languages are used to develop different kinds of applications. C and C++ have been widely used for systems programming and for systems in which performance is very critical. At the same time, working with C and C++ affect the productivity of application development. Some other programming languages, such as Ruby and Python, offer rapid application development that enables better productivity. Although the server-side JavaScript platform Node.js is good for building lightweight JSON APIs and real-time applications, it gets a fail when CPU-intensive programming tasks are executed. Another set of programming languages is used for building native mobile applications. Programming languages such as Objective C and Swift are restricted for use only with mobile application development. Various programming languages are used for a variety of use cases, such as systems programming, distributed computing, web application development, enterprise applications, and mobile application development.

The greatest practical benefit of using Go is that it can be used to build a variety of applications, including systems that require high performance, and also for rapid application development scenarios. Although Go was initially designed as a systems programming language, it is also used for developing enterprise business applications and powerful back-end servers. Go provides high performance while keeping high productivity for application development, thanks to its minimalistic and pragmatic design. The Go ecosystem (which includes Go tooling, the Go standard library, and the Go third-party library) provides essential tools and libraries for building a variety of Go applications. The Go Mobile project adds support for building native mobile applications for both Android and iOS platforms, enabling more opportunities with Go.

In the era of cloud computing, Go is a modern programming language that can be used to build system-level applications; distributed applications; networking programs; games; web apps; RESTful services; back-end servers; native mobile applications; and cloud-optimized, next-generation applications. Go is the choice of many revolutionary innovative systems such as Docker and Kubernetes. A majority of tools on the software containerization ecosystem are being written in Go.

▓ **Note**   Docker is a revolutionary software container platform, and Kubernetes is a container cluster manager. Both are written in Go.

Go Ecosystem

Go is not just a simple programming language; it is also an ecosystem that provides essential tools and features for writing a variety of efficient software systems. The Go ecosystem contains the following components:

- Go language

- Go libraries

- Go tooling

Go language provides essential syntax and features that allows you to write your programs. These programs leverage libraries for reusable pieces of functionality and tooling for formatting code, compiling code, running tests, installing programs, and creating documentations.

Libraries play a key role in the Go ecosystem because Go is designed to be a modular programming language for writing highly maintainable and composable applications. Libraries provide reusable pieces of functionality distributed as *packages*. You can use packages in Go to write software components in a modular and reusable manner to be shared across Go programs, and can easily maintain your applications. The design philosophy of a Go application is to write small pieces of software components through packages and then compose Go applications with these smaller packages. Libraries are available from the standard library and third-party libraries. When you install Go packages from the standard library, they are installed into the Go installation directory. When you install Go, the environment variable GOROOT will be automatically added to your system for specifying the Go installation directory. The standard library includes a larger set of packages that provide a wide range of functionality for writing real-world applications. For example, "net/http", a package from the standard library, can be used to write powerful web application and RESTful services.

▓ **Note**   For documentation about packages from the standard library, go to http://golang.org/pkg/.

If you need extra functionality not available from the Go standard library, you can leverage third-party libraries provided by the Go developer community, which is very enthusiastic about developing and providing many useful third-party Go packages. For example, if you want to work with the MongoDB database, you can leverage a third-party package called "mgo".

Go tooling is an important component in the Go ecosystem, which provides a number of tooling-support services: building, testing, and installing Go programs; formatting Go code; creating documentation; fetching and installing Go packages; and so on.

Installing the Go Tools

It is easy to install Go on your computers. It provides binary distributions for the FreeBSD, Linux, Mac OS X, and Windows operating systems (OSs); and the 32-bit (386) and 64-bit (amd64) x86 processor architectures. The binary distributions are available at http://golang.org/dl/. (If a binary distribution is not available for your combination of OS and architecture, you can install Go from the source.)

Figure 1-1 shows the installer packages and archived sources for Mac, Windows, and Linux platforms, which are listed on the download page of the Go web site. Go provides installers for both Mac and Windows OSs. A package installer is available for Mac X OS that installs the Go distribution to /usr/local/go and puts the /usr/local/go/bin directory in the PATH environment variable.

Stable versions

go1.5.1 ▾

File name	Kind	OS	Arch	Size	SHA1 Checksum
go1.5.1.src.tar.gz	Source			11MB	0df564746d105f4180c2b576a1553ebca9d9a124
go1.5.1.darwin-amd64.tar.gz	Archive	OS X	64-bit	74MB	02451b1f3b2c715edc5587174e35438982663672
go1.5.1.darwin-amd64.pkg	Installer	OS X	64-bit	74MB	857b77a85ba111af1b0928a73cca52136780a75d
go1.5.1.freebsd-amd64.tar.gz	Archive	FreeBSD	64-bit	74MB	78ac27b7c009142ed0d86b899f1711bb9811b7e1
go1.5.1.linux-386.tar.gz	Archive	Linux	32-bit	66MB	6ce7328f84a863f341876658538dfdf10aff86ee
go1.5.1.linux-amd64.tar.gz	Archive	Linux	64-bit	74MB	46eecd290d8803887dec718c691cc243f2175fe0
go1.5.1.windows-386.zip	Archive	Windows	32-bit	70MB	bb071ec45ef39cd5ed9449b54c5dd083b8233bfa
go1.5.1.windows-386.msi	Installer	Windows	32-bit	58MB	034065452b7233b2a570d4be1218a97c475cded0
go1.5.1.windows-amd64.zip	Archive	Windows	64-bit	79MB	7815772347ad3e11a096d927c65bfb15d5b0f490
go1.5.1.windows-amd64.msi	Installer	Windows	64-bit	64MB	0a439f49b546b82f85adf84a79bbf40de2b3d5ba

Figure 1-1. *Go binary distributions for multiple OSs*

In Mac OS, you can also install Go using Homebrew (http://brew.sh/). The following command installs Go on a Mac OS:

```
brew install go
```

An MSI installer is available for the Windows OS that installs Go distribution in c:\Go. The installer also puts the c:\Go\bin directory in the PATH environment variable. Figure 1-2 shows the package installer running for Mac OS.

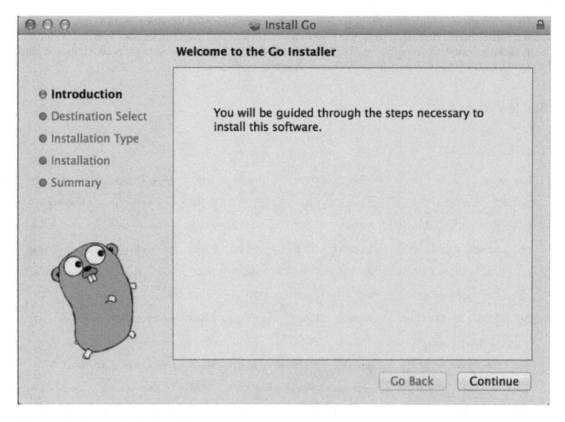

Figure 1-2. Go installer for Mac OS

As mentioned earlier, a successful installation of Go sets up the GOROOT environment variable with the location in which the Go tools are installed: /usr/local/go (or c:\Go under Windows).

You can also install Go tools in a custom location. When you do so, manually configure the environment variable GOROOT with the location in which you installed the Go tools on your system.

■ **Note**   The complete instructions for downloading and installing Go tools are available at http://golang.org/doc/install.

Checking the Installation

You can test the Go installation by typing some Go commands in the terminal window. To verify the installation of Go tools, open the terminal and type the following command:

```
go version
```

Here is the result that shows in a Mac X system:

```
go version go1.4.1 darwin/amd64
```

Here is the result that shows in a Windows system:

```
go version go1.4.1 windows/amd64
```

The following command provides help for Go tools:

```
go help
```

Setting up a Work Environment

Go follows some conventions that organize code in a specific way and help to compile, install, and share Go code more easily. This section discusses how to organize Go code as packages in a workspace.

Go Workspace

Go programs must be kept in a directory hierarchy called a *workspace*, which is simply a root directory of the Go programs.

A workspace contains three subdirectories at its root:

- src: This directory contains Go source files organized into packages.

- pkg: This directory contains Go package objects.

- bin: This directory contains executable commands (executable programs).

When you start working with Go, the initial step is to set up a workspace in which Go programs reside. You must create a directory with three subdirectories for setting up the Go workspace. A Go developer writes Go programs as packages into the src directory. Go source files are organized into directories called packages, in which a single directory is used for a single package. You can write two types of packages in Go:

- Packages resulting in executable programs

- Packages resulting in a shared library

The Go tool builds Go packages and installs the resulting binaries into the pkg directory if it is a shared library, and into the bin directory if it is an executable program. So the pkg and bin directories are used for storing the output of the packages based on the package type. Keep in mind that you can have multiple workspaces for your Go programs (Go developers typically use a single workspace for their Go programs).

GOPATH Environment Variable

You write Go programs in the workspace, which you should manually specify so that Go runtime knows the workspace location. You can set the workspace location by using the GOPATH environment variable. To get started working with Go, create a workspace and set the GOPATH environment variable.

Code Organization Paths

You write Go programs as packages into the GOPATH src directory. A single directory is used for a single package. Go is designed to easily work with remote repositories such as GitHub and Google Code. When you maintain your programs in a remote source repository, use the root of that source repository as your base path.

For example, if you have a GitHub account at github.com/user, it should be your base path. Let's say you write a package named "mypackage" at github.com/user; your code organization path will be at %GOPATH%/src/github.com/user/mypackage. When you import this package to other programs, the path for importing the package will be github.com/user/mypackage. If you maintain the source in your local system, you can directly write programs under the GOPATH src directory. Suppose that you write a package named mypackage on a local system; your code organization path will be at %GOPATH%/src/mypackage, and the path for importing the package will be mypackage.

Writing Go Programs

Once you create a workspace and set the GOPATH environment variable, you can start working with Go. Let's write few simple programs in Go to get started.

Writing a Hello World Program

Let's start by writing a Hello World program, as shown in Listing 1-1.

Listing 1-1. Hello World Program in Go

```
1 package main
2 import "fmt"
3 func main() {
4       fmt.Println("Hello, world")
5 }
```

Line 1: Go programs are organized as packages, and the package name here is specified as main. If you name a package main, it has a special meaning in Go: the resulting binary will be an executable program.

Line 2: The "fmt" package, which provides the functionality for format and print data, is imported from the standard library. The keyword import is used for importing packages.

Line 3: The keyword func is used to define a function. The function main will be the entry point of an executable program and will be executed when the application runs. The package main will have one main function.

Line 4 The function Println is provided by the package fmt to print the data. Note that the name of the Println function started with an uppercase letter. In Go, all identifiers that start with an uppercase letter are exported to other packages so they will be available to call in other packages.

Let's compile and run the sample program using the Go tool. Navigate to the package directory and then type the run command to run the program. Suppose that the location of the package directory is at github.com/user/hello:

```
cd $GOPATH/src/github.com/user/hello
go run main.go
```

The preceding command simply prints the phrase "Hello, world". The run command compiles the source and runs the program. You can also use the build and install commands with the Go tool to build and install Go programs that produce binary executables to be run later.

The build command compiles the package and puts the resulting binary into the package folder:

```
cd $GOPATH/src/github.com/user/hello
go build
```

The name of the resulting binary is the same as the directory name. If you write this program in a directory named hello, the resulting binary will be hello (or hello.exe under Windows). After compiling the source with the build command, you can run the program by typing the binary name.

The install command compiles the package and installs the resulting binary into the bin directory of GOPATH:

```
cd $GOPATH/src/github.com/user/hello
go install
```

You can run this command from any location on your system:

```
go install github.com/user/hello
```

The name of the resulting binary is the same as the directory name. You can now run the program by typing the binary from the bin directory of GOPATH:

```
$GOPATH/bin/hello
```

If you have added $GOPATH/bin to your PATH environment variable, just type the binary name from any location on your system:

```
hello
```

Writing a Library

In Go, you can write two types of programs: executable programs and reusable libraries. The previous sample program was an executable program. Let's write a shared library to provide a reusable piece of code to other programs. Create a package directory at the location $GOPATH/src/github.com/shijuvar/go-web-book/chapter1/calc.

Listing 1-2 shows a simple package that provides the functionality for adding and subtracting two values.

Listing 1-2. Shared Library Program in Go

```
1 package calc
2
3 func Add(x, y int) int {
4       return x + y
5 }
6 func Subtract(x, y int) int {
7       return x - y
8 }
```

Line 1: The package name is specified as calc. The name of the package and package directory must be same.

Line 3: A function named Add is defined with the keyword func. The name of this function starts with an uppercase letter, so the Add function will be exported to other packages. If the name of the function starts with a lowercase letter, it is not exported to other packages, and accessibility will be limited to the same package. Unlike programming in C++, Java, and C#, you don't need to use private and public keywords to specify the accessibility of identifiers. You can see the simplicity of the Go language throughout the language features. The Add method takes two integer parameters and returns an integer value.

Line 6: The Subtract function is similar to the Add function, but subtracts values between two integer types.

Let's build and install the package. Navigate to the package directory in the terminal window and type the following command:

```
go install
```

The install command compiles the source and installs the resulting binary into the pkg folder of GOPATH (see Figure 1-3). In the pkg directory, the calc package will be installed at the location github.com/shijuvar/go-web-book/chapter1/calc under the platform-specific directory.

pkg ▸ windows_amd64 ▸ github.com ▸ shijuvar ▸ go-web-book ▸ chapter1

Name	Date modified	Type
☐ calc.a	31-01-2015 07:02	A File

Figure 1-3. *Install command installing calc package into pkg folder*

The install command behaves a bit differently depending on whether you are creating an executable program or a reusable library. When you run install for executable programs the resulting binary will be installed into the bin directory of GOPATH while it will be installed into the pkg directory of GOPATH for libraries.

Now you can reuse this package from any program residing in the GOPATH. Code reusability in Go is very easy with packages. You have created your first library package. Let's reuse the package code from another executable program (see Listing 1-3).

Listing 1-3. Reusing the calc Package in a Go Program

```
1 package main
2
3 import (
4         "fmt"
5         "github.com/shijuvar/go-web-book/chapter1/calc"
6 )
7
8 func main() {
9         var x, y int = 10, 5
10        fmt.Println(calc.Add(x, y))
11        fmt.Println(calc.Subtract(x, y))
12 }
```

Line 1: Create an executable program.

Lines 3 to 6: These lines import the "fmt" package from the standard library and the "calc" package from your own library. You can use a single import statement to import multiple packages. The path for the packages from the standard library uses short paths such as the "fmt" package. For your own packages, you must specify the full path when importing the packages. Using the full path for external packages avoids name conflicts among packages, and you can use the same name for multiple external packages in which the package path would be different.

Line 8: The function main, entry point of the package main.

Line 9: Declaring two variables, x and y, with the int data type. Go uses the var keyword to declare variables in which you can declare multiple variables in a single statement. If you assign values to variables along with the variable declarations, you can use a shorter statement:

```
x,y:=10,5
```

When you use Go's shorter statement for declaring variables, you don't need to specify the variable type because the Go compiler can infer the type, based on the value you assign to the variable. Go provides the productivity of a dynamically typed language while keeping it as a statically typed language. The Go compiler can also do type inference with the var statement:

```
var x,y=10,5
```

Lines 10 to 11: You call the exported functions of the calc package and reuse the functionality provided by the library.

To run the program, type the following command from the program directory:

```
go run main.go
```

Testing Go Code

The Go ecosystem provides all the essential tools for developing Go applications, including the capability for testing Go code without leveraging any external library or tool. The "testing" package from the standard library provides the features for writing automated tests, and Go tooling provides support for running automated tests. When you develop software systems, writing automated tests for application code is an important practice to ensure quality and improve maintainability. If your code is covered by tests, you can fearlessly refactor your application code.

Let's write some tests for the calc package created in the previous section. You create a source file with a name ending in _test.go, in which you write tests by adding functions starting with "Test" and taking one argument of type *testing.T.

In the calc package directory, create a new source file named calc_test.go that contains the code shown in Listing 1-4.

Listing 1-4. Testing the calc Package

```
1 package calc
2
3 import "testing"
4
5 func TestAdd(t *testing.T) {
6        var result int
7        result = Add(15,10)
8        if result!= 25 {
9                t.Error("Expected 25, got ", result)
10       }
11 }
12 func TestSubtract(t *testing.T) {
13       var result int
14       result = Subtract(15,10)
```

```
15      if result!= 5 {
16              t.Error("Expected 5, got ", result)
17      }
18 }
```

Line 1: Specifies the package name as calc.

Line 3: Imports the "testing" package from the standard library, which provides the essential functionality for writing tests and works with the Go test command.

Line 5: Adds a test named "TestAdd" with signature func (t *testing.T) for verifying the functionality Add function in the calc package.

Line 12: Adds a test named "TestSubtract" with signature func (t *testing.T) for verifying the functionality Subtract function in the calc package.

To run the tests with the Go tool, type the following command from the package directory:

```
go test
```

The go test command identifies and execute tests in the package files, based on the conventions used for testing. It will show the following result:

PASS
ok   github.com/shijuvar/go-web-book/chapter1/calc   0.310s

Using Go Playground

Go Playground is a tool that allows you to write and run Go programs from your web browser (see Figure 1-4). By using this tool, you can write and run Go programs without having to install Go on your system.

Figure 1-4. Go Playground

■ **Note**   The browser-based Go Playground tool is available at https://play.golang.org/.

Go Playground can also be used to share Go code with other developers. Clicking the Share button provides a sharable URL for sharing your code with others.

Using Go Mobile

You already know that Go can be used as a general-purpose programming language for building a variety of applications. It can also be used for building native mobile applications for both Android and iOS. The Go Mobile project provides tools and libraries for building native mobile applications. It includes a command-line tool called gomobile to help you build these applications.

You can follow two development strategies to include Go into your mobile stack:

- Develop native mobile applications entirely written in Go

- Develop SDK applications by generating bindings from a Go package and invoking them from Java (on Android) and Objective-C (on iOS).

The first strategy is to use Go everywhere in your mobile project by using the packages and tools provided by Go Mobile. Here you can use Go to develop both Android and iOS applications. In the second strategy, you can reuse a Go library package from a mobile application without making significant changes to your existing application. In this strategy, you can share a common code base for both Android and iOS applications. You can write the common functionality once in Go as a library package and put it to the platform-specific code by invoking the Go package through bindings.

■ **Note**   You can find out more about the Go Mobile project at `https://github.com/golang/mobile`.

Go as a Language for Web and Microservices

The primary focus of this book is web development using Go. In modern computing, a digital transformation is happening, in which HTTP APIs (often RESTful APIs) are becoming the backbone for web applications, mobile applications, Big Data solutions, and the Internet of Things (IoT). These web-based APIs, which are powering the back ends for many modern applications, enable developers to integrate among various applications.

There has recently been a monolithic architecture approach for developing larger applications, in which a single application includes all the logical components for running the application. These applications are very hard to maintain and scale due to tight coupling among various logical components. To solve various problems found in monolithic application architecture, developers prefer a microservices architectural style, in which a monolithic application is broken into a suite of small services (microservices), each running as an independent unit. The independent service pieces communicate by using either RESTful APIs or message brokers. Go is gradually becoming a preferred language for building RESTful APIs and microservices.

Go may not be the language choice for building traditional web applications in which application logic and UI rendering logic reside in a server-side application. It is, however, the language choice for building modern web applications in which an API, often a RESTful API, is developed as the server-side implementation. By consuming these back-end services, you can build your front-end web applications. A Single Page Application (SPA) architecture has been widely used for building these web applications. The back-end services can also be used for building mobile applications.

Go provides an HTTP package that allows you to build high-performance web applications and RESTful services by leveraging the built-in concurrency mechanism provided by Go. In Go, you can quickly build an HTTP server with fewer lines of code and start listening at a given HTTP port. By default, each HTTP request to the web server will be processed concurrently using a goroutine, which is a mechanism in Go to concurrently run functions independently of other functions. You can run millions of goroutines in a single server that enables you to build massively scalable web applications and web APIs in Go.

The simplicity of Go is also reflected in Go web programming that enables lots of developer productivity. When you build web-based systems in other programming languages, you may have to use a full-fledged web framework such as Rails for Ruby, Django for Python, or ASP.NET MVC for C#. In Go, lots of web frameworks are available as third-party packages. But without using a full-fledged web framework, you can build highly scalable web systems by simply using built-in Go packages and a few lightweight libraries available as third-party packages.

■ **Note** In Chapter 9, you will learn how to build a scalable web API in Go without using a web framework.

Microservices architecture, in which independently running services have been widely used to communicate over RESTful APIs, was previously discussed. Go is a great choice for building these RESTful services and is also becoming the language of choice for building independent services (microservices) in the microservices architecture because of the simplicity of its language, concurrency capability, performance, and capability to develop distributed applications.

Microservices architecture is a distributed application architecture, and Go is a great choice for building distributed systems. Some technologies such as Node.js are great for building lightweight RESTful APIs, but simply fail when they are used to build distributed applications. Go is the perfect language of choice for applications with microservices architecture, in which Go can be used for all components of the application architecture, including small services running as independent units, RESTful services to communicate among independent services, and message brokers to communicate among independent services using asynchronous protocols such as AMQP.

Summary

Go is a modern, statically typed, natively compiled, garbage-collected programming language that allows you to write high-performance applications while enabling a greater level of productivity with its simple syntax and pragmatic design. In Go, concurrency is a built-in feature at the core language level that allows you to write highly efficient software systems for modern computers. The Go ecosystem includes the language, libraries, and tools that provide all the essential features for developing a wide variety of applications. The Go Mobile project includes packages and tools for building native mobile applications for Android and iOS. Go is a great programming language for building scalable, web-based, back-end systems and microservices.

CHAPTER 2

■ ■ ■

Go Fundamentals

Chapter 1 furnished an overview of the Go programming language and discussed how it is different from other programming languages. In this chapter, you will learn Go fundamentals for writing reusable code using packages and how to work with arrays and collections. You will also learn Go language fundamentals such as defer, panic, and recover, and about Go's unique error-handling capabilities.

Packages

For a Go developer, the design philosophy for developing applications is to develop reusable pieces of smaller software components and build applications by composing these components. Go provides modularity, composability, and code reusability through its package ecosystem. Go encourages you to write maintainable and reusable pieces of code through packages that enable you to compose your applications with these smaller packages. Go packages are a vital concept that allow you to achieve many of the Go design principles. Like other features of Go, packages are designed with simplicity and pragmatism.

Go source files are organized into directories called packages, and the name of the package must be the name of the directory containing the Go source files. You organize Go source files with the .go extension into directories in which the package name will be same for the source files that belong to a directory. Packages from the standard library belong to the GOROOT directory, which is the Go installation directory. You write Go programs in the GOPATH directory as packages that are easily reusable from other packages.

■ **Note** The documentation on standard library packages is available at http://golang.org/pkg/. Visit http://godoc.org/ for documentation on packages of both standard library and third-party libraries.

Package main

In Go, you can write two types of programs: executable programs and a shared library. When you write executable programs, you must give main as the package name to make the package an executable program: the package main tells the Go compiler that the package should compile as an executable program. The executable programs in Go are often referred to as *commands* in the official Go documentation. The entry point of the executable program is the main function of the main package; the main function in the package main is the entry point of the executable program. When you write packages as shared libraries, there are no main packages or main functions in the package.

15

Listing 2-1 is the code block for package main.

Listing 2-1. Package main with the main Function

```
package main

import (
    "fmt"
)

func main() {
    fmt.Println("Hello World!")
}
```

When you build the preceding program using the Go tool, the Go compiler generates an executable binary as the output. As mentioned earlier, if you want to build executable programs in Go, you must write a package main with a function main as the entry point for your programs.

Package Alias

When you write Go packages, you don't have to worry about package ambiguity; you can even use the same package names as those of the standard library. When you import your own packages from the GOPATH location, you refer the full path of the package location to avoid package name ambiguity. You can use two packages with the same name from two different locations, but you should avoid name ambiguity when referencing from your programs. The package alias helps you avoid name ambiguity when you reference multiple packages with the same name.

Listing 2-2 is an example program that uses the package alias to reference packages.

Listing 2-2. Using the Package Alias to Avoid Name Ambiguity

```
package main
import (
    mongo "lib/mongodb/db"
    mysql "lib/mysql/db"
)
func main() {
    mongo.Get() //calling method of package "lib/mongodb/db"
    mysql.Get() //calling method of package "lib/mysql/db"
}
```

Two packages are imported with the same name, db, but they are referenced with different aliases, and their exported identifiers are accessed using an alias name.

Function init

When you write packages, you may need to provide some initialization logic for the packages, such as initializing package variables, initializing database objects, and providing some bootstrapping logic for the packages. The init function, which helps provide initialization logic into packages, is executed at the beginning of the execution.

Listing 2-3 is an example program that uses the init function to initialize a database session object.

Listing 2-3. Using the init Function

```
package db

import (
    "gopkg.in/mgo.v2"
)
var Session *mgo.Session //Database Session object
func init() {
    // initialization code here
    Session, err := mgo.Dial("localhost")
}
func get() {
        //logic for get that uses Session object
}
func add() {
        //logic for add that uses Session object
}
func update() {
        //logic for update that uses Session object
}
func delete() {
        //logic for delete that uses Session object
}
```

In this code block, a MongoDB session object is created in the init function. When you import the package db into other packages, the function init will be invoked at the beginning of the execution in which the initialization logic for the package is included. Suppose that you reference the package db from a main package; the init function will be invoked before the main function executes.

Using a Blank Identifier

In some scenarios, you may need to reference a package to invoke only its init method to execute the initialization logic in the referenced package, but not to use other identifiers. Suppose that you want the init function of package db (refer to Listing 2-3) to be invoked from the package main, but not use other functions. You reference the package db in package main to invoke the init function for initializing the database session object. The Go compiler shows an error if none of the identifiers of package is referencing from the package where you imported a package, but not referencing any package identifiers. Keep in mind that you can't directly call the init function by explicitly referencing it; it gets automatically invoked when you reference the packages. When you reference packages, the init functions of these packages will be invoked at the beginning of the execution.

If you want to reference a package only for invoking its init method, you can use a blank identifier (_) as the package alias name. The compiler ignores the error of not using the package identifier, but still invokes the init function, as shown in Listing 2-4.

Listing 2-4. Using a Blank Identifier (_) to Call Only the init Method

```
package main
import (
            "fmt"
        _ "lib/mongodb/db"
)
func main() {
  //implementation here
}
```

In Listing 2-4, the db package was imported with a package alias as a blank identifier (_). Here you want the init function of package db to be invoked, but not use other package identifiers.

Importing Packages

Go source files are organized into directories as packages that provide code reusability into other packages. If you want to reuse package code into other shared libraries and executable programs, you must import the packages into your programs. You can import packages into your Go programs by using the keyword import. The statement import tells the Go compiler that you want to reference the code provided by that particular package. When you import a package into a program, you can reuse all the exported identifiers of the referenced packages. If you want to export variables, constants, and functions to be used with other programs, the name of the identifier must start with an uppercase letter. See Listing 2-5.

Listing 2-5. The import Statement to the imports Package

```
import (
    "bytes"
    "fmt"
    "unicode"
)
```

In this listing, the packages bytes, fmt, and unicode are imported. The idiomatic way to import multiple packages in Go is to write the import statements in an import block, as shown here.

When a package is imported, the Go compiler will search the GOROOT directory and then look for the GOPATH directory if it can't find the package in GOROOT. If the Go compiler can't find a package in either the GOROOT or GOPATH location, it will generate an error when you try to build your program.

Install Third-Party Packages

The Go developer community is very enthusiastic about providing many useful third-party packages through code-sharing web sites such as github.com and code.google.com. You can import and reuse these third-party packages by using the Go tools. The go get command fetches packages from remote repositories.

The following go get command fetches the third-part package negroni and installs it into the GOPATH location:

go get github.com/codegangsta/negroni

The go get command fetches the package and dependent packages recursively from the repository location. Once the package is fetched into the GOPATH, you can import and reuse these packages from all the programs located in the GOPATH location. In many other developer ecosystems, you have to import these packages at a project level; you have to install packages for each individual project separately. When you import a package in Go, you actually import from a common location: the GOPATH pkg directory, so you can appreciate the simplicity and pragmatism in many of the Go features, including the package ecosystem.

Writing Packages

Let's write a sample package to reuse with other programs. Listing 2-6 is a simple package that swaps characters' case from upper- to lowercase or lower- to uppercase.

Listing 2-6. Library Package

```
package strcon

import (
    "bytes"
    "unicode"
)

// Swap characters case from upper to lower or lower to upper.
func SwapCase(str string) string {

    buf := &bytes.Buffer{}

    for _, r := range str {
        if unicode.IsUpper(r) {
            buf.WriteRune(unicode.ToLower(r))
        } else {
            buf.WriteRune(unicode.ToUpper(r))
        }
    }

    return buf.String()
}
```

The package is named strcon. The idiomatic way to provide a package name is to give short and simple lowercase names without underscores or mixed capital letters. The package names of the standard library are a great reference for naming packages.

Let's build and install the package strcon to be used with other programs. The package provides a method named SwapCase that swaps the character case of a string from upper- to lowercase or lower- to uppercase. Reuse the packages bytes and unicode from the standard library to swap character case. Because the name of the SwapCase method starts with an uppercase letter, it will be exported to other programs when this package is referenced package. The SwapCase method iterates through a string and changed the case of each character:

```
for _, r := range str {
    if unicode.IsUpper(r) {
        buf.WriteRune(unicode.ToLower(r))
    } else {
        buf.WriteRune(unicode.ToUpper(r))
    }
}
```

The keyword range allows you to iterate through arrays and collections. By iterating through a string value, you can extract each character as a value and swap the character case. On the left side of the range block, you can provide two variables for getting the key and value of each item in the collection. In this code block, the value for getting the character value is used, but you don't use the key in the program. In this context, you can use a blank identifier (_) to avoid compiler errors. It is common practice to use a blank identifier with range whenever you want to ignore a key or value variable declaration from the left side.

With the following command at the location of the package directory, build the package and install it on the pkg subdirectory of GOPATH:

go install

Let's write a sample program to reuse the code of the strconv package (see Listing 2-7).

Listing 2-7. Reusing the strconv Package in main.go

```
package main

import (
    "fmt"
    "strcon"
)

func main() {
    s := strconv.SwapCase("Gopher")
    fmt.Println("Converted string is :", s)
}
```

We import the package strcon to reuse the code for swapping character case in a string. Let's run the program by typing the following command in the terminal from the package directory:

go run main.go

You should see the following result when running the program:

gOPHER

Because the program in Listing 2-7 is written in package main, the Go build command generates an executable binary into the package directory. The Go install command builds the package and installs the resulting binary into the GOPATH bin subdirectory.

Go Tool

The Go tool is a very important component of the Go ecosystem. In the previous sections, you used the Go tool to build and run Go programs. In the terminal, type the go command without any parameters to get documentation on the commands provided by the Go tool.

Here is the documentation on Go commands:

```
Go is a tool for managing Go source code.

Usage:

        go command [arguments]

The commands are:

        build       compile packages and dependencies
        clean       remove object files
        doc         show documentation for package or symbol
        env         print Go environment information
        fix         run go tool fix on packages
        fmt         run gofmt on package sources
        generate    generate Go files by processing source
        get         download and install packages and dependencies
        install     compile and install packages and dependencies
        list        list packages
        run         compile and run Go program
        test        test packages
        tool        run specified go tool
        version     print Go version
        vet         run go tool vet on packages

Use "go help [command]" for more information about a command.

Additional help topics:

        c           calling between Go and C
        buildmode   description of build modes
        filetype    file types
        gopath      GOPATH environment variable
        environment environment variables
        importpath  import path syntax
        packages    description of package lists
        testflag    description of testing flags
        testfunc    description of testing functions

Use "go help [topic]" for more information about that topic.
```

For documentation on any specific command type:

```
go help [command]
```

Here is the command for getting documentation for the install command:

go help install

Here is the documentation for the install command:

```
usage: go install [build flags] [packages]

Install compiles and installs the packages named by the import paths,
along with their dependencies.

For more about the build flags, see 'go help build'.
For more about specifying packages, see 'go help packages'.

See also: go build, go get, go clean.
```

Formatting Go Code

The Go tool provides the fmt command to format Go code. It is a good practice to format Go programs before committing source files into version control systems. The go fmt command applies predefined styles to the source code for format source files, which ensures the right placement of curly brackets, ensures the proper usage of tabs and spaces, and alphabetically sorts package imports. The go fmt command can be applied at the package level or on a specific source file.

Listing 2-8 shows the import block before applying go fmt.

Listing 2-8. import Package Block Before go fmt

```
import (
        "log"
        "net/http"
        "encoding/json"
)
```

Listing 2-9 shows the import block after applying go fmt:

Listing 2-9. import Package Block After go fmt

```
import (
        "encoding/json"
        "log"
        "net/http"
)
```

The import package block rearranges in an alphabetical order after the go fmt command executes.

■ **Note** The idiomatic way of writing the import block is to start with standard library packages in alphabetical order and follow with custom packages in alphabetical order by using one line space between standard library packages and custom packages.

Go Documentation

Documentation is a huge part of making software accessible and maintainable. It must be well-written and accurate, of course, but it must also be easy to write and maintain. Ideally, the documentation should be coupled to the code so it evolves along with the code. The easier it is for programmers to produce good documentation, the better the situation for everyone.

Go provides the godoc tool, which provides documentation for Go packages. It parses Go source code, including comments, and generates documentation as HTML or plain text. In short, the godoc tool generates the documentation from the comments included in the source files. If you want to access the documentation from the command prompt, type:

godoc [**package**]

For example, if you want to get documentation for the fmt package, type the following command in the terminal:

godoc fmt

This command displays the fmt package documentation onto the terminal.

The godoc tool also provides browsable documentation on a web interface. To access the documentation through a web-based interface, start the web server provided by the godoc tool. Type the following command in the terminal:

godoc -http=:3000

This command starts a web server at port 3000, which allows you to access the documentation on the web browser. You can then easily navigate to the package documentation from both the standard library and the GOPATH location. See Figure 2-1.

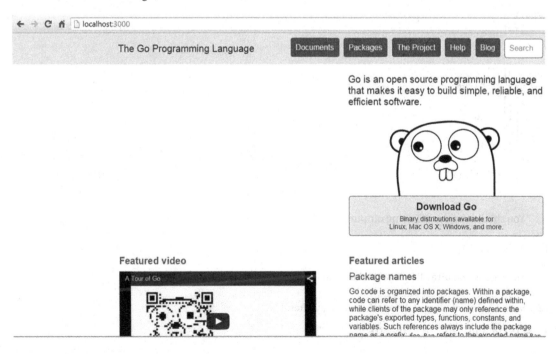

Figure 2-1. Accessing godoc documentation from a web browser

Working with Collections

When you work with real-world applications, you have to leverage various data structures to manage application data. When you persist application data into database systems, you might be using the values of data structure objects that hold the application data. When you read data from databases, you might be putting the data into various forms of data structures for other uses, such as rendering the user interface. Collections are the data structures that can hold collections of data structures that include built-in and user-defined types. Go provides three types of data structures to manage data collections: arrays, slices, and maps.

Arrays

An *array* is a fixed-length data type that contains the sequence of elements of a single type. An array is declared by specifying the data type and the length.

Listing 2-10 is a code block that declares an array.

Listing 2-10. Declaring an Integer Array of Five Elements

```
var x [5]int
```

An array x is declared for storing five elements of the int type, so the array x will be composed of five integer elements.

Listing 2-11 is an example program that declares an array and assigns values.

Listing 2-11. Declaring an Array and Assigning Values

```
package main

import (
    "fmt"
)

func main() {
    var x [5]int
    x[0] = 10
    x[1] = 20
    x[2] = 30
    x[3] = 40
    x[4] = 50
    fmt.Println(x)
}
```

You should see the following output:

```
[10 20 30 40 50]
```

You can use an array literal to declare and initialize arrays, as shown in Listing 2-12.

Listing 2-12. Initializing an Array with an Array Literal

```
x := [5]int{10, 20, 30, 40, 50}
```

You can also initialize an array with a multiline statement (see Listing 2-13).

Listing 2-13. Array Declaration with a Multiline statement

```
x := [5]int{
    10,
    20,
    30,
    40,
    50,
}
```

Note that a comma has been added, even after the last element, because Go requires it. Doing so enables usability benefits such as being able to easily remove or comment one element from the initialization block without removing a comment.

When you declare arrays using an array literal, you can use ... instead of specifying the length. The Go compiler can identify the length of the array, based on the elements you have specified in the array declaration.

Listing 2-14 is a code block that declares and initializes an array with ....

Listing 2-14. Initializing an Array with ...

```
x := [...]int{10, 20, 30, 40, 50}
```

When arrays are initialized using an array literal, you can initialize values for specific elements. Listing 2-15 is an example program that assigns values for a specific location.

Listing 2-15. Initializing Values for Specific Elements

```
package main

import "fmt"

func main() {
    x := [5]int{2: 10, 4: 40}
    fmt.Println(x)
}
```

You should see the following output:

```
[0 0 10 0 40]
```

In Listing 2-15, a value of 10 is assigned to the third element (index 2) and a value of 40 is assigned to the fifth element (index 4).

Slices

A *slice* is a data structure that is very similar to an array, but has no specified length. It is an abstraction built on top of an array type that provides a more convenient way of working with collections. Unlike regular arrays, slices are dynamic arrays in which the length of the slices can be changed at a later stage as data increases or shrinks. Slices are very useful data structures when the number of elements to be stored into a collection can't be predicted.

When you develop applications in Go, you often see slices in the code. If you want to read a database table and put data into a collection type, use slices instead of arrays because you can't predict the length of the collection. Slices provide a built-in function called append, which can append elements to a slice quickly.

Listing 2-16 is a code block that declares a nil slice.

Listing 2-16. Declaring a Nil Slice

```
var x []int
```

A slice x is declared without specifying the length. It will create a nil slice of integers with a length of zero. Because slices are dynamic arrays, you can modify their length later on.

There are several ways to create and initialize slices in Go: you can use the built-in function make or a slice literal.

Creating a Slice with the make Function

When you declare a slice with the make function, you can explicitly specify the length and capacity of a slice.

Listing 2-17 is a code block that declares a slice with a length of 5 and a capacity of 10.

Listing 2-17. Specifying Length and Capacity in a Slice with the make Function

```
x := make([]int, 5,10)
```

If the slice capacity is not specified, the capacity is the same as the length.

Listing 2-18 is a code block that declares a slice without specifying capacity.

Listing 2-18. Specifying Length in a Slice with the make Function

```
 x := make([]int, 5)
```

ryry

Creating a Slice with Slice Literal

One common approach for creating and initializing a slice is to use a slice literal, which doesn't require specifying length within the [ ] operator. The initial length and capacity are taken from the number of elements that are initialized.

Listing 2-19 is a code block that declares and initializes a slice by using a slice literal.

Listing 2-19. Initializing a Slice with a Slice Literal

```
x:= []int{10, 20, 30, 40, 50}
```

This code creates and initializes a slice with a length of 5 and a capacity of 5.

When you create a slice with a slice literal, you can also initialize a slice for a specific length without providing all the elements, as shown in Listing 2-20.

Listing 2-20. A Slice Initializes for a Specific Length Without Providing Elements

```
x := []int{4: 0}
```

This code creates a slice with a length of 5 and a capacity of 5. There is a zero value provided for the index 4.

You can create empty slices with a slice literal, as shown in Listing 2-21.

Listing 2-21. Creating an Empty Slice

```
x:= []int{}
```

This code creates an empty slice with zero elements of value. Empty slices are useful when you want to return empty collections from functions.

Slice Functions

Go provides two built-in functions to easily work with slices: append and copy. The append function creates a new slice by taking an existing slice and appending all the following elements into it.

Listing 2-22 shows an example of append.

Listing 2-22. Slice with the append Function

```
package main

import "fmt"

func main() {
    x := []int{10,20,30}
    y := append(x, 40, 50)
    fmt.Println(x, y)
}
```

You should see the following output:

```
[10 20 30] [10 20 30 40 50]
```

The copy function creates a new slice by copying elements from an existing slice into another slice. Listing 2-23 shows an example of the copy function.

Listing 2-23. Slice with the copy Function

```
package main

import "fmt"

func main() {
    x := []int{10, 20, 30}
    y := make([]int, 2)
    copy(y, x)
    fmt.Println(x, y)

}
```

You should see the following output:

```
[10 20 30] [10 20]
```

After running this program, slice x has [10, 20, 30], and slice y has [10, 20]. Because the length of slice y is 2, it copies the first two elements from slice x. If you specify the length of slice y as 3, it will copy all three elements from slice x.

Length and Capacity

As discussed in previous sections, a slice has a length and capacity that you can specify when it is declared. The length of the slice is the number of elements referred to by the slice; the capacity is the number of elements in the underlying array. A slice can't hold values beyond its capacity; if you try to add more elements, a runtime error will occur. A slice can be grown by using the append function. When you add elements using the append function, it checks to see whether the capacity is sufficient. Otherwise, it automatically increases the capacity. You can get the length value by using the len function and the capacity value by using the cap function.

Listing 2-24 illustrates length and capacity.

Listing 2-24. Slice Length and Capacity

```go
package main

import "fmt"

func main() {
        x := make([]int, 2, 5)
        x[0] = 10
        x[1] = 20
        fmt.Println(x)
        fmt.Println("Length is", len(x))
        fmt.Println("Capacity is", cap(x))
        x = append(x, 30, 40, 50)
        fmt.Println(x)
        fmt.Println("Length is", len(x))
        fmt.Println("Capacity is", cap(x))
        fmt.Println(x)
        x = append(x, 60)
        fmt.Println("Length is", len(x))
        fmt.Println("Capacity is", cap(x))
        fmt.Println(x)
}
```

In this code, slice x with length as 2 and capacity as 5 is declared. Two more elements are then appended into slice x. This time, the capacity is sufficient for slice x, but when you try to append one more element into slice x, the slice automatically grows with more capacity.

When you run the program, you should get the following output:

```
[10 20]
Length is 2
Capacity is 5
[10 20 30 40 50]
Length is 5
Capacity is 5
[10 20 30 40 50]
Length is 6
Capacity is 12
[10 20 30 40 50 60]
```

In this output, the slice capacity gets increased to 12 when the append function is used for the second time.

Iterating Over Slices

Go provides a keyword range, which can be used to iterate over collections. The keyword range iterates over a collection of elements, which returns two values for each iteration. The first value is the index position of the element; the second value is a copy of the value contained in the index position.

Listing 2-25 is an example of using range to iterate over a slice.

Listing 2-25. Iterating Over Slice

```go
package main

import "fmt"

func main() {
    x := []int{10, 20, 30, 40, 50}
    for k, v := range x {
        fmt.Printf("Index: %d Value: %d\n", k, v)
    }
}
```

You should see the following output:

```
Index: 0 Value: 10
Index: 1 Value: 20
Index: 2 Value: 30
Index: 3 Value: 40
Index: 4 Value: 50
```

Maps

A *map* is a data structure that provides an unordered collection of key-value pairs. (A data structure similar to a map is a hash table or dictionary in other programming languages.) Remember that a map is an unordered collection, so you can't predict the data order when it is iterated over the collection.

There are several ways to create and initialize maps in Go. Similar to slices, the built-in function make or the map literal can be used to create and initialize maps.

Listing 2-26 is an example program that creates and initializes a map and iterates it over the collection.

Listing 2-26. Creating a Map and Iterating it Over a Collection

```go
package main

import "fmt"

func main() {
    dict := make(map[string]string)
    dict["go"] = "Golang"
    dict["cs"] = "CSharp"
    dict["rb"] = "Ruby"
    dict["py"] = "Python"
    dict["js"] = "JavaScript"
    for k, v := range dict {
        fmt.Printf("Key: %s Value: %s\n", k, v)
    }
}
```

A map named dict is declared, where the string type is specified for the key (type within the [ ] operator) and value:

```go
dict := make(map[string]string)
```

Values are assigned to the map with the given key (here the key "go" is for the value "Golang"):

```go
dict["go"] = "Golang"
```

Finally, iterate over the collection using the range and print key and value of each element in the collection:

```go
for k, v := range dict {
    fmt.Printf("Key: %s Value: %s\n", k, v)
}
```

You should see the following output:

```
Key: cs Value: CSharp
Key: rb Value: Ruby
Key: py Value: Python
Key: js Value: JavaScript
Key: go Value: Golang
```

■ **Note** The data order will vary every time because a map is an unordered collection.

You can access the value of an element from a map by providing the key (see Listing 2-27):

Listing 2-27. Accessing the Value of an Element from a Map

```
lan, ok := dict["go"]
```

When an element is accessed by providing a key, it will return two values: The first value is the result (the value of the element); the second is a Boolean value that indicates whether the lookup was successful. Go provides a convenient way to write this, as shown in Listing 2-28.

Listing 2-28. Accessing the Element Value from a Map in an Idiomatic Way

```
if lan, ok := dict["go"]; ok {
    fmt.Println(lan, ok)
 }
```

Defer, Panic, and Recover

Go is a minimalist programming language that comes with essential features to develop applications. Although minimal, Go provides all the capabilities to develop highly reliable applications. For example, the language features defer, panic, and recover let you properly clean up your objects by explicitly panicking your application and then recovering from the panic.

Defer

If you have used try/catch/finally blocks in any programming language such as C# and Java, you may have used the finally block to clean up the resources that are allocated in a try block. The statements of a finally block run when the execution flow of control leaves a try statement. This finally block will invoke even when the flow of control goes to a catch block due to a handled exception. Using defer, you can implement cleanup code in Go, which is more efficient than using a finally block in other languages. Though you would primarily use defer for implementing cleanup code, it is not used only for that purpose. For example, by using conjunction with recover, you regain control from a panicking function.

A defer statement pushes a function call (or a code statement) onto a list. The list of saved "function calls" is executed after the surrounding function returns. The last added functions are invoked first from the list of deferred functions. Suppose you add function f1 first, then f2, and finally f3 onto the deferred list; the order of the execution will be f3, f2, and then f1.

Listing 2-29 is a code block that uses defer to clean up a database session object.

Listing 2-29. Defer Statements for Cleaning up Resources

```
session, err := mgo.Dial("localhost") //MongoDB Session object
defer session.Close()
c := session.DB("taskdb").C("categories")
//code statements using session object
```

This code block creates a session object for a MongoDB database. In the next line, the code statement session.Close() is added onto the deferred list to clean up the resources of the database session object after returning the surrounding function. You can add any number of code statements and functions onto the deferred list.

Panic

The panic function is a built-in function that lets you stop the normal flow of control and panic a function. When you call panic from a function, it stops the execution of the function, any deferred functions are executed, and the caller function gets a panicking function. Keep in mind that all deferred functions are executed normally before the execution stops. When developing applications, you will rarely call the panic function because your responsibility is to provide proper error messages rather than stopping the normal control flow. But in some scenarios, you may need to call the panic function if there are no possibilities to continue the normal flow of control. For example, if you can't connect to a database server, it doesn't make any sense to continue executing the application.

Listing 2-30 is the code block that calls panic if there is an error while connecting to a database.

Listing 2-30. Using the panic Function to Panic a Function

```
session, err := mgo.Dial("localhost") // Create MongoDB Session object
if err != nil {
        panic(err)
}
defer session.Close()
```

This code block tries to establish a connection to a MongoDB database and create a session object. You call panic if there is an error while establishing a connection to the database. It stops the execution, and the caller function gets a panicking function.

Recover

The recover function is a built-in function that is typically used inside deferred functions that regain control of a panicking function. The recover function is useful only inside deferred functions because the differing statements are the only way to execute something when a function is panicking.

Listing 2-31 is an example program that demonstrates panic recovery.

Listing 2-31. Recovering from a Panicking Function Using recover

```
package main

import "fmt"

func doPanic() {
        defer func() {
                if e := recover(); e != nil {
                    fmt.Println("Recover with: ", e)
                }
        }()
        panic("Just panicking for the sake of demo")
        fmt.Println("This will never be called")
}

func main() {
        fmt.Println("Starting to panic")
        doPanic()
        fmt.Println("Program regains control after panic recover")
}
```

In the preceding program, the function doPanic is called from the main function. Inside the function doPanic, an anonymous function has been added to the deferred list, in which recover is called to regain control from the panicking function. For the sake of the demo, the panic function is called by providing a string value. When a function is panicking, any deferred functions are executed. Because the recover function is called inside the deferred function, control of the program execution is regained. When recover is called, the value provided by the panic function is received.

■ **Note**   Statements provided after the panic call in the doPanic function don't execute, but statements after the call to the doPanic function in the main function do execute as control is regained from the panicked function.

You should see the following output:

```
Starting to panic
Recover with:  Just panicking for the sake of demo
Program regains control after panic recover
```

Error Handling

Error handling in Go is different from that of other programming languages. Most programming languages use a try/catch block to handle exceptions; in Go, a function can return multiple values. By leveraging this feature, functions in Go typically return a value of a built-in error type, along with other values returned from a function. An idiomatic way to return an error value is to provide the value after other values return. When you look on the standard library packages, you can see that many functions return an error value. So when you call the functions of standard library packages, you can see whether the error value is nil. If a non-nil error value returns, you can identify that you are getting an exception. You can use the same approach for Go functions where you can return multiple values from a function including an error value.

Listing 2-32 is the code block that demonstrates error handling by calling the standard library function.

Listing 2-32. Error Handling in Go

```
f, err := os.Open("readme.ext")
if err != nil {
    log.Fatal(err)
}
```

In this code block, the function Open of the os package is called to open a file. The function Open returns two values: the File object and the error value. If the function returns a non-nil error value, there is an error, and the file won't open. Here the error value is logged if an error occurred.

Listing 2-33 is a custom function that returns multiple values, including an error value.

Listing 2-33. Defining Functions with an Error Value

```
func GetById(id string) (models.Task, error) {
    var task models.Task
    // Implementation here
    return task,nil // multiple return values
}
```

When you write functions to provide an error value, you can return a nil value if any error has occurred. The `caller` function can check whether the error value is nil; if the error value is not nil, the function receives an error.

Listing 2-34 is the code block that demonstrates how to call a function that provides an error value.

Listing 2-34. A caller Function Checks the Error Value

```
task, err:= GetById ("105")
if err != nil {
    log.Fatal(err)
}
//Implementation here if error is nill
```

Summary

This chapter discussed Go packages, which are important features in the Go ecosystem. Go provides modularity, composability, and code reusability through its package ecosystem. Go source files are organized into directories called packages. In Go, you can write two types of packages: package main that results in an executable program (often known as a command in Go documentation) and shared library packages that reuse code with other packages. You can give package aliases to avoid name ambiguity when referencing packages with the same name. The package's init function can be used to initialize packages variables and for other initialization logic. You don't need to explicitly call the init function; it is automatically executed at the beginning of the execution.

The Go tool is a command-line tool that provides various commands for functionalities such as compiling, formatting, testing and running Go code.

Go provides three types of data structures to manage collections of data: arrays, slices, and maps. An array is a fixed-length data type that contains a sequence of elements of a single type. A slice is a dynamic array that can be grown at a later stage as data increases or shrinks. Go provides two built-in functions for manipulating slices: append and copy. A map is a data structure that provides an unordered collection of key-value pairs.

Go provides the defer keyword for cleaning up resources. A defer statement pushes a function call onto a list of deferred functions, which is executed after the surrounding function returns. The panic function allows you to stop the normal flow of control and panic a function. The recover function, which regains control of a panicking function, is useful only inside deferred functions.

Error handling in Go differs from that of most other programming languages. Because Go functions can return multiple values, an error value can be returned from functions. So from caller functions, you can easily check whether the function returns an error value and then provide code implementations accordingly.

CHAPTER 3

■ ■ ■

User-Defined Types and Concurrency

The type system is one of the most important features of a programming language; types allow you to organize and store your application data. When choosing a programming language, it is important to take its type system into consideration. Go enforces simplicity throughout the language design.

Go is a static type language in which you can use built-in types and user-defined types for storing application data. Go provides several built-in types, such as `int`, `float64`, `string`, and `bool`. Chapter 2 discussed arrays, slices, and maps, which are the composite types made up of other types using built-in types and user-defined types. For example, the composite type `map[string]float64` represents a collection of `float64` values, in which each value of the `float64` type can be added to the collection with a key of type `string`, where values can be retrieved with the corresponding key value. Apart from built-in types, you can create your own types by combining one or more built-in or user-defined types. Go provides an interface type in its type system that allows you to develop programs with a greater level of extensibility.

User-defined Types with Structs

Go's type system was designed with simplicity and pragmatism in mind, which avoids a lot of complexity when data structures for applications are designed. The object-oriented approach of Go is completely different from other programming languages. If you are coming from programming languages such as C++, Java, and C#, you will realize that the object-oriented approach of Go is different and unique, although you may miss some features of those languages. When you look at Go's type system and its user-defined types, you should look at the language with a fresh mind so you can enjoy and appreciate the simplicity and power that can be leveraged to solve real-world problems.

Go does not provide classes in its type system; it has structs, which are analogous to classes. A struct can be considered as a lightweight version of a class, but the design of the struct is unique because it focuses on real-world practices. Structs in Go let you create user-defined concrete types; they are a collection of fields or properties that can be used for storing complex data. You can use structs for storing application domain models.

Creating a Struct Type

Let's create a struct type for representing a person's information (see Listing 3-1).

Listing 3-1. Declaring a Struct with a Group of Fields

```
type Person struct {
        FirstName, LastName string
        Dob                 time.Time
        Email, Location     string
}
```

Create a user-defined type with the keyword struct:

```
type Person struct
```

Because the type identifier starts with an uppercase letter, the Person type will be exported into other packages. You specify the struct fields within the body of the Person type. Because the fields FirstName and LastName use the same data type, you can declare both variables in a single statement:

```
FirstName, LastName string
```

Creating Instances of Struct Types

A struct type named Person has been defined. Let's create an instance of a Person type and assign the values to the fields (see Listing 3-2).

Listing 3-2. Creating a Struct Instance

```
var p Person
p.FirstName="Shiju"
p.LastName="Varghese"
p.Dob= time.Date(1979, time.February, 17, 0, 0, 0, 0, time.UTC)
p.Email= "shiju@email.com"
p.Location="Kochi"
```

An instance of a Person type is created, and field values have been assigned one by one. You can also use a struct literal to create a struct type instance (see Listing 3-3).

Listing 3-3. Creating a Struct Instance Using a Struct Literal

```
p:= Person {
    FirstName : "Shiju",
    LastName : "Varghese",
    Dob : time.Date(1979, time.February, 17, 0, 0, 0, 0, time.UTC),
    Email : "shiju@email.com",
    Location : "Kochi",
}
```

You can create a Person type instance by using a struct literal. When you create struct type instances using struct literals, you can split the assignment of struct fields into multiple lines, which enhances the readability of your code block. When you create struck instances this way, you have to put an extra comma at the end of the last assignment, which enables you to easily rearrange the assignment order of the struct fields without worrying about removing a comma for the last assignment and adding a comma for all other fields. Now you have to insert a comma for every struct type field, regardless of whether it is the last field.

You can create struct instances in a more efficient way if you know the order of the struct fields (see Listing 3-4).

Listing 3-4. Creating a Struct Instance Using a Struct Literal

```
p:= Person {
    "Shiju",
    "Varghese",
    time.Date(1979, time.February, 17, 0, 0, 0, 0, time.UTC),
    "shiju@email.com",
    "Kochi",
}
```

This is a very convenient way of creating struct type instances if you know the struct type field order. You can also create struct instances with a single-line statement.

Listing 3-5 shows an example of creating a struct instance by specifying a few fields using a struct literal and assigning remaining fields later.

Listing 3-5. Creating a Struct Instance by Specifying a Few Fields

```
p:= Person { FirstName :"Shiju", LastName : "Varghese" }
p.Dob= time.Date(1979, time.February, 17, 0, 0, 0, 0, time.UTC)
p.Email= "shiju@email.com"
p.Location="Kochi"
```

Adding Behavior to a Struct Type

Go's type system allows you to add behavior to struct types. Like classes of other object-oriented languages, structs in Go allow you to define fields along with operations. Let's add a couple of behaviors to the Person type (see Listing 3-6).

Listing 3-6. Struct Type with Behaviors

```
type Person struct {
    FirstName, LastName string
    Dob                 time.Time
    Email, Location     string
}

//A person method
func (p Person) PrintName() {
    fmt.Printf("\n%s %s\n", p.FirstName, p.LastName)
}

//A person method
func (p Person) PrintDetails() {
    fmt.Printf("[Date of Birth: %s, Email: %s, Location: %s ]\n", p.Dob.String(), p.Email,
    p.Location)
}
```

Two methods have been added to the Person type: PrintName and PrintDetails. A method in Go is a function that is declared with a receiver. Although a method looks like a normal function, it has a receiver. You can specify the method receiver between the func keyword and the name of the function. In Listing 3-6, the Person struct was added as the receiver into the functions PrintName and PrintDetails. When this is done, functions are attached to the Person type to call as methods. This allows you to call the functions using the dot (.) operator from the struct type instance, just as you call instance methods of classes in traditional object-oriented language.

Here, the method with the Person receiver type is declared:

```go
func (p Person) PrintName() {
    fmt.Printf("\n%s %s\n", p.FirstName, p.LastName)
}

//A person method
func (p Person) PrintDetails() {
    fmt.Printf("[Date of Birth: %s, Email: %s, Location: %s ]\n", p.Dob.String(), p.Email,
    p.Location)
}
```

Calling Struct Methods

Let's create an instance of a Person type and call the methods provided by the type (see Listing 3-7).

Listing 3-7. Calling Struct Methods

```go
p := Person{
        "Shiju",
        "Varghese",
        time.Date(1979, time.February, 17, 0, 0, 0, 0, time.UTC),
        "shiju@email.com",
        "Kochi",
}
p. PrintName()
p. PrintDetails()
```

You should see the following output:

```
Shiju Varghese
[Date of Birth: 1979-02-17 00:00:00 +0000 UTC, Email: shiju@email.com, Location: Kochi ]
```

Pointer Method Receivers

In Go, you can define methods using both pointer and nonpointer method receivers. Listing 3-7 used nonpointer receivers for the methods PrintName and PrintDetails. If you want to modify the data of a receiver from the method, the receiver must be a pointer, as shown in Listing 3-8.

Listing 3-8. Receiver Method with Pointer

```go
//A person method with pointer receiver
func (p *Person) ChangeLocation(newLocation string) {
    p.Location= newLocation
}
```

A ChangeLocation function is attached to a pointer receiver. Here the location from the method itself is modified. Suppose that you add this new method to the Person struct listed in Listing 3-7. Let's create a Person type instance and call its methods (see Listing 3-9).

Listing 3-9. Calling Methods of a Pointer Receiver

```
p := &Person{
                "Shiju",
                "Varghese",
                time.Date(1979, time.February, 17, 0, 0, 0, 0, time.UTC),
                "shiju@email.com",
                "Kochi",
        }
        p.ChangeLocation("Santa Clara")
        p.PrintName()
        p.PrintDetails()
```

You should see the following output:

```
Shiju Varghese
[Date of Birth: 1979-02-17 00:00:00 +0000 UTC, Email: shiju@email.com, Location: Santa Clara ]
```

Because you want to call a pointer receiver method, you can create the Person type instance by providing the ampersand (&) operator. When you call the ChangeLocation method, it changes the value of the Location field, so when calling the PrintDetails method, you get the modified value. The value of the Location field would not have changed if the ChangeLocation method were a nonpointer method.

When you call a pointer receiver method, you pass by reference as opposed to passing by value (used with a nonpointer receiver). This makes sense when you want to modify the state (value of the fields) of the receiver within the methods. If the struct has a pointer receiver on some its methods, it is better to use it for the rest of the methods because it enables better consistency and predictability for the struct behaviors.

Let's modify the program to define all methods of the Person struct with a pointer receiver to keep consistency among all its methods (see Listing 3-10).

Listing 3-10. Person Struct with Pointer Receiver Methods

```
package main

import (
        "fmt"
        "time"
)

func main() {
        p := &Person{
                "Shiju",
                "Varghese",
                time.Date(1979, time.February, 17, 0, 0, 0, 0, time.UTC),
                "shiju@email.com",
                "Kochi",
        }
        p.ChangeLocation("Santa Clara")
        p.PrintName()
        p.PrintDetails()

}
```

```
type Person struct {
        FirstName, LastName string
        Dob                 time.Time
        Email, Location     string
}

//A person method with pointer receiver
func (p *Person) PrintName() {
        fmt.Printf("\n%s %s\n", p.FirstName, p.LastName)
}

//A person method with pointer receiver
func (p *Person) PrintDetails() {
        fmt.Printf("[Date of Birth: %s, Email: %s, Location: %s ]\n", p.Dob.String(),
p.Email, p.Location)
}

//A person method with pointer receiver
func (p *Person) ChangeLocation(newLocation string) {
        p.Location = newLocation
}
```

Type Composition

Go's design philosophy is to be a simple language while focusing on real-world practices; it simply ignores many academic thoughts to maintain it as a minimalistic language. You saw the simplicity of Go's type system in previous sections. The major decision about its type system is that although it does not support inheritance, it supports composition through type embedding. Go encourages you to use composition over inheritance.

■ **Note**   Composition is a design philosophy in which smaller components are combined into larger components.

The Person type was defined in the previous section. You can create bigger and more concrete types by embedding the Person type. In Listing 3-11, two more types are created by embedding the Person type.

Listing 3-11.   Type Embedding for Composition

```
type Admin struct {
        Person //type embedding for composition
        Roles  []string
}

type Member struct {
    Person //type embedding for composition
    Skills []string
}
```

The Person type is embedded into Admin and Member types so that all Person fields and methods will be available in these new types.

Let's create a sample program to understand the functionality of type embedding (see Listing 3-12).

Listing 3-12. Example Program for Type Composition

```go
package main

import (
        "fmt"
        "time"
)

type Person struct {
        FirstName, LastName string
        Dob                 time.Time
        Email, Location     string
}

//A person method
func (p Person) PrintName() {
        fmt.Printf("\n%s %s\n", p.FirstName, p.LastName)
}

//A person method
func (p Person) PrintDetails() {
        fmt.Printf("[Date of Birth: %s, Email: %s, Location: %s ]\n", p.Dob.String(),
        p.Email, p.Location)
}

type Admin struct {
        Person //type embedding for composition
        Roles  []string
}

type Member struct {
        Person //type embedding for composition
        Skills []string
}

func main() {
        alex := Admin{
                Person{
                        "Alex",
                        "John",
                        time.Date(1970, time.January, 10, 0, 0, 0, 0, time.UTC),
                        "alex@email.com",
                        "New York"},
                []string{"Manage Team", "Manage Tasks"},
        }
        shiju := Member{
                Person{
                        "Shiju",
                        "Varghese",
                        time.Date(1979, time.February, 17, 0, 0, 0, 0, time.UTC),
                        "shiju@email.com",
                        "Kochi"},
```

```
            []string{"Go", "Docker", "Kubernetes"},
    }
    //call methods for alex
    alex.PrintName()
    alex.PrintDetails()
    //call methods for shiju
    shiju.PrintName ()
    shiju.PrintDetails()
}
```

A Person type was created with a few fields and two methods. Two more types were then created—Admin and Member—by embedding the Person type. These new types have all the properties and methods provided by the Person type. Instances of Admin and Member types can be created by simply embedding the Person type, as shown here:

```
alex := Admin{
            Person{
                    "Alex",
                    "John",
                    time.Date(1970, time.January, 10, 0, 0, 0, 0, time.UTC),
                    "alex@email.com",
                    "New York"},
            []string{"Manage Team", "Manage Tasks"},
    }
    shiju := Member{
            Person{
                    "Shiju",
                    "Varghese",
                    time.Date(1979, time.February, 17, 0, 0, 0, 0, time.UTC),
                    "shiju@email.com",
                    "Kochi"},
            []string{"Go", "Docker", "Kubernetes"},
    }
```

Because all Person type methods are available to Admin and Member types, you can call the methods as shown in the following code:

```
//call methods for alex
        alex.PrintName()
        alex.PrintDetails()
        //call methods for shiju
        shiju.PrintName()
        shiju.PrintDetails()
```

You should see the following output:

```
Alex John
[Date of Birth: 1970-01-10 00:00:00 +0000 UTC, Email: alex@email.com, Location: New York ]
Shiju Varghese
[Date of Birth: 1979-02-17 00:00:00 +0000 UTC, Email: shiju@email.com, Location: Kochi ]
```

Type composition with type embedding provides the practical benefits of using inheritance, coupled with better maintainability.

Overriding Methods of Embedded Type

In Listing 3-11, the Person type was embedded into Admin and Member types and called the methods provided by the Person type. Suppose that you want to override the PrintDetails method in Admin and Member because these types have additional fields: Roles and Skills. The methods of embedded types can be overridden, as shown in Listing 3-13.

Listing 3-13. Overriding the Embedded Type Method

```
type Admin struct {
        Person //type embedding for composition
        Roles  []string
}

//overrides PrintDetails
func (a Admin) PrintDetails() {
        //Call person PrintDetails
        a.Person.PrintDetails()
        fmt.Println("Admin Roles:")
        for _, v := range a.Roles {
                fmt.Println(v)
        }
}

type Member struct {
        Person //type embedding for composition
        Skills []string
}

//overrides PrintDetails
func (m Member) PrintDetails() {
        //Call person PrintDetails
        m.Person.PrintDetails()
        fmt.Println("Skills:")
        for _, v := range m.Skills {
                fmt.Println(v)
        }
}
```

The PrintDetails method is overridden to include additional information held by each type. When this method is overridden, you can call the PrintDetails method of the embedded type to get basic information provided by the embedded type and then provide additional information held by the types:

```
func (m Member) PrintDetails() {
        //Call person PrintDetails
        m.Person. PrintDetails()
        fmt.Println("Skills:")
        for _, v := range m.Skills {
                fmt.Println(v)
        }
}
```

43

The statement m.Person.PrintDetails() calls the PrintDetails method of the Person type. Let's run the modified program with the code shown in Listing 3-14.

Listing 3-14. Running the Program with Method Overriding

```
alex := Admin{
            Person{
                  "Alex",
                  "John",
                  time.Date(1970, time.January, 10, 0, 0, 0, 0, time.UTC),
                  "alex@email.com",
                  "New York"},
            []string{"Manage Team", "Manage Tasks"},
      }
      shiju := Member{
            Person{
                  "Shiju",
                  "Varghese",
                  time.Date(1979, time.February, 17, 0, 0, 0, 0, time.UTC),
                  "shiju@email.com",
                  "Kochi"},
            []string{"Go", "Docker", "Kubernetes"},
      }
      //call methods for alex
      alex.PrintName()
      alex.printDetails()
      //call methods for shiju
      shiju.PrintName()
      shiju.PrintDetails()
```

You should see the following output:

```
Alex John
[Date of Birth: 1970-01-10 00:00:00 +0000 UTC, Email: alex@email.com, Location: New York ]
Admin Roles:
Manage Team
Manage Tasks

Shiju Varghese
[Date of Birth: 1979-02-17 00:00:00 +0000 UTC, Email: shiju@email.com, Location: Kochi ]
Skills:
Go
Docker
Kubernetes
```

Working with Interfaces

In Go's type system, you can create concrete types and interface types. (Concrete types were discussed in previous sections of this chapter.) The interface is one of the greatest features of the Go language because it provides contracts to user-defined concrete types, which allows you to define behaviors for your objects. Let's create an interface type to specify the behavior for Person objects (see Listing 3-15).

Listing 3-15. Defining the Interface Type

```
type User interface {
    PrintName()
    PrintDetails()
}
```

An interface type named User was defined with two behaviors: PrintName and PrintDetails. Let's have a look at the Person type:

```
type Person struct {
        FirstName, LastName string
        Dob                 time.Time
        Email, Location     string
}
```

```
//A person method
func (p Person) PrintName() {
        fmt.Printf("\n%s %s\n", p.FirstName, p.LastName)
}
```

```
//A person method
func (p Person) PrintDetails() {
        fmt.Printf("[Date of Birth: %s, Email: %s, Location: %s ]\n", p.Dob.String(),
p.Email, p.Location)
}
```

The most surprising thing about interface is that you don't need to explicitly implement it into concrete types; instead, just define the methods in the concrete types based on the interface type specification. The Person type has already implemented the User Interface into the Person type. The Person type has implemented the PrintName and PrintDetails methods, which were defined in the user interface type. In programming languages such as C# and Java, you must explicitly implement the interface type into concrete types. Go provides lot of productivity while keeping itself as a static type language.

Listing 3-16 shows a sample program that describes interface and its concrete types:

Listing 3-16. Example Program with Interface

```
package main

import (
        "fmt"
        "time"
)

type User interface {
        PrintName()
        PrintDetails()
}
```

```go
type Person struct {
        FirstName, LastName string
        Dob                 time.Time
        Email, Location     string
}

//A person method
func (p Person) PrintName() {
        fmt.Printf("\n%s %s\n", p.FirstName, p.LastName)
}

//A person method
func (p Person) PrintDetails() {
        fmt.Printf("[Date of Birth: %s, Email: %s, Location: %s ]\n", p.Dob.String(),
        p.Email, p.Location)
}

func main() {
        alex := Person{
                "Alex",
                "John",
                time.Date(1970, time.January, 10, 0, 0, 0, 0, time.UTC),
                "alex@email.com",
                "New York",
        }
        shiju := Person{
                "Shiju",
                "Varghese",
                time.Date(1979, time.February, 17, 0, 0, 0, 0, time.UTC),
                "shiju@email.com",
                "Kochi",
        }
        users := []User{alex, shiju}
        for _, v := range users {
                v.printName()
                v.PrintDetails()
        }
}
```

An interface type and a concrete type were created based on the behavior defined by the interface type. In the main function, two Person objects were created; then a slice of the user interface type with the two Person objects was created. Finally, you iterated through the collection and call methods defined in the interface type: PrintName and PrintDetails.

You should see the following output:

```
Alex John
[Date of Birth: 1970-01-10 00:00:00 +0000 UTC, Email: alex@email.com, Location: New York ]
Shiju Varghese
[Date of Birth: 1979-02-17 00:00:00 +0000 UTC, Email: shiju@email.com, Location: Kochi ]
```

Let's combine the different features of user-defined types that have been discussed in this chapter by writing the example program shown in Listing 3-17.

Listing 3-17. Example Program with Interface, Composition, and Method Overriding

```go
package main

import (
        "fmt"
        "time"
)

type User interface {
        PrintName()
        PrintDetails()
}

type Person struct {
        FirstName, LastName string
        Dob                 time.Time
        Email, Location     string
}

//A person method
func (p Person) PrintName() {
        fmt.Printf("\n%s %s\n", p.FirstName, p.LastName)
}

//A person method
func (p Person) PrintDetails() {
        fmt.Printf("[Date of Birth: %s, Email: %s, Location: %s ]\n", p.Dob.String(),
        p.Email, p.Location)
}

type Admin struct {
        Person //type embedding for composition
        Roles  []string
}

//overrides PrintDetails
func (a Admin) PrintDetails () {
        //Call person PrintDetails
        a.Person. PrintDetails ()
        fmt.Println("Admin Roles:")
        for _, v := range a.Roles {
                fmt.Println(v)
        }
}

type Member struct {
        Person //type embedding for composition
        Skills []string
}
```

```go
//overrides PrintDetails
func (m Member) PrintDetails () {
        //Call person PrintDetails
        m.Person. PrintDetails()
        fmt.Println("Skills:")
        for _, v := range m.Skills {
                fmt.Println(v)
        }
}

type Team struct {
        Name, Description string
        Users             []User
}

func (t Team) GetTeamDetails() {
        fmt.Printf("Team: %s  - %s\n", t.Name, t.Description)
        fmt.Println("Details of the team members:")
        for _, v := range t.Users {
                v.PrintName()
                v.PrintDetails()
        }
}

func main() {
        alex := Admin{
                Person{
                        "Alex",
                        "John",
                        time.Date(1970, time.January, 10, 0, 0, 0, 0, time.UTC),
                        "alex@email.com",
                        "New York"},
                []string{"Manage Team", "Manage Tasks"},
        }
        shiju := Member{
                Person{
                        "Shiju",
                        "Varghese",
                        time.Date(1979, time.February, 17, 0, 0, 0, 0, time.UTC),
                        "shiju@email.com",
                        "Kochi"},
                []string{"Go", "Docker", "Kubernetes"},
        }
        chris := Member{
                Person{
                        "Chris",
                        "Martin",
                        time.Date(1978, time.March, 15, 0, 0, 0, 0, time.UTC),
                        "chris@email.com",
                        "Santa Clara"},
                []string{"Go", "Docker"},
        }
```

```
        team := Team{
                "Go",
                "Golang CoE",
                []User{alex, shiju, chris},
        }
        //get details of Team
        team.GetTeamDetails()
}
```

You should see the following output:

```
Team: Go  - Golang CoE
```

Here are details of the team members:

```
Alex John
[Date of Birth: 1970-01-10 00:00:00 +0000 UTC, Email: alex@email.com, Location: New York ]
Admin Roles:
Manage Team
Manage Tasks

Shiju Varghese
[Date of Birth: 1979-02-17 00:00:00 +0000 UTC, Email: shiju@email.com, Location: Kochi ]
Skills:
Go
Docker
Kubernetes

Chris Martin
[Date of Birth: 1978-03-15 00:00:00 +0000 UTC, Email: chris@email.com, Location: Santa Clara
]
Skills:
Go
Docker
```

In addition to the types defined in Listing 3-16, two more concrete types of the interface type were added (User - Admin and Member), in which the Person type was embedded. The PrintName and PrintDetails methods were modified for both Admin and Member types. Finally, a new struct type (Team) was created, composed of two string fields and a slice of the user interface type, in which you can add Person, Admin, or Member type objects. In the GetTeamDetails method, you iterate through the Users collection, which is made of Admin and Member types, and call the PrintName and PrintDetails methods:

```
type Team struct {
        Name, Description string
        Users             []User
}
```

```
func (t Team) GetTeamDetails() {
        fmt.Printf("Team: %s  - %s\n", t.Name, t.Description)
        fmt.Println("Deteails of the team members:")
        for _, v := range t.Users {
                v.PrintName()
                v.PrintDetails()
        }
}
```

This program shows the power of using the interface type. When the Team type object was created, a slice of user interface was provided, composed with two Member type objects and one Admin type object for the Users field. Objects of different types for the Users field were provided because these objects are the implementation of interface User.

An interface, which adds extensibility and maintainability to your programs, is a contract that lets you write programs depending on abstractions instead of concrete implementations. In the example program, the Users field was defined with a slice of the user interface type so that you can provide objects of any type to provide the implementations of the contract defined in the user interface. If you define a slice of the Member type as the type for the Users property, you would be limited to providing Member type objects as the value for the Users field.

Concurrency

When larger applications are developed, multiple tasks might be needed to complete program execution. Other programs are composed of many smaller subprograms. When you develop these kinds of applications, you can achieve performance improvements if you can execute these tasks and subprograms concurrently. Let's say you are developing a web-based, back-end API in which many concurrent users are accessing the API. If you can concurrently execute these concurrent web requests on the web server, you can dramatically improve the performance and efficiency of the system.

When you develop web applications and web APIs, managing a large set of concurrent users is really a challenge. Go is designed to solve the challenges of modern programming and larger systems. It provides support for concurrency at the core language level and implements concurrency directly into its language and runtime. This helps you easily build high-performance systems.

Many programming environments provide concurrency support with the help of an extra library, but not as a built-in feature of the core language. Concurrency is one of the major selling points of the Go language, along with its simplicity and pragmatism. In Go, concurrency is implemented by using two unique features: goroutines and channels.

Goroutines

In Go, a goroutine is the primary mechanism for running programs concurrently. Goroutines let you run functions concurrently with other functions, and you can run a function as a goroutine to access the concurrency capability of Go. When you create a function as a goroutine, it works as an independent task unit that runs concurrently with other goroutines. In short, a goroutine is a lightweight thread managed by the Go runtime.

The most powerful capability of Go's concurrency is that everything related to concurrency is fully managed by the Go runtime, but not the OS resources. Go runtime has a powerful piece of software component called the *scheduler* that controls and manages everything related to the scheduling and running of goroutines. Because the Go runtime has the full control over the concurrent tasks running with goroutines, it enables high performance and better control to your applications when you leverage the concurrency capabilities of Go.

To invoke a function as a goroutine, use the keyword go:

go function()

Because goroutines are treated as independent units that are running concurrently, ensure that all goroutines are getting executed before the main program is terminated. You can achieve this by using the WaitGroup type provided by the sync standard library package.

Listing 3-18 is an example program in which two goroutines are launched and executed before terminating the program.

Listing 3-18. Concurrency with Goroutines

```go
// This sample program demonstrates how to create goroutines
package main

import (
    "fmt"
    "math/rand"
    "sync"
    "time"
)

// wg is used to wait for the program to finish goroutines.
var wg sync.WaitGroup

func main() {

    // Add a count of two, one for each goroutine.
    wg.Add(2)

    fmt.Println("Start Goroutines")
    //launch a goroutine with label "A"
    go printCounts("A")
    //launch a goroutine with label "B"
    go printCounts("B")
    // Wait for the goroutines to finish.
    fmt.Println("Waiting To Finish")
    wg.Wait()
    fmt.Println("\nTerminating Program")
}

func printCounts(label string) {
    // Schedule the call to WaitGroup's Done to tell we are done.
    defer wg.Done()
    // Randomly wait
    for count := 1; count <= 10; count++ {
        sleep := rand.Int63n(1000)
        time.Sleep(time.Duration(sleep) * time.Millisecond)
        fmt.Printf("Count: %d from %s\n", count, label)
    }
}
```

When you run the program, you see the following output. It will vary each time because of the random wait during the program execution:

```
Start Goroutines
Waiting To Finish
Count: 1 from A
Count: 1 from B
Count: 2 from B
Count: 2 from A
Count: 3 from B
Count: 3 from A
Count: 4 from A
Count: 5 from A
Count: 4 from B
Count: 6 from A
Count: 5 from B
Count: 7 from A
Count: 6 from B
Count: 7 from B
Count: 8 from A
Count: 8 from B
Count: 9 from B
Count: 9 from A
Count: 10 from A
Count: 10 from B
Terminating Program
```

A function named printCounts is created that is called two times as a goroutine:

```
//launch a goroutine with label "A"
 go printCounts("A")
//launch a goroutine with label "B"
  go printCounts("B")
```

To ensure that all goroutines are executed before the program is terminated, use WaitGroup, which is provided by the sync package:

```
var wg sync.WaitGroup
```

In the main function, add a count of 2 into the WaitGroup for the two goroutines:

```
wg.Add(2)
```

Launch two goroutines by using the keyword go:

```
//launch a goroutine with label "A"
  go printCounts("A")
//launch a goroutine with label "B"
  go printCounts("B")
```

In the printCounts function, the values from 1 to 10 are printed. For the sake of the demo, the execution is randomly delayed.

```
func printCounts(label string) {
// Schedule the call to WaitGroup's Done to tell we are done.
    defer wg.Done()
    // Randomly wait
    for count := 1; count <= 10; count++ {
        sleep := rand.Int63n(1000)
        time.Sleep(time.Duration(sleep) * time.Millisecond)
        fmt.Printf("Count: %d from %s\n", count, label)
    }
}
```

In the beginning of the printCounts function, the Done method of the WaitGroup type is scheduled to call to tell the main program that the goroutine has executed. The Done method of the WaitGroup type is scheduled to call using the keyword defer (as discussed in Chapter 2). This keyword allows you to schedule other functions to be called when the function returns. In this example, the Done method will be invoked when the goroutine is executed, which ensures that the value of WaitGroup is decremented so the main function can check whether any goroutine is yet to be executed. In the main function, the Wait method of WaitGroup is called, which will check the count of WaitGroup and will block the program until it becomes zero. When the Done method of WaitGroup is called, the count will be decremented by one. At the beginning of the execution, the count is added as 2. When Wait is called, it will wait for the count to turn zero, thereby ensuring that both the goroutines are executed before the program terminates. When the count becomes zero, the program terminates:

```
wg.Wait()
```

GOMAXPROCS and Parallelism

The Go runtime scheduler manages the goroutine execution by leveraging the number of OS threads to attempt goroutine executions simultaneously. The value for the OS threads is taken from the GOMAXPROCS environment variable. Prior to Go 1.5, the default setting of GOMAXPROCS was 1, meaning that goroutines were running on a single OS thread by default. (Keep in mind that Go runtime can execute thousands of goroutines on a single OS thread.) With Go 1.5, the default setting of GOMAXPROCS was changed to the number of CPUs available, as determined by the NumCPU function provided by the runtime package. This default behavior lets the Go programs leverage all available CPU cores for running goroutines in parallel. The value of the GOMAXPROCS can be set by explicitly using the GOMAXPROCS environment variable or by calling runtime.GOMAXPROCS from within a program.

The simultaneous execution of goroutines is achieved by raising the GOMAXPROCS setting. This behavior is parallelism. *Concurrency* is not parallelism; concurrency in Go is designing a program by breaking it into goroutines (as subprograms or tasks) that can be executed independently by leveraging available resources. *Parallelism* is about doing lots of computations at once. In parallelism, more CPU cores are leveraged to enable the simultaneous execution of goroutines as much as possible.

In many cases, parallelism can provide better performance because the Go runtime can run goroutines in parallel by leveraging all the available compute resources of a computer. Remember that running goroutines in parallel can't always provide better performance because it depends on your program context. Sometimes concurrency can outperform parallelism because parallelism may put more strain on the OS's resources.

You can control the GOMAXPROCS setting in your program based on the context of your applications. Listing 3-19 is a code block that modifies the GOMAXPROCS to one from its default setting:

Listing 3-19. Explicitly Set GOMAXPROCS Setting

```
import "runtime"
// Set the value of GOMAXPROCS.
runtime.GOMAXPROCS(1)
```

■ **Note** Check out Rob Pike's excellent presentation, "Concurrency Is Not Parallelism" to understand the difference between concurrency and parallelism: www.youtube.com/watch?v=cN_DpYBzKso

---

Channels

Listing 3-18 created two goroutines that were running independently and didn't need to communicate with each other. However, sometimes there is a need for communication among goroutines for sending and receiving data, hence the need for synchronization among goroutines. In many programming environments, communication among concurrent programs is complex or limited with features. Go allows you to communicate among goroutines using channels that enable the synchronization of goroutine execution.

The built-in make function is used to declare a channel with the help of the keyword chan, followed by the type for specifying the type of data you are using for exchanging data:

count := make(chan int)

A channel of integer type is declared, so integer values will be passed into channels. There are two types of channels available for synchronization of goroutines:

- Buffered channels
- Unbuffered channels

Listing 3-20 is the code block that declares unbuffered and buffered channels.

Listing 3-20. Declaring Unbuffered and Buffered Channels

```
// Unbuffered channel of integers.
count := make(chan int)
// Buffered channel of integers for buffering up to 10 values.
count:= make(chan int, 10)
```

When buffered channels are declared, the capacity of channels to hold the data must be specified. If you try to send more data than its capacity, you get an error.

Unbuffered Channel

Unbuffered channels provide synchronous communication among goroutines, which ensures message delivery among them. With unbuffered channels, message sending is permitted only if there is a corresponding receiver that is ready to receive the messages. In this case, both sides of the channel have to wait until the other side is ready for sending and receiving messages. With buffered channels, a limited number of messages can be sent into the channel without a corresponding concurrent receiver for receiving those messages. After the messages are sent into buffered channels, those messages from the channel are received. Unlike unbuffered channels, message delivery can't be guaranteed with buffered channels.

The <- operator is used to send values into channels (see Listing 3-21).

Listing 3-21. Sending Values into a Channel

```
// Buffered channel of strings.
messages := make(chan string, 2)
// Send a message into the channel.
messages <- "Golang"
```

To receive messages from channels, the <- operator is used as a unary operator (see Listing 3-22).

Listing 3-22. Receiving Values from a Channel

```
// Receive a string value from the channel.
value := <-messages
```

Listing 3-23 is an example program that demonstrates how to communicate and synchronize data among goroutines using unbuffered channels.

Listing 3-23. Example Program with Unbuffered Chanel

```
package main

import (
    "fmt"
    "sync"
)

// wg is used to wait for the program to finish.
var wg sync.WaitGroup

func main() {

    count := make(chan int)
    // Add a count of two, one for each goroutine.
    wg.Add(2)

    fmt.Println("Start Goroutines")
    //launch a goroutine with label "A"
    go printCounts("A", count)
    //launch a goroutine with label "B"
    go printCounts("B", count)
    fmt.Println("Channel begin")
    count <- 1
    // Wait for the goroutines to finish.
    fmt.Println("Waiting To Finish")
    wg.Wait()
    fmt.Println("\nTerminating Program")
}
```

```go
func printCounts(label string, count chan int) {
    // Schedule the call to WaitGroup's Done to tell we are done.
    defer wg.Done()
    for {
        //Receives message from Channel
        val, ok := <-count
        if !ok {
            fmt.Println("Channel was closed")
            return
        }
        fmt.Printf("Count: %d received from %s \n", val, label)
        if val == 10 {
            fmt.Printf("Channel Closed from %s \n", label)
            // Close the channel
            close(count)
            return
        }
        val++
        // Send count back to the other goroutine.
        count <- val
    }
}
```

The output can vary when you run the program. You should see output similar to the following:

```
Start Goroutines
Channel begin
Count: 1 received from A
Count: 2 received from B
Waiting To Finish
Count: 3 received from A
Count: 4 received from B
Count: 5 received from A
Count: 6 received from B
Count: 7 received from A
Count: 8 received from B
Count: 9 received from A
Count: 10 received from B
Channel Closed from B
Channel was closed
Terminating Program
```

In this program, two goroutines synchronize and communicate using an unbuffered channel. A channel of integer values for exchanging data among goroutines is used. In the main function, the unbuffered channel count is declared for exchanging messages between two goroutines. A count of two is added into WaitGroup for the two goroutines. Then two goroutines are launched with passing the channel:

```go
count := make(chan int)
// Add a count of two, one for each goroutine.
 wg.Add(2)
//launch a goroutine with label "A"
  go printCounts("A", count)
```

```
//launch a goroutine with label "B"
  go printCounts("B", count)
```

Inside the printCounts function, an endless for loop is used and returns from the function when the value 10 is received from the channel. After launching two goroutines, the channel is started by sending a value of 1, which it will receive from the goroutine. The unbuffered channel blocks the receiver until the message is available into the channel.

The following code block in the printCounts function blocks until the value is sent into the channel:

```
//Receive messages from Channel
  val, ok := <-count
```

When values are received from channels, two variables on the left side of the assignment can be used: the data from the channel and a Boolean value to indicate whether the channel is available. We return from the function if the channel is closed.

```
if !ok {
        fmt.Println("Channel was closed")
        return
    }
```

The channel is closed when the value 10 is received from the channel. If the received value of the channel is less than 10, the value is incremented, and a new value is sent into the channel. This process blocks the sender until a receiver receives the value from the channel.

```
if val == 10 {
    fmt.Printf("Channel Closed from %s \n", label)
    // Close the channel
    close(count)
    return
}
val++
// Send count back to the other goroutine.
count <- val
```

The most important thing about the unbuffered channel is that a receive on the channel blocks the goroutine until the channel gets the data, and a send on the channel blocks the goroutine until a receiver receives the data, thus ensuring message delivery among goroutines. If you look at the program output you will clearly understand the functionality of channels.

Buffered Channels

An unbuffered channel provides a synchronous way of data communication among goroutines that ensures guaranteed message delivery. A buffered channel is different from this approach. Unlike an unbuffered channel, it is created by specifying the number of values it can contain. Buffered channels accept the specified number of values before they are received.

Listing 3-24 is a basic example program that demonstrates a buffered channel.

Listing 3-24. Example Program with a Buffered Channel

```
package main

import "fmt"

func main() {
        messages := make(chan string, 2)
        messages <- "Golang"
        messages <- "Gopher"
        //Recieve value from buffered channel
        fmt.Println(<-messages)
        fmt.Println(<-messages)
}
```

You should see the following output:

```
Golang
Gopher
```

Listing 3-24 is a simple example program that demonstrates a buffer channel without having any goroutines. It creates a `messages` channel for buffering up to two string values. Values are sent into the channel until its capacity of two. Because this channel is buffered, values can be sent without depending on a receiver receiving them. If you try to add more values than its capacity, you will get an error. Once the values are sent into the buffered channel, they can be received from the channel.

Summary

Go's type system has two fundamental types: concrete types and interface types. You can create concrete types by using built-in types such as `bool`, `int`, `string`, and `float64`. You can also create composite types such as arrays, slices, maps and channels, and your own user-defined types.

Structs are used to create user-defined types in Go. Structs are analogous to classes in classical object-oriented languages, but the struct design is unique when compared with other languages. A struct is a lightweight version of a class. Go's type system does not support inheritance. Instead, you can compose your types using type embedding.

The interface type is a powerful feature; it enables you to provide lots of extensibility and composability when you build software systems. Interface provides contracts to user-defined concrete types. In Go, you don't need to explicitly implement interfaces into concreate types; you can implement interfaces into concrete types by simply providing the implementation of methods into your concrete types based on the definition of methods defined in the interface type.

Concurrency in Go is the capability to run functions concurrently with other functions. Concurrency is a built-in feature of the Go language, and the Go runtime manages the execution of concurrent functions using a scheduler. Concurrency in Go is implemented with two features: goroutines and channels. A goroutine is a function that can run concurrently with other functions, working as an independent unit. Channels are used to synchronize goroutines to send and receive messages. In Go, you can create two type of channels: buffered channels and unbuffered channels. Unbuffered channels block receivers of goroutines until the data is available on a channel and block senders of goroutines until a receiver is available. Buffered channels block a sender only when the buffer is filled to capacity.

In Chapters 2 and 3, you learned the basics of the Go programming language. From Chapter 4 onward, you will learn about web programming in Go and how to develop web applications and RESTful services.

CHAPTER 4

■ ■ ■

Getting Started with Web Development

The previous three chapters discussed the fundamentals of the Go programming language and the Go ecosystem. Because the primary focus of this book is to explore web development in Go, the rest of the chapters will explore web development in Go with a practical perspective.

Go is a great technology stack for building scalable, web-based, back-end systems for mobile and web applications, although it might not be the best choice for building traditional web applications in which all kind of processing and rendering of view templates execute on the server side. This doesn't mean that Go is not good for developing traditional web applications, but it is an ideal choice for building back-end systems for SPAs and mobile applications in which you can use Go to build APIs on the server side. In the era of mobile APIs, RESTful APIs are becoming the backbone of modern applications, and server-side web development is moving toward REST APIs. Go is great environment choice for building these kind of APIs for powering as a back end for web and mobile applications. In the past, I used C# and Node.js for building back-end APIs for mobile apps, but now I highly recommend Go for developing web APIs.

This chapter takes a look at the fundamentals of building web applications in Go. For a web developer, the Go standard library provides everything for developing web systems. By simply leveraging the standard library, you can build highly scalable web applications and web APIs in Go.

net/http Package

When you think about building web applications and web APIs, or simply building HTTP servers in Go, the most important package is net/http, which comes from the Go standard library and provides all essential functionalities necessary for developing full-fledged web applications. The design philosophy of Go is to develop bigger programs by composing small pieces of components. The net/http package provides a greater level of composability and extensibility so you can easily replace or extend functionalities of the standard library with your own package or a third-party package. In other programming environments such as Ruby, you use a full-fledged web application framework such as Rails to develop web applications. In Go, you can find many full-fledged web application frameworks such as Beego, Revel, and Martini. But the idiomatic way of developing web applications in Go is to leverage standard library packages as the fundamental pieces of the programming block, along with other libraries (not frameworks) that are compatible with the http package. For web development, net/http and html/template are the major packages provided by the standard library. By simply using these two packages, you can build fully functional web applications without leveraging any third-party packages.

■ **Note**   You should start web development with standard library packages before diving into third-party packages and frameworks so that you understand Go's web development ecosystem. If you start web development with third-party packages and frameworks, you will miss many core fundamentals because these frameworks provide lots of spoon-feeding kinds of functionalities and syntactic sugars.

The http package provides implementations for HTTP clients and servers, including various structs and functions for client and server implementations. Various functionalities of the http package will be explored throughout this chapter.

Processing HTTP Requests

The Web is based on a request-response paradigm. In this model (see Figure 4-1), HTTP clients send a request for some data to the web server, the request is processed, and the server and sends a response back to the HTTP clients.

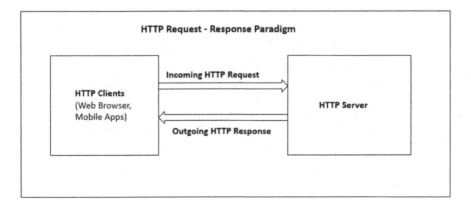

Figure 4-1. *HTTP request-response paradigm*

The most important thing about this communication model is that HTTP is a stateless layer, which means that each request to the HTTP server is treated as an independent transaction that does not remember any previous requests and cannot persist data between the requests. So the communication consists of independent pairs of requests and responses. If you are building web APIs, the web server processes the HTTP requests and sends the response in either XML or JSON format. If you are building web applications, the web server processes the HTTP requests and sends the response as HTML web pages, which will be rendered in a web browser.

The net/http library has two major components for processing HTTP requests (discussed in the following sections):

- ServeMux
- Handler

ServeMux

The ServeMux is a multiplexor (or simply an HTTP request router) that compares incoming HTTP requests against a list of predefined URI resources and then calls the associated handler for the resource requested by the HTTP client.

Handler

The ServeMux provides a multiplexor and calls corresponding handlers for HTTP requests. Handlers are responsible for writing response headers and bodies. In Go, any object can become a handler, thanks to Go's excellent interface implementation provided by its type system. If any object satisfies the implementation of the http.Handler interface, it can be a handler for serving HTTP requests.

Listing 4-1 shows the definition of the http.Handler interface.

Listing 4-1. http.Handler Interface

```
type Handler interface {
    ServeHTTP(ResponseWriter, *Request)
}
```

The ServeHTTP method has two arguments: an http.ResponseWriter interface and a pointer to an http.Request struct. The ResponseWriter interface writes response headers and bodies into the HTTP response. You can use Request to extract information from the incoming HTTP requests. For example, if you want to read querystring values, use the Request object.

The http package provides several functions that implement the http.Handler interface and are used as common handlers:

- FileServer

- NotFoundHandler

- RedirectHandler

- StripPrefix

- TimeoutHandler

Building a Static Web Server

Let's build a static web server in Go using the common handler function FileServer, which returns a handler object that can be used for building static web servers.

Figure 4-2 illustrates the folder structure of a static web site.

Figure 4-2. *Folder structure of a static web site*

A static web site application is created in the GOPATH location with the folder structure specified in Figure 4-2. The implementation of the static web server is written in the main.go source file, and the static contents are put into the public folder that provides the contents for the static web site.

Listing 4-2 shows the implementation in main.go that provides a static web server by serving the contents of public folder.

Listing 4-2. Static Web Server Using the FileServer Function

```
package main

import (
    "net/http"
)

func main() {
    mux := http.NewServeMux()
    fs := http.FileServer(http.Dir("public"))
    mux.Handle("/", fs)
    http.ListenAndServe(":8080", mux)
}
```

In the main function, the http.NewServeMux function is called to create an empty ServeMux object. The http.FileServer function is then called to create a new handler for serving the static contents of a public folder in the web site. The ServeMux.Handle function is called to register the URL path "/" with the handler created with the http.FileServer function. Finally, the http.ListenAndServe function is called to create a HTTP server that starts listening at :8080 for incoming requests. The address and ServeMux objects are passed into the ListenAndServe function.

Listing 4-3 shows the signature of the ListenAndServe function.

Listing 4-3. ListenAndServe Signature

```
func ListenAndServe(addr string, handler Handler) error
```

The ListenAndServe function listens on the TCP network address and then calls Serve with http.Handler to handle requests on incoming connections. The second argument of the ListenAndServe function is an http.Handler, but a ServeMux object was passed. The ServeMux type also has a ServeHTTP method, which means that it satisfies the http.Handler interface so that a ServeMux object can be passed as a second argument for the ListenAndServe function. Keep in mind that an instance of a ServeMux is an implementation of the http.Handler interface. If you pass nil as the second argument for ListenAndServe, a DefaultServeMux will be used for the http.Handler. DefaultServeMux is an instance of ServeMux, so it is also a handler.

When you run the program, you can access the static web page "about.html" by navigating to http://localhost:8080/about.html (see Figure 4-3). The about.html page was put into the public folder for serving as static content.

About Shiju

Shiju Varghese is a Solutions Architect focused on building highly scalable Cloud solutions with a special interest in APIs, Microservices, Containerization and Distributed apps. He currently specializes in Golang, Google Cloud, Microsoft Azure and Docker.

Figure 4-3. *Accessing the static web site*

Creating Custom Handlers

In Go, any object can be an implementation of http.Handler if it can provide a method with the signature ServeHTTP(http.ResponseWriter, *http.Request).

Listing 4-4 creates a custom handler by implementing the http.Handler interface.

Listing 4-4. Creating a Custom Handler

```
type messageHandler struct {
    message string
}

func (m *messageHandler) ServeHTTP(w http.ResponseWriter, r *http.Request) {
    fmt.Fprintf(w, m.message)
}
```

A struct named messageHandler is created. To make this type implement Handler, a method with the signature ServeHTTP(http.ResponseWriter, *http.Request) is implemented. As discussed in Chapter 3, you don't need to specify a keyword to implement an interface into a type; you can implement an interface type into concrete types by providing the methods based on the method signature defined by the interface. The receiver method is added as a messageHandler type into the ServeHTTP function to make it a method of the messageHandler struct. In the ServeHTTP method, a string message is returned as the HTTP response, taking data from the struct field message.

Let's write a program to use the custom handler (see Listing 4-5).

Listing 4-5. Using a Custom Handler Type

```
package main

import (
    "fmt"
    "log"
    "net/http"
)

type messageHandler struct {
    message string
}
```

```go
func (m *messageHandler) ServeHTTP(w http.ResponseWriter, r *http.Request) {
    fmt.Fprintf(w, m.message)
}

func main() {
    mux := http.NewServeMux()

    mh1 := &messageHandler{"Welcome to Go Web Development"}
    mux.Handle("/welcome", mh1)

    mh2 := &messageHandler{"net/http is awesome"}
    mux.Handle("/message", mh2)

    log.Println("Listening...")
    http.ListenAndServe(":8080", mux)
}
```

In the main function, instances of the messageHandler struct (the & symbol is used to yield a pointer) are created and then ServeMux.Handle is called to register handlers with the messageHandler struct instances. If there are requests for the URL path "/welcome" and "/message", the ServeHTTP method of messageHandler does all processing at the server. You can also reuse the custom handlers. In the example, messageHandler is used as the handler for two URL paths.

Using Functions as Handlers

Listing 4-5 created a struct type and made it a handler by implementing the ServeHTTP method with the appropriate method signature. The custom handler can even be reused for multiple URL paths. Although it works for some scenarios, making handlers this way is bit verbose because you have to define structs and then provide implementations for the ServeHTTP method. And in many contexts, you may want to use normal functions as handlers.

http.HandlerFunc type

Instead of creating custom handler types by implementing the http.Handler interface, you can use the http.HandlerFunc type to serve as an HTTP handler. You can convert any function into a HandlerFunc type if the function has the signature func(http.ResponseWriter, *http.Request). The HandlerFunc type works as an adapter that allows you to use normal functions as HTTP handlers. The HandlerFunc type has a built-in method ServeHTTP(http.ResponseWriter, *http.Request), so it also satisfies the http.Handler interface and can work as an HTTP handler.

Listing 4-6 is an example program that uses the HandlerFunc type to create HTTP handlers.

Listing 4-6. Using the HandlerFunc Type to Create Ordinary Functions as Handlers

```go
package main

import (
    "fmt"
    "log"
    "net/http"
)
```

```go
func messageHandler(w http.ResponseWriter, r *http.Request) {
    fmt.Fprintf(w, "Welcome to Go Web Development")
}

func main() {
    mux := http.NewServeMux()

    // Convert the messageHandler function to a HandlerFunc type
    mh := http.HandlerFunc(messageHandler)
    mux.Handle("/welcome", mh)

    log.Println("Listening...")
    http.ListenAndServe(":8080", mux)
}
```

When you run the program, navigate to http://localhost:8080/welcome for the output.

In the main function, an instance of HandlerFunc is created by converting the messageHandler function and then adding it to ServeMux.Handle to handle the requests to the "/welcome" URL path. With the HandlerFunc type, you can easily use ordinary functions as HTTP handlers.

In Listing 4-5, the custom handler was reused for multiple URL paths because it provides a reusable "message" field that provides a string value to the handlers. Listing 4-6 could not provide values for "message", so the value for the message string has to be hard-coded. In many scenarios, you have to provide some values to the handler functions.

Suppose that you want to pass a database connection object into a handler function to reuse it inside the handler function. You can write a function with an argument for receiving some values, and then define and return another function to work as an http.Handler inside the function. In Go, you can create functions inside the function, and it is also supports closure. Handler logic can be implemented into a closure.

Listing 4-7 is an example program that writes handler logic with a closure.

Listing 4-7. Writing Handler Logic into a Closure

```go
package main

import (
    "fmt"
    "log"
    "net/http"
)

//Handler logic into a Closure
func messageHandler(message string) http.Handler {
    return http.HandlerFunc(func(w http.ResponseWriter, r *http.Request) {
        fmt.Fprintf(w, message)
    })
}
func main() {
    mux := http.NewServeMux()

    mux.Handle("/welcome", messageHandler("Welcome to Go Web Development"))
    mux.Handle("/message", messageHandler("net/http is awesome"))

    log.Println("Listening...")
    http.ListenAndServe(":8080", mux)
}
```

This program works the same way as Listing 4-5. The messageHandler function returns an http.Handler. Within the messageHandler function, http.HandlerFunc is returned by calling an anonymous function that has the signature func(http.ResponseWriter, *http.Request) so that it satisfies the http.Handler, and the messageHandler function can return http.Handler. As discussed in the previous section, the http.HandlerFunc type is an implementation of http.Handler. Here, a closure is formed with the variable "message", and the function is put inside the messageHandler function. This approach is useful when you are working on real-world applications; you can use this approach to provide values of application context level types into handler functions.

ServeMux.HandleFunc Function

In the previous section, a normal function was converted into a HandlerFunc type and used as an HTTP handler by registering it with ServeMux.Handle. Because ordinary functions are frequently used as HTTP handlers in this way, the http package provides a shortcut method: ServeMux.HandleFunc. The HandleFunc registers the handler function for the given pattern. (This is just a shortcut method for your convenience.) It internally (inside the http package) converts into a HandlerFunc type and registers the handler into ServeMux.

Listing 4-8 is an example program that uses ServeMux.HandleFunc.

Listing 4-8. Using ServeMux.HandleFunc

```
package main

import (
    "fmt"
    "log"
    "net/http"
)

func messageHandler(w http.ResponseWriter, r *http.Request) {
    fmt.Fprintf(w, "Welcome to Go Web Development")
}

func main() {
    mux := http.NewServeMux()

    // Use the shortcut method ServeMux.HandleFunc
    mux.HandleFunc("/welcome", messageHandler)

    log.Println("Listening...")
    http.ListenAndServe(":8080", mux)
}
```

When you run the program, navigate to http://localhost:8080/welcome for the output.

DefaultServeMux

In the example programs in this chapter, the ServeMux object was created by calling the function http.NewServeMux. DefaultServeMux is same as the ServeMux objects from the previous programs. DefaultServeMux is the default ServeMux used by the Serve method, and the ServeMux object is instantiated when the http package is used.

Here is the code statement from Go source:

```
var DefaultServeMux = NewServeMux()
```

Listing 4-9 shows the source of the NewServeMux function from Go source.

Listing 4-9. NewServeMux Function from Go Source

```
// NewServeMux allocates and returns a new ServeMux.
func NewServeMux() *ServeMux { return &ServeMux{m: make(map[string]muxEntry)} }
```

The http package provides a couple of shortcut methods for working with DefaultServeMux: http.Handle and http.HandleFunc. The http.Handle function registers the handler for the given pattern in DefaultServeMux, and http.HandleFunc registers the handler function for the given pattern in DefaultServeMux. So these functions are just shortcuts to use ServeMux.Handle and ServeMux.HandleFunc in DefaultServeMux. The ListenAndServe function uses DefaultServeMux if the second parameter is set as nil instead of providing an http.Handler object.

Let's rewrite the program in Listing 4-8 to use with DefaultServeMux (see Listing 4-10).

Listing 4-10. Using DefaultServeMux

```
package main

import (
    "fmt"
    "log"
    "net/http"
)

func messageHandler(w http.ResponseWriter, r *http.Request) {
    fmt.Fprintf(w, "Welcome to Go Web Development")
}

func main() {

    http.HandleFunc("/welcome", messageHandler)

    log.Println("Listening...")
    http.ListenAndServe(":8080", nil)
}
```

When you run the program, navigate to http://localhost:8080/welcome for the output. When you use the http.Handle and http.HandleFunc functions, you can pass a nil value as the second parameter for calling ListenAndServe because handler and handler functions register into DefaultServeMux through the http.Handle and http.HandleFunc functions.

http.Server Struct

In previous examples, http.ListenAndServe was called to run HTTP servers, which does not allow you to customize HTTP server configuration. The http package provides a struct named Server that enables you to specify HTTP server configuration.

Listing 4-11 shows the Server struct.

Listing 4-11. http.Server Struct

```
type Server struct {
    Addr           string
    Handler        Handler
    ReadTimeout    time.Duration
    WriteTimeout   time.Duration
    MaxHeaderBytes int
    TLSConfig      *tls.Config
    TLSNextProto   map[string]func(*Server, *tls.Conn, Handler)
    ConnState      func(net.Conn, ConnState)
    ErrorLog       *log.Logger
}
```

This struct allows you to configure many values, including error logger for the server, maximum duration before timing out read of the request, maximum duration before timing out write of the response, and maximum size of request headers.

Listing 4-12 is an example program that uses the Server struct to customize server behavior.

Listing 4-12. Using the http.Server Struct

```
package main

import (
    "fmt"
    "log"
    "net/http"
    "time"
)

func messageHandler(w http.ResponseWriter, r *http.Request) {
    fmt.Fprintf(w, "Welcome to Go Web Development")
}

func main() {

    http.HandleFunc("/welcome", messageHandler)

    server := &http.Server{
        Addr:           ":8080",
        ReadTimeout:    10 * time.Second,
        WriteTimeout:   10 * time.Second,
        MaxHeaderBytes: 1 << 20,
    }
    log.Println("Listening...")
    server.ListenAndServe()
}
```

The server behavior is customized by creating a Server type object and calling the Server ListenAndServe method. In previous examples, the http.ListenAndServe function was used to start the HTTP server. When the http.ListenAndServe function is called, it internally creates a Server type instance and calls the ListenAndServe method.

Listing 4-13 is the implementation of http.ListenAndServe from Go source.

Listing 4-13. Implementation of http.ListenAndServe

```
func ListenAndServe(addr string, handler Handler) error {
        server := &Server{Addr: addr, Handler: handler}
        return server.ListenAndServe()
}
```

Gorilla Mux

The http.ServeMux is an HTTP request multiplexer that works well for most common scenarios. It was used in the example programs as the request multiplexer. If you want more power for your request multiplexer, you might consider a third-party routing package that is compatible with standard http.ServeMux. For example, if you want to specify RESTful resources with proper HTTP endpoints and HTTP methods, it is difficult to work with the standard http.ServeMux.

The mux package from the Gorilla web toolkit (github.com/gorilla/mux) is a powerful request router that allows you to configure the multiplexer in your own way. This package is very useful when you build RESTful services and it implements the http.Handler interface so it is compatible with the standard http.ServeMux. With the mux package, requests can be matched based on URL host, path, path prefix, schemes, header and query values, and HTTP methods. You can also use custom matchers and routes as subrouters with this package.

To install the mux package, run the following command in the terminal:

```
go get github.com/gorilla/mux
```

Let's configure routes with the mux package (see Listing 4-14).

Listing 4-14. Routing with the mux Package

```
func main() {
        r := mux.NewRouter().StrictSlash(false)
        r.HandleFunc("/api/notes", GetNoteHandler).Methods("GET")
        r.HandleFunc("/api/notes", PostNoteHandler).Methods("POST")
        r.HandleFunc("/api/notes/{id}", PutNoteHandler).Methods("PUT")
        r.HandleFunc("/api/notes/{id}", DeleteNoteHandler).Methods("DELETE")

        server := &http.Server{
                Addr:    ":8080",
                Handler: r,
        }
        server.ListenAndServe()
}
```

Here a mux.Router object is created by calling the NewRouter function and then specifying the routes for the resources. You can match with HTTP methods when specifying URI patterns, so it is useful when building RESTful applications. Because the mux package implements the http.Handler interface, you can easily work with the http standard package. It provides lot of extensibility so that you can easily replace or extend many of its functionalities with your own packages and third-party packages.

Unlike other web-programming ecosystems, the idiomatic way of web development in Go is to use standard library packages and third-party packages if required to extend the capabilities of existing functionalities. When you choose third-party packages, it is important to choose those that are compatible with the standard library package. The mux package is a great example for this approach, which is compatible with the http package because it provides the http.Handler interface.

Building a RESTful API

This chapter discussed the fundamentals of web development in Go, including `http.ServeMux` and `http.Handler` for processing and serving HTTP requests. You also learned about the `mux` third-party package, which can be used as a replacement for `http.ServeMux` and is compatible with the `http` package. Let's now build a simple JSON-based REST API with the `mux` package as the request multiplexer, which will help you understand many real-world practices for building web systems in Go (see Listing 4-15).

■ **Note** Representational State Transfer (REST): If you want to know more about REST, I recommend that you read Martin Fowler's article, "Richardson Maturity Model: Steps Toward the Glory of REST." Access it here: http://martinfowler.com/articles/richardsonMaturityModel.html

---

Listing 4-15. JSON-based RESTful API

```go
package main

import (
    "encoding/json"
    "log"
    "net/http"
    "strconv"
    "time"

    "github.com/gorilla/mux"
)

type Note struct {
    Title       string    `json:"title"`
    Description string    `json:"description"`
    CreatedOn   time.Time `json:"createdon"`
}

//Store for the Notes collection
var noteStore = make(map[string]Note)

//Variable to generate key for the collection
var id int = 0

//HTTP Post - /api/notes
func PostNoteHandler(w http.ResponseWriter, r *http.Request) {
    var note Note
    // Decode the incoming Note json
    err := json.NewDecoder(r.Body).Decode(&note)
    if err != nil {
        panic(err)
    }
```

```go
        note.CreatedOn = time.Now()
        id++
        k := strconv.Itoa(id)
        noteStore[k] = note

        j, err := json.Marshal(note)
        if err != nil {
            panic(err)
        }
        w.Header().Set("Content-Type", "application/json")
        w.WriteHeader(http.StatusCreated)
        w.Write(j)
}

//HTTP Get - /api/notes
func GetNoteHandler(w http.ResponseWriter, r *http.Request) {
        var notes []Note
        for _, v := range noteStore {
            notes = append(notes, v)
        }
        w.Header().Set("Content-Type", "application/json")
        j, err := json.Marshal(notes)
        if err != nil {
            panic(err)
        }
        w.WriteHeader(http.StatusOK)
        w.Write(j)
}

//HTTP Put - /api/notes/{id}
func PutNoteHandler(w http.ResponseWriter, r *http.Request) {
        var err error
        vars := mux.Vars(r)
        k := vars["id"]
        var noteToUpd Note
        // Decode the incoming Note json
        err = json.NewDecoder(r.Body).Decode(&noteToUpd)
        if err != nil {
            panic(err)
        }
        if note, ok := noteStore[k]; ok {
            noteToUpd.CreatedOn = note.CreatedOn
            //delete existing item and add the updated item
            delete(noteStore, k)
            noteStore[k] = noteToUpd
        } else {
            log.Printf("Could not find key of Note %s to delete", k)
        }
        w.WriteHeader(http.StatusNoContent)
}
```

```go
//HTTP Delete - /api/notes/{id}
func DeleteNoteHandler(w http.ResponseWriter, r *http.Request) {
    vars := mux.Vars(r)
    k := vars["id"]
    // Remove from Store
    if _, ok := noteStore[k]; ok {
        //delete existing item
        delete(noteStore, k)
    } else {
        log.Printf("Could not find key of Note %s to delete", k)
    }
    w.WriteHeader(http.StatusNoContent)
}


//Entry point of the program
func main() {
    r := mux.NewRouter().StrictSlash(false)
    r.HandleFunc("/api/notes", GetNoteHandler).Methods("GET")
    r.HandleFunc("/api/notes", PostNoteHandler).Methods("POST")
    r.HandleFunc("/api/notes/{id}", PutNoteHandler).Methods("PUT")
    r.HandleFunc("/api/notes/{id}", DeleteNoteHandler).Methods("DELETE")

    server := &http.Server{
        Addr:    ":8080",
        Handler: r,
    }
    log.Println("Listening...")
    server.ListenAndServe()
}
```

Data Model and Data Store

Listing 4-15 built a simple REST API with basic CRUD operations against the data model Note struct:

```go
type Note struct {
    Title       string    `json:"title"`
    Description string    `json:"description"`
    CreatedOn   time.Time `json:"createdon"`
}
```

For the JSON-based API, the struct fields are encoded into JSON to serve as the response to HTTP clients. You can easily encode a struct as JSON and decode JSON as a struct by using the standard library package encoding/json. If you need a representation for the elements of JSON different from struct fields, you can map the struct fields with the elements you want for JSON encoding:

```go
Title       string    `json:"title"`
Description string    `json:"description"`
CreatedOn   time.Time `json:"createdon"`
```

Here the struct fields are represented in uppercase letters; encode these fields in lowercase letters for JSON representation.

This sample does not use any database storage, so a map is used as the persistence storage for the sake of the demo. An integer variable id is used to generate a key for the map:

```
//Store for the Notes collection
var noteStore = make(map[string]Note)

//Variable to generate key for the map
var id int = 0
```

Configuring the Multiplexer

You can use a mux package as the multiplexer and configure it with corresponding handler functions. Use "/api/notes" as the base endpoint for representing the Notes resources. Because mux provides support for mapping with HTTP methods, you can easily represent resources in a RESTful way:

```
//Entry point of the program
func main() {
    r := mux.NewRouter().StrictSlash(false)
    r.HandleFunc("/api/notes", GetNoteHandler).Methods("GET")
    r.HandleFunc("/api/notes", PostNoteHandler).Methods("POST")
    r.HandleFunc("/api/notes/{id}", PutNoteHandler).Methods("PUT")
    r.HandleFunc("/api/notes/{id}", DeleteNoteHandler).Methods("DELETE")

    server := &http.Server{
        Addr:    ":8080",
        Handler: r,
    }
    log.Println("Listening...")
    server.ListenAndServe()
}
```

Table 4-1 shows the configurations used with the multiplexer. The multiplexer calls corresponding handler functions if the URI and HTTP methods match with a predefined list of configurations.

Table 4-1. *Multiplexer Configurations*

URI	HTTP Method	Handler Function
/api/notes	Get	GetNoteHandler
/api/notes	Post	PostNoteHandler
/api/notes/{id}	Put	PutNoteHandler
/api/notes/{id}	Delete	DeleteNoteHandler

Handler Functions for CRUD Operations

Let's have a look at the handler function for HTTP Get to get Note resource values:

```
//HTTP Get - /api/notes
func GetNoteHandler(w http.ResponseWriter, r *http.Request) {
    var notes []Note
    for _, v := range noteStore {
        notes = append(notes, v)
    }
    w.Header().Set("Content-Type", "application/json")
    j, err := json.Marshal(notes)
    if err != nil {
        panic(err)
    }
    w.WriteHeader(http.StatusOK)
    w.Write(j)
}
```

Here you iterate through the noteStore map, and the values are appended into a Note slice. By using the Marshal function of the json package, the Note slice is encoded as JSON.

ResponseWriter is used for writing response headers and bodies. Here the header is written using the WriteHeader method of ResponseWriter, and the response body is written using the Write method of ResponseWriter. When you call the API endpoint "/api/notes" with the HTTP Get method, you see the output in the format shown in Figure 4-4.

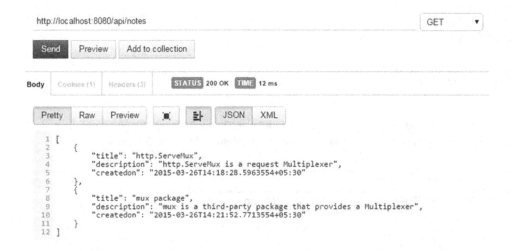

Figure 4-4. *HTTP Get for the Notes resource*

In Figure 4-4, you get the Note collection as JSON. Here the Postman REST API client tool is used to test the REST API example. Postman is a Chrome app that allows you to test your APIs. (Because it is a Chrome app, it runs only on the Chrome browser, however). With Postman, you can quickly construct HTTP requests to an API server, save them for later use, and analyze the responses sent by the API server. Postman is a very useful tool that can be used to test REST APIs without building a client application. To get more details, visit the Postman web site at www.getpostman.com.

Let's have a look at the handler function for HTTP Post for creating a new Note resource:

```
//HTTP Post - /api/notes
func PostNoteHandler(w http.ResponseWriter, r *http.Request) {
    var note Note
    // Decode the incoming Note json
    err := json.NewDecoder(r.Body).Decode(&note)
    if err != nil {
        panic(err)
    }

    note.CreatedOn = time.Now()
    id++
    k := strconv.Itoa(id)
    noteStore[k] = note

    j, err := json.Marshal(note)
    if err != nil {
        panic(err)
    }
    w.Header().Set("Content-Type", "application/json")
    w.WriteHeader(http.StatusCreated)
    w.Write(j)
}
```

A pointer to the http.Request object is used to get information about HTTP Request. Here the incoming JSON data is accessed from Request.Body and decoded into the Note resource using the json package. The NewDecoder function creates a Decoder object, and its Decode method decodes the JSON string into the given type (the Note type in this example). The id variable is incremented to generate a key value for the noteStore map. The string type is used as the key for the noteStore map, so the int type is converted to string using the strconv.Itoa function. The new Note resource is added into the noteStore map with the key created with the id variable. Finally, the response is sent as JSON data for the newly created Note resource with the appropriate response header back to the HTTP client. json.Marshal is used to convert the Note object into JSON data.

Figure 4-5 shows testing of HTTP Post for the resource "/api/nodes". You see the newly created resource in the body with the HTTP status code 201 that represents the HTTP status "Created".

Figure 4-5. *HTTP Post for the Notes resource*

The endpoint "/api/notes/{id}" is used for the Note resource HTTP Put and HTTP Delete operations. In this example, the value of id is used as the key of the noteStore map. To retrieve this value from the request object, mux.Vars() is called:

```
vars := mux.Vars(r)
k := vars["id"]
```

The Vars function of the mux package returns the route variables for the current request. With a route value of id, the Note object is retrieved from the noteStore map, and the value of CreatedOn is copied to the Note object.

Here the existing Note object is removed and added into the noteStore map for the sake of update functionality. Everything else is implemented the same way as the HTTP Post operation:

```
//HTTP Put - /api/notes/{id}
func PutNoteHandler(w http.ResponseWriter, r *http.Request) {
    var err error
    vars := mux.Vars(r)
    k := vars["id"]
    var noteToUpd Note
    // Decode the incoming Note json
    err = json.NewDecoder(r.Body).Decode(&noteToUpd)
    if err != nil {
        panic(err)
    }
```

```
    if note, ok := noteStore[k]; ok {
        noteToUpd.CreatedOn = note.CreatedOn
        //delete existing item and add the updated item
        delete(noteStore, k)
        noteStore[k] = noteToUpd
    } else {
        log.Printf("Could not find key of Note %s to delete", k)
    }
    w.WriteHeader(http.StatusNoContent)
}
```

Similar to the HTTP Put operation for the Note resource, the route value of id is taken and the Note object is removed from the noteStore map by using the key value from the route variable id:

```
//HTTP Delete - /api/notes/{id}
func DeleteNoteHandler(w http.ResponseWriter, r *http.Request) {
    vars := mux.Vars(r)
    k := vars["id"]
    // Remove from Store
    if _, ok := noteStore[k]; ok {
        //delete existing item
        delete(noteStore, k)
    } else {
        log.Printf("Could not find key of Note %s to delete", k)
    }
    w.WriteHeader(http.StatusNoContent)
}
```

This example application demonstrated the fundamental concepts for building RESTful APIs in Go by using its standard library package net/http and the mux third-party package.

Summary

Go is a great technology stack for building web-based, back-end systems; and is especially excellent for building RESTful APIs. The net/http package from the standard library provides the fundamental blocks for building web applications in Go. The Go philosophy discourages using bigger frameworks for building web applications; it encourages the use of the net/http package as the fundamental block to use third-party packages and your own packages to extend the functionalities provided by the net/http package.

The http package has two major components for processing HTTP requests: http.ServeMux and http.Handler. http.ServeMux is a request multiplexor that compares incoming HTTP requests against a list of predefined URI resources and calls the associated handler for the resource requested by HTTP clients. Handlers are responsible for writing response headers and bodies. By using third-party packages such as mux, you can extend the capabilities of http.ServeMux.

The final section of this chapter explored the fundamental pieces of web development in Go by showing the development of a JSON-based RESTful API.

CHAPTER 5

■ ■ ■

Working with Go Templates

Chapter 4 discussed the fundamentals of web development in Go using the standard library package net/http. A JSON-based web API was created by using the standard library package net/http as the primary web programming block and the third-party package Gorilla mux as the HTTP request multiplexer. This chapter shows you how to develop web applications in Go; the standard library package html/template is used for rendering web pages.

This chapter begins with the fundamentals of Go templates and includes how to develop full-fledged web applications by leveraging the html/template package.

text/template Package

Using templates is a great way to build dynamic contents; you provide data at runtime to generate dynamic contents with a predefined format. The Go standard library package html/template allows you to build dynamic HTML pages by combining static contents with dynamic contents where it parses the templates with the data structure that is provided at runtime.

You will have a look at the standard library package text/template before diving into the html/template package. The html/template package provides the same interface as the text/template package; the only difference between the two is that the html/template package parses the template and generates the output in HTML, and the text/template package generates the output in text format. You can start with the text/template package to understand the syntax of Go templates and can easily work with the html/template without any syntactical difference. The text/template package allows you to build data-driven templates for generating textual output.

Working with text/template

Templates are parsed against the data structure provided at runtime. Commands in the template refer to elements of the data structure. For example, struct fields can be mapped with template commands. The commands in the templates are delimited by {{ and }}.

To work with text/template, it to the list of imports:

```
import (
        "text/template"
)
```

Listing 5-1 is an example program that generates textual output with struct object fields.

Listing 5-1. Applying Struct Fields into a Template

```go
package main

import (
    "log"
    "os"
    "text/template"
)

type Note struct {
    Title       string
    Description string
}

const tmpl = `Note - Title: {{.Title}}, Description: {{.Description}}`

func main() {
    //Create an instance of Note struct
    note := Note{"text/templates", "Template generates textual output"}

    //create a new template with a name
    t := template.New("note")

    //parse some content and generate a template
    t, err := t.Parse(tmpl)
    if err != nil {
        log.Fatal("Parse: ", err)
        return
    }
    //Applies a parsed template to the data of Note object
    if err := t.Execute(os.Stdout, note); err != nil {
        log.Fatal("Execute: ", err)
        return
    }
}
```

You should get the following output:

```
Note - Title: text/templates, Description: Template generates textual output
```

In the previous listing, a struct named Note is declared, and a template is declared as a string constant:

```go
const tmpl = `Note - Title: {{.Title}}, Description: {{.Description}}`
```

In the template, the Title and Description fields of the Note struct are mapped so the textual output with the values of the Note object can be rendered when the template is executed. The template block {{ . }} is a context-aware block that will be executed based on the execution context. Here the Note object is provided when the template is executed, so the names after the dot (.) maps the field names of the Note object.

A new template with the name "note" is created. The New function returns the type *Template:

```
t := template.New("note")
```

The Parse method parses a string into a template:

```
t, err := t.Parse(tmpl)
```

Here the template is parsed from a string that has declared with a constant variable. To parse the template from template files, use the ParseFiles method of *Template:

```
func (t *Template) ParseFiles(filenames ...string) (*Template, error)
```

The ParseGlob method parses the template definitions in the files identified by the pattern. Here is a sample for parsing all template definition files in a folder with the extension .tmpl:

```
t, err := template.ParseGlob("templates/*.tmpl")
```

The previous code block parses all template definitions in the folder templates if the files have an extension of .tmpl.

The Execute method applies a parsed template to the specified data object (here a Note object) and writes the output to an output writer. If an error occurs during the template execution or between writing its output, execution stops, but partial results may already have been written to the output writer:

```
err1 := t.Execute(os.Stdout, note)
```

Here's a summary of the steps for generating the textual output using text/template:

1. Declare a template for mapping with a data object.

2. Create a template (*Template) by calling the template.New function.

3. Parses a string into a template by calling the Parse method.

4. Executes the parsed template with the specified data object for rendering the textual contents with the values of the data object.

In the previous program, a simple struct object was applied to the template for generating the output. Let's have a look at how to apply a collection of objects to templates for generating the textual output.

Listing 5-2 is an example program that renders a text template with a collection object.

Listing 5-2. Applying a Slice of Objects into a Template

```
package main

import (
        "log"
        "os"
        "text/template"
)
```

```go
type Note struct {
        Title       string
        Description string
}

const tmpl = `Notes are:
{{range .}}
        Title: {{.Title}}, Description: {{.Description}}
{{end}}
`

func main() {
        //Create slice of Note objects
        notes := []Note{
                {"text/template", "Template generates textual output"},
                {"html/template", "Template generates HTML output"},
        }

        //create a new template with a name
        t := template.New("note")

        //parse some content and generate a template
        t, err := t.Parse(tmpl)
        if err != nil {
                log.Fatal("Parse: ", err)
                return
        }

        //Applies a parsed template to the slice of Note objects
        if err := t.Execute(os.Stdout, notes); err!=nil {
                log.Fatal("Execute: ", err)
                return
        }
}
```

You should get the following output:

```
Notes are:

        Title: text/templates, Description: Template generates textual output

        Title: html/templates, Description: Template generates HTML output
```

A template definition is declared as a string constant:

```go
const tmpl = `Notes are:
{{range .}}
    Title: {{.Title}}, Description: {{.Description}}
{{end}}
`
```

In this listing, the slice of the Note struct as the data object is provided. Here the template definition block {{.}} represents the collection object where we can iterate through the collection using the action {{range .}}. All control structures (if, with, or range) definitions must close with {{end}}.

Define Named Templates

Template definitions can be defined with a define and end action. The define action names the template being created by providing a string constant, which will be useful when you work with nested template definitions. (Nested templates will be used later in this chapter when you build a web application.) Listing 5-3 is an example program.

Listing 5-3. Defining a Template Definition

```
package main

import (
    "log"
    "os"
    "text/template"
)

func main() {
    t, err := template.New("test").Parse(`{{define "T"}}Hello, {{.}}!{{end}}`)
    err = t.ExecuteTemplate(os.Stdout, "T", "World")
    if err != nil {
        log.Fatal("Execute: ", err)
    }
}
```

You should get the following output:

Hello World!

In the preceding program, a template definition is defined with a name "T". The ExecuteTemplate method is used to execute a named template "T" by applying the string data "World" that will be mapped with template definition block {{.}}. Keep in mind that the define action must be closed with an end action in which you can provide the template definition between the define and end action.

Declaring Variables

Variables can be declared in template definitions that can be referenced in the template definitions for later use. To declare a variable, use $variable inside the {{ }} block. Listing 5-4 is an example.

Listing 5-4. Declaring a Variable and Referencing it Later

```
{{ $note := "Sample Note"}}
{{ $note }}
```

Here a $note variable is declared and referenced later by simply specifying the variable name. The {{ $note }} command prints the value of the $note variable.

When you declare a variable with a range action, the variable value would be successive elements of the each iteration. A range action can declare two variables for a key and value element, separated by a comma (see Listing 5-5).

Listing 5-5. Declaring Variables with a range Action

```
{{range $key,$value := . }}
```

If you use a range action with a map, the $key variable is the store key of the map, and the $value variable is the store value element of each iteration.

Using Pipes

When you work with Go templates, you can perform actions one after another by using pipes: each pipeline's output becomes the input of the following pipe. Listing 5-6 shows an example.

Listing 5-6. Using a Pipe in a Template

```
{{ eq $a $b | if }} a nnd b are equal{{ end }}
```

Here an output value is printed if the values of variables $a and $b are equal.

Building HTML Views Using html/template

When you build web applications, you have to render the view (UI) templates with the application data. The standard library package html/template lets you build user interfaces of dynamic web applications in Go. When you build web applications, you can define view templates by combining Go template syntax with HTML, CSS, and JavaScript, which can be rendered as web pages at runtime by providing the application data using various data structures.

The html/template package provides the same interface as text/template, but the output of the template definitions is HTML. html/template not only generates HTML but also guards against certain code injections while rendering the HTML pages. When you render HTML views for your web applications, you must use html/template instead of text/template.

The greatest advantage of using html/template is that it does the HTML encoding safely with a proper security model. Listing 5-7 shows a program that protects against a script injection.

Listing 5-7. html/template Protecting Against Script Injection

```
package main

import (
    "html/template"
    "log"
    "os"
)

func main() {
    t, err := template.New("test").Parse(`{{define "T"}}Hello, {{.}}!{{end}}`)
    err = t.ExecuteTemplate(os.Stdout, "T", "<script>alert('XSS Injection')</script>")
```

```
    if err != nil {
        log.Fatal("Execute: ", err)
    }
}
```

You should get the following output:

Hello, <script>alert('XSS Injection')</script>!

The template securely encodes the output where it replaces the script blocks with corresponding text.

Building a Web Application

In this section, you learn how to use `html/template` for building HTML views by building a simple web application.

Figure 5-1 shows the folder structure of the web application that you will build in the next section. You will write the application in the GOPATH location. All template definition files are put into the `templates` folder, and static files such as CSS and JS files are put into the `public` folder.

Figure 5-1. Folder Structure of the Example Web Application

`html/template` must first be added to the list of imports (see Listing 5-8).

Listing 5-8. List of Imports in main.go

```
import (
        "html/template"
        "log"
        "net/http"
        "strconv"
        "time"

        "github.com/gorilla/mux"
)
```

Data Structure and Data Store

In the example web application shown in Listing 5-9, a struct type is used as the data structure, and CRUD operations are performed against the struct type. A map type is used as the store for persisting struct objects with a key. The key will be generated by incrementing a variable id.

Listing 5-9. Data Structure and Data Store in main.go

```
type Note struct {
    Title       string
    Description string
    CreatedOn   time.Time
}

//Store for the Notes collection
var noteStore = make(map[string]Note)

//Variable to generate key for the collection
var id int = 0
```

main function

Listing 5-10 shows the entry point of the program in which the HTTP request multiplexer is configured and starts the HTTP server.

Listing 5-10. Entry Point of the Program in main.go

```
//Entry point of the program
func main() {

    r := mux.NewRouter().StrictSlash(false)
    fs := http.FileServer(http.Dir("public"))
    r.Handle("/public/", fs)
    r.HandleFunc("/", getNotes)
    r.HandleFunc("/notes/add", addNote)
    r.HandleFunc("/notes/save", saveNote)
    r.HandleFunc("/notes/edit/{id}", editNote)
    r.HandleFunc("/notes/update/{id}", updateNote)
    r.HandleFunc("/notes/delete/{id}", deleteNote)

    server := &http.Server{
        Addr:    ":8080",
        Handler: r,
    }
    log.Println("Listening...")
    server.ListenAndServe()
}
```

Views and Template Definition Files

The web application provides the following HTML pages:

- Index shows the list of Note objects.

- Add is used to create a new Note.

- Edit is used to edit an existing Note object.

Four template definition files are created to render the HTML views:

- index.html: Template definition file for generating contents for the Index page.

- add.html: Template definition file for generating contents for the Add page.

- edit.html: Template definition file for generating contents for the Edit page.

- base.html: A nested template definition file used for generating all pages of the web application. You provide the appropriate content page for rendering each web page.

Listing 5-11 is the template definition file for base.html.

Listing 5-11. Template Definition in base.html

```
{{define "base"}}
<html>
  <head>{{template "head" .}}</head>
  <body>{{template "body" .}}</body>
</html>
{{end}}
```

Here a template called base is defined, in which the two templates are embedded. To render web pages, the base template is called every time the named templates "head" and "body" are provided from the content pages. For example, when the Index page is rendered, the template definition files from base.html and index.html are parsed, and the nested template defined in the "base" in base.html is executed and takes the contents for "head" and "body" from index.html.

Initializing View Templates

Template definition files have to be parsed before templates execute. Parsing the template definition files is a one-time activity; the files do not need to be parsed each time the templates execute. Here the files are parsed and put into a map in which each element represents the template file for rendering a particular page. Three HTML pages have to be generated, so three items are put into the map. The template definition files are parsed in the init function and are parsed with the Must helper function. Must is a helper that wraps a call to a function returning (*Template, error) and panics if the error is non-nil.

Listing 5-12 parses the template files with the Must helper function and puts it into the map.

Listing 5-12. Compiling View Template Files in init in main.go

```go
var templates map[string]*template.Template

//Compile view templates
func init() {
    if templates == nil {
        templates = make(map[string]*template.Template)
    }
    templates["index"] = template.Must(template.ParseFiles("templates/index.html",
    "templates/base.html"))
    templates["add"] = template.Must(template.ParseFiles("templates/add.html",
    "templates/base.html"))
    templates["edit"] = template.Must(template.ParseFiles("templates/edit.html",
    "templates/base.html"))
}
```

For each content page, the appropriate content file is parsed along with base.html. Listing 5-13 is a helper function that renders individual web pages.

Listing 5-13. Helper Function that Renders Templates in main.go

```go
//Render templates for the given name, template definition and data object
func renderTemplate(w http.ResponseWriter, name string, template string, viewModel interface{}) {
    // Ensure the template exists in the map.
    tmpl, ok := templates[name]
    if !ok {
        http.Error(w, "The template does not exist.", http.StatusInternalServerError)
    }
    err := tmpl.ExecuteTemplate(w, template, viewModel)
    if err != nil {
        http.Error(w, err.Error(), http.StatusInternalServerError)
    }
}
```

Here the parameter name is used as the key for retrieving the template file from the map, while the parameter template is used for providing the template name when we execute the template. The renderTemplate function provides the type interface{} as the type for the data object, so you can pass any type as the data object for applying into the template. The type interface{} is known as an "empty interface" that can hold values of any type. This type is very useful when you pass values to a function parameter when you don't know the type that you pass at runtime or you want to provide values of any type.

Rendering the Index Page

Let's render the Index page to show the list of Note objects. Listing 5-14 is the template definition in index.html.

Listing 5-14. Template Definition in index.html

```
{{define "head"}}<title>Index</title>{{end}}
{{define "body"}}
<h1>Notes List</h1>
```

```
<p>
<a href="/notes/add" >Add Note</a>
</p>
<div>
<table border="1">
    <tr>
        <th>Title</th>
        <th>Description</th>
        <th>Created On</th>
        <th>Actions</th>
    </tr>
    {{range $key,$value := . }}
    <tr>
        <td> {{$value.Title}}</td>
        <td>{{$value.Description}}</td>
        <td>{{$value.CreatedOn}}</td>
        <td>
            <a href="/notes/edit/{{$key}}" >Edit</a> |
            <a href="/notes/delete/{{$key}}" >Delete</a>
        </td>
    </tr>
{{end}}
</table>
</div>
{{end}}
```

Named definitions of two templates are defined: head and body. Both will be used by the base template defined in base.html. When the Index page is executed, the map object that contains the object of the Note struct in each element is passed. The range action is used to iterate through the map object. In the range action, two variables are declared for the key and value element that is referenced inside the range action. A range action must be closed with an end action.

When users request the route "/", the Index page is rendered by calling the getNotes request handler in main.go. Listing 5-15 shows the getNotes function.

Listing 5-15. Handler Function for Route "/" in main.go

```
func getNotes(w http.ResponseWriter, r *http.Request) {
    renderTemplate(w, "index", "base", noteStore)
}
```

In the getNotes handler function, the renderTemplate helper function is called for rendering the Index page. To call renderTemplate, the http.ResponseWriter object is provided as the io.Writer, the index for getting the parsed template for executing the Index page, the base for specifying the template definition to be executed, and the map object as the data object to apply to the template definitions.

When templates["index"] is called, you get the compiled template that was parsed by using the template definition files index.html and base.html. The base template definition is finally executed from the parsed template that is a nested template in which it takes the template definition from head and page defined in the index.html file.

Figure 5-2 shows the Index page with the list of Note objects.

Title	Description	Created On	Actions
text/template	Template generates textual output	2015-04-12 22:18:19.7258713 +0530 IST	Edit | Delete
html/template	Template generates HTML output	2015-04-12 22:20:13.1980519 +0530 IST	Edit | Delete

Figure 5-2. *Index page*

Note that Figure 5-2 shows the final result of the application after implementing all handler functions for the example web application. For the sake of the demo, a couple of values were added into the noteStore object.

Rendering the Add Page

The Add page is used to add new Note objects. add.html is used to provide contents for the head and body sections (see Listing 5-16).

Listing 5-16. Template Definitions in add.html

```
{{define "head"}}<title>Add Note</title>{{end}}
{{define "body"}}
<h1>Add Note</h1>
<form action="/notes/save" method="post">
    <p>Title:<br> <input type="text" name="title"></p>
    <p>Description:<br> <textarea rows="4" cols="50" name="description"></textarea> </p>
    <p><input type="submit" value="submit"/> </p>
</form>
{{end}}
```

When the HTTP server gets the request for the "/notes/add" route, it calls the addNote handler function (see Listing 5-17).

Listing 5-17. Handler Function for "/notes/add" in main.go

```
func addNote(w http.ResponseWriter, r *http.Request) {
    renderTemplate(w, "add", "base", nil)
}
```

The Add page is used to add a new Note object when you don't need to provide any data object to the template definition. So nil is passed as the data object. The string "add" is provided as the key of the map object for getting the parsed template, which was parsed by using the template definition files add.html and base.html, for rendering the Add page.

Figure 5-3 shows the Add page that provides the user interface for creating a new Note.

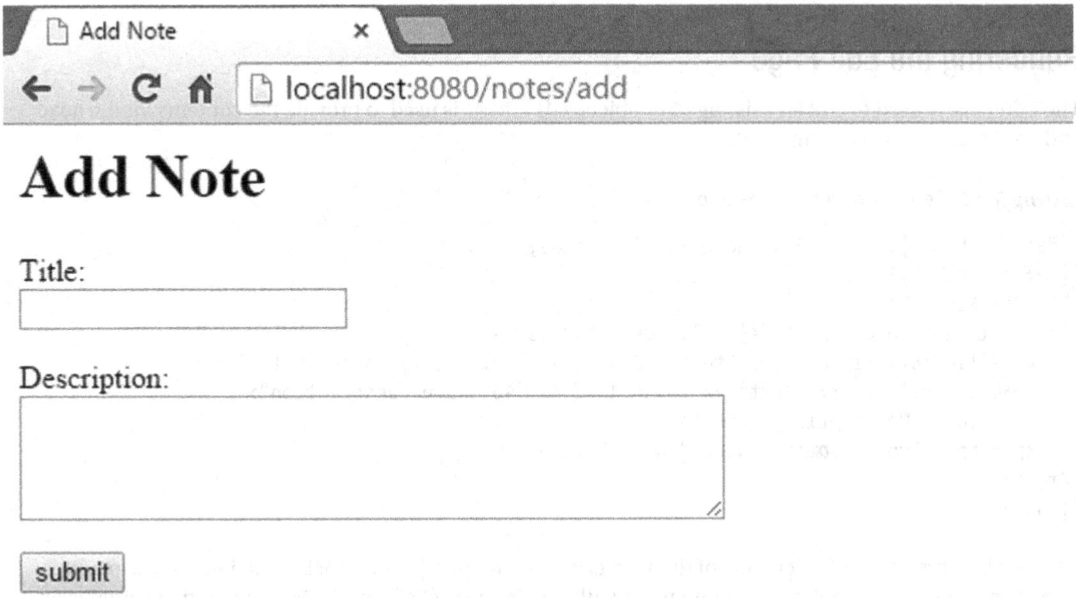

Figure 5-3. *Add page*

When the user submits the HTML form, an HTTP POST request is sent to the server for a URL "/notes/save" that will be handled by the handler function shown in Listing 5-18.

Listing 5-18. Handler Function to Save a New Note Object in main.go

```
//Handler for "/notes/save" for save a new item into the data store
func saveNote(w http.ResponseWriter, r *http.Request) {

    r.ParseForm()
    title := r.PostFormValue("title")
    desc := r.PostFormValue("description")
    note := Note{title, desc, time.Now()}
    //increment the value of id for generating key for the map
    id++
    //convert id value to string
    k := strconv.Itoa(id)
    noteStore[k] = note
    http.Redirect(w, r, "/", 302)
}
```

The saveHandler function parses the form values from the *http.Request object by calling the ParseForm method; then form field values are read by calling PostFormValue("element_name"). In Listing 5-18, the values are read from the HTML form elements title and description. The value of id is incremented for generating a key for the noteStore map object, and finally the newly added Note object is added into the noteStore map object with the key that was generated. The request is redirected to "/" for redirecting to the Index page, in which the newly added data can be seen.

Rendering the Edit Page

The Edit page is used to edit an existing Note object. edit.html is used to provide the contents for the head and body sections (see Listing 5-19).

Listing 5-19. Template Definitions in edit.html

```
{{define "head"}}<title>Edit Note</title>{{end}}
{{define "body"}}
<h1>Edit Note</h1>
<form action="/notes/update/{{.Id}}" method="post">
    <p>Title:<br> <input type="text" value="{{.Note.Title}}" name="title"></p>
    <p>Description:<br> <textarea rows="4" cols="50" name="description">
        {{.Note.Description}}</textarea> </p>
    <p><input type="submit" value="submit"/></p>
</form>
{{end}}
```

In edit.html, the data elements of the Note object are mapped with HTML form field values to edit an existing item. This template definition maps with the data object of the EditNote struct that contains an id for the item to be edited, along with the Note object for editing the fields of the Note object. When the template for rendering the Edit page is executed, an instance of the EditNote struct is provided as the data object (see Listing 5-20).

Listing 5-20. Data Model for Editing an Item

```
//View Model for edit
type EditNote struct {
    Note
    Id string
}
```

When the HTTP server gets the request for the "/notes/edit/{id}" route, it calls the editNote handler function (see Listing 5-21).

Listing 5-21. Handler Function for "/notes/edit/{id}" in main.go

```
//Handler for "/notes/edit/{id}" to edit an existing item
func editNote(w http.ResponseWriter, r *http.Request) {
    var viewModel EditNote
    //Read value from route variable
    vars := mux.Vars(r)
    k := vars["id"]
```

```
    if note, ok := noteStore[k]; ok {
        viewModel = EditNote{note, k}
    }else {
        http.Error(w, "Could not find the resource to edit.", http.StatusBadRequest)
    }
    renderTemplate(w, "edit", "base", viewModel)
}
```

An EditNote struct instance is provided as the data object to the template definition. The string "edit" is provided as the key of the map object for getting the parsed template, which was parsed by using template definition files edit.html and base.html, for rendering the Edit page.

Figure 5-4 shows the Edit page that provides the user interface to edit an existing Note.

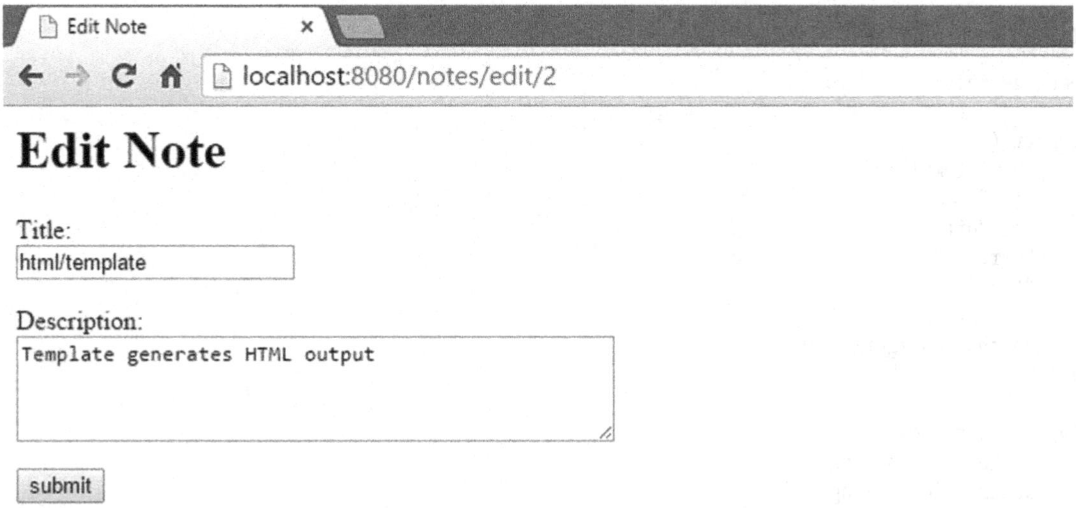

Figure 5-4. *Edit page*

When the user submits the HTML form after editing the values of the Note object, an HTTP POST request is sent to the server for a URL "/notes/update/{id}" that will be handled by the handler function shown in Listing 5-22.

Listing 5-22. Handler for "/notes/update/{id}" to Update an Existing Item in main.go

```
//Handler for "/notes/update/{id}" which update an item into the data store
func updateNote(w http.ResponseWriter, r *http.Request) {
    //Read value from route variable
    vars := mux.Vars(r)
    k := vars["id"]
    var noteToUpd Note
    if note, ok := noteStore[k]; ok {
        r.ParseForm()
        noteToUpd.Title = r.PostFormValue("title")
        noteToUpd.Description = r.PostFormValue("description")
        noteToUpd.CreatedOn = note.CreatedOn
```

```
        //delete existing item and add the updated item
        delete(noteStore, k)
        noteStore[k] = noteToUpd
    } else {
        http.Error(w, "Could not find the resource to update.", http.StatusBadRequest)
    }
    http.Redirect(w, r, "/", 302)
}
```

Similar to adding a new Note object in Listing 5-18, the form field values from the *http.Request object are parsed, and the values of the Note object are updated. The request is then redirected to "/" for redirecting to the Index page, in which the updated values can be seen.

The full source of main.go is provided in Listing 5-23.

Listing 5-23. main.go

```go
package main

import (
    "html/template"
    "log"
    "net/http"
    "strconv"
    "time"

    "github.com/gorilla/mux"
)

type Note struct {
    Title       string
    Description string
    CreatedOn   time.Time
}

//View Model for edit
type EditNote struct {
    Note
    Id string
}

//Store for the Notes collection
var noteStore = make(map[string]Note)

//Variable to generate key for the collection
var id int = 0

var templates map[string]*template.Template
```

```go
//Compile view templates
func init() {
    if templates == nil {
        templates = make(map[string]*template.Template)
    }
    templates["index"] = template.Must(template.ParseFiles("templates/index.html",
    "templates/base.html"))
    templates["add"] = template.Must(template.ParseFiles("templates/add.html",
    "templates/base.html"))
    templates["edit"] = template.Must(template.ParseFiles("templates/edit.html",
    "templates/base.html"))
}

//Render templates for the given name, template definition and data object
func renderTemplate(w http.ResponseWriter, name string, template string, viewModel
interface{}) {
    // Ensure the template exists in the map.
    tmpl, ok := templates[name]
    if !ok {
        http.Error(w, "The template does not exist.", http.StatusInternalServerError)
    }
    err := tmpl.ExecuteTemplate(w, template, viewModel)
    if err != nil {
        http.Error(w, err.Error(), http.StatusInternalServerError)
    }
}

//Handler for "/notes/save" for save a new item into the data store
func saveNote(w http.ResponseWriter, r *http.Request) {

    r.ParseForm()
    title := r.PostFormValue("title")
    desc := r.PostFormValue("description")
    note := Note{title, desc, time.Now()}
    //increment the value of id for generating key for the map
    id++
    //convert id value to string
    k := strconv.Itoa(id)
    noteStore[k] = note
    http.Redirect(w, r, "/", 302)
}

//Handler for "/notes/add" for add a new item
func addNote(w http.ResponseWriter, r *http.Request) {
    renderTemplate(w, "add", "base", nil)
}
```

```go
//Handler for "/notes/edit/{id}" to edit an existing item
func editNote(w http.ResponseWriter, r *http.Request) {
    var viewModel EditNote
    //Read value from route variable
    vars := mux.Vars(r)
    k := vars["id"]
    if note, ok := noteStore[k]; ok {
        viewModel = EditNote{note, k}
    } else {
        http.Error(w, "Could not find the resource to edit.", http.StatusBadRequest)
    }
    renderTemplate(w, "edit", "base", viewModel)
}

//Handler for "/notes/update/{id}" which update an item into the data store
func updateNote(w http.ResponseWriter, r *http.Request) {
    //Read value from route variable
    vars := mux.Vars(r)
    k := vars["id"]
    var noteToUpd Note
    if note, ok := noteStore[k]; ok {
        r.ParseForm()
        noteToUpd.Title = r.PostFormValue("title")
        noteToUpd.Description = r.PostFormValue("description")
        noteToUpd.CreatedOn = note.CreatedOn
        //delete existing item and add the updated item
        delete(noteStore, k)
        noteStore[k] = noteToUpd
    } else {
        http.Error(w, "Could not find the resource to update.", http.StatusBadRequest)
    }
    http.Redirect(w, r, "/", 302)
}

//Handler for "/notes/delete/{id}" which delete an item form the store
func deleteNote(w http.ResponseWriter, r *http.Request) {
    //Read value from route variable
    vars := mux.Vars(r)
    k := vars["id"]
    // Remove from Store
    if _, ok := noteStore[k]; ok {
        //delete existing item
        delete(noteStore, k)
    } else {
        http.Error(w, "Could not find the resource to delete.", http.StatusBadRequest)
    }
    http.Redirect(w, r, "/", 302)
}
```

```
//Handler for "/" which render the index page
func getNotes(w http.ResponseWriter, r *http.Request) {
    renderTemplate(w, "index", "base", noteStore)
}

//Entry point of the program
func main() {

    r := mux.NewRouter().StrictSlash(false)
    fs := http.FileServer(http.Dir("public"))
    r.Handle("/public/", fs)
    r.HandleFunc("/", getNotes)
    r.HandleFunc("/notes/add", addNote)
    r.HandleFunc("/notes/save", saveNote)
    r.HandleFunc("/notes/edit/{id}", editNote)
    r.HandleFunc("/notes/update/{id}", updateNote)
    r.HandleFunc("/notes/delete/{id}", deleteNote)

    server := &http.Server{
        Addr:    ":8080",
        Handler: r,
    }
    log.Println("Listening...")
    server.ListenAndServe()
}
```

In this example, a full web application was completed in Go by leveraging the standard library package html/template for rendering the user interfaces with dynamic data. Template definition files are parsed and put into a map object so that you can easily get the parsed template files whenever you want to execute the templates. This approach allows you to avoid parsing the template files every time the templates are executed, which improves web application performance. By leveraging the various techniques shown in this example application, you can build real-world web applications.

Summary

This chapter showed how to work with Go templates by developing a web application. When you work with data-driven web applications, you have to leverage templates to render HTML pages in which you can combine static contents with dynamic contents by applying a data object to the templates.

The html/template package is used to render HTML pages. It also provides a security mechanism against various code injections while rendering the HTML output. Both html/template and text/template provide the same interface for the template authors, in which html/template generates HTML output, and text/template generates textual output. By leveraging the standard library packages net/http and html/template, you can build full-fledged web applications in Go.

CHAPTER 6

■ ■ ■

HTTP Middleware

The last two chapters explored various aspects of building web applications and web APIs. This chapter takes a look at HTTP middleware, which simplifies development efforts when real-world web applications are built. The Go developer community has not been too interested in adopting full-fledged web application frameworks for building web applications. Instead, they prefer to use standard library packages such as the fundamental block, along with a few essential third-party libraries such as Gorilla mux. Writing and using HTTP middleware is an essential approach for staying with this strategy. You can implement many cross-cutting behaviors such as security, HTTP request and response logging, compressing HTTP responses, and caching as middleware components; and these middleware components can be applied to many application handlers or across-the-application handlers.

Introduction to HTTP Middleware

When you build web applications, you might need some shared functionality to be executed for some or all HTTP request handlers. For example, let's say that you want to log all HTTP requests into a web server; implementing logic for logging for every HTTP request handler would be a tedious job. It would be great to use special kinds of handlers to implement shared behaviors and to be applied to some or all of the application handlers. By using HTTP middleware, you can implement this kind of functionality into your web applications. Using HTTP middleware handlers is a great way to implement shared behaviors into your applications.

Middleware is a pluggable and self-contained piece of code that wraps a web application. It can be used to implement shared behaviors into HTTP request handlers. The middleware components can be plugged into applications to work as another layer in the request-handling cycle, which can execute some logic before or after HTTP request handlers. For example, to log all HTTP requests, you can write logging middleware that can decorate into the request handlers, in which it does apply the logging functionality for each HTTP request to the web server. It doesn't affect your application logic because it is an independent piece of code. You can decorate the middleware components into HTTP request handlers whenever you need to, and you can remove them whenever you don't need them.

Here are some example scenarios in which you can use middleware:

- Logging HTTP requests and responses

- Compressing HTTP responses

- Writing common response headers

- Creating database session objects

- Implementing security and validating authentication credentials

Writing HTTP Middleware

The Go standard library package net/http provides functions such as StripPrefix and TimeoutHandler, which are similar to middleware: they wrap request handlers and provide additional implementations in the request-handling cycle. Both StripPrefix and TimeoutHandler take http.Handler as a parameter, along with other parameters, and return an http.Handler so that you can easily wrap this into normal handlers to execute some additional logic. The StripPrefix function takes a string prefix and an http.Handler as parameters, and returns a handler that serves HTTP requests by removing the given prefix from the request URL's path (see Listing 6-1).

Listing 6-1. Using StripPrefix to Wrap the http.FileServer Handler

```
package main

import (
        "net/http"
)

func main() {
        // To serve a directory on disk (/public) under an alternate URL
        // path (/public/), use StripPrefix to modify the request
        // URL's path before the FileServer sees it:
        fs := http.FileServer(http.Dir("public"))
        http.Handle("/public/", http.StripPrefix("/public/", fs))
}
```

The StripPrefix function wraps the http.FileServer handler and provides extra functionality because it modifies the request URL's path by removing the given prefix from the request URL's path and invoking the given handler object.

Listing 6-2 is the Go source code for the StripPrefix function.

Listing 6-2. Source of StripPrefix from the net/http Library

```
func StripPrefix(prefix string, h Handler) Handler {
        if prefix == "" {
                return h
        }
        return HandlerFunc(func(w ResponseWriter, r *Request) {
                if p := strings.TrimPrefix(r.URL.Path, prefix); len(p) < len(r.URL.Path) {
                        r.URL.Path = p
                        h.ServeHTTP(w, r)
                } else {
                        NotFound(w, r)
                }
        })
}
```

The StripPrefix function returns an http.Handler object by converting an anonymous function with the signature func(w ResponseWriter, r *Request), into the HandlerFunc func. When you write wrapper handler functions, you can execute additional logic before or after the normal handler function. In the StripPrefix function, the http library executes the logic before executing the normal handler. The function invokes the given handler (the application handler or another wrapper handler) by calling the ServeHTTP method:

```
if p := strings.TrimPrefix(r.URL.Path, prefix); len(p) < len(r.URL.Path) {
        r.URL.Path = p
        h.ServeHTTP(w, r)
} else {
        NotFound(w, r)
}
```

You can easily write HTTP middleware in the same way as the http package implements wrapper handler functions. You can write middleware functions by implementing functions with the signature func(http.Handler) http.Handler. If you want to pass any values into the middleware functions, you can provide the same as function parameters along with http.Handler, as the StripPrefix function does in the http package.

How to Write HTTP Middleware

The fundamental steps of writing HTTP middleware are as follows:

1.   Write a function with http.Handler as a function parameter so that you can pass other middleware handlers and normal application handlers as the function parameter. You can invoke the handler functions by calling the ServeHTTP method within the middleware functions.

2.   Return http.Handler from the middleware function to chain with other middleware handlers and wrap with normal application handlers. Because middleware functions return http.Handler, you can register this with the ServeMux object.

Listing 6-3 shows the pattern for writing HTTP middleware.

Listing 6-3. Pattern for Writing Middleware

```
func middlewareHandler(next http.Handler) http.Handler {
  return http.HandlerFunc(func(w http.ResponseWriter, r *http.Request) {
    // Middleware logic goes here before executing application handler
    next.ServeHTTP(w, r)
    // Middleware logic goes here after executing application handler
  })
}
```

Writing a Logging Middleware

Let's write an HTTP middleware to log all HTTP requests so that this behavior can be applied into multiple application handlers.

Listing 6-4 is an example of logging middleware.

Listing 6-4. Logging Middleware

```go
package main

import (
    "fmt"
    "log"
    "net/http"
    "time"
)

func loggingHandler(next http.Handler) http.Handler {
    return http.HandlerFunc(func(w http.ResponseWriter, r *http.Request) {
        start := time.Now()
        log.Printf("Started %s %s", r.Method, r.URL.Path)
        next.ServeHTTP(w, r)
        log.Printf("Completed %s in %v", r.URL.Path, time.Since(start))
    })
}
func index(w http.ResponseWriter, r *http.Request) {
    log.Println("Executing index handler")
    fmt.Fprintf(w, "Welcome!")
}
func about(w http.ResponseWriter, r *http.Request) {
    log.Println("Executing about handler")
    fmt.Fprintf(w, "Go Middleware")
}
func iconHandler(w http.ResponseWriter, r *http.Request) {
}
func main() {
    http.HandleFunc("/favicon.ico", iconHandler)
    indexHandler := http.HandlerFunc(index)
    aboutHandler := http.HandlerFunc(about)
    http.Handle("/", loggingHandler(indexHandler))
    http.Handle("/about", loggingHandler(aboutHandler))
    server := &http.Server{
        Addr: ":8080",
    }
    log.Println("Listening...")
    server.ListenAndServe()
}
```

Run this program and make a request to "/" and "/about". You should get a log output similar to this:

```
2015/04/25 19:40:10 Started GET /
2015/04/25 19:40:10 Executing index handler
2015/04/25 19:40:10 Completed / in 0
2015/04/25 19:40:18 Started GET /about
2015/04/25 19:40:18 Executing about handler
2015/04/25 19:40:18 Completed /about in 1.0005ms
```

In the previous program, loggingHandler is the HTTP middleware that decorates into the application handlers for the "/" and "/about" routes. Middleware allows you to reuse the shared behavior functionality onto multiple handlers. In the logging middleware handler, the log messages are written before and after executing the application handler. The middleware function logs the HTTP method and URL path of the requests before invoking the application handler, and logs the time it takes to execute the application handler after executing the application handler. By calling next.ServeHTTP(w, r), the middleware function can execute the application handler function:

```go
func loggingHandler(next http.Handler) http.Handler {
    return http.HandlerFunc(func(w http.ResponseWriter, r *http.Request) {
        start := time.Now()
        log.Printf("Started %s %s", r.Method, r.URL.Path)
        next.ServeHTTP(w, r)
        log.Printf("Completed %s in %v", r.URL.Path, time.Since(start))
    })
}
```

The application handler functions are converted to the HandlerFunc func type and passed into the logging middleware handler function:

```go
indexHandler := http.HandlerFunc(index)
aboutHandler := http.HandlerFunc(about)
http.Handle("/", loggingHandler(indexHandler))
http.Handle("/about", loggingHandler(aboutHandler))
```

Controlling the Flow of HTTP Middleware

Because HTTP middleware handler functions take http.Handler as a function parameter and return an http.Handler, you can easily chain with other middleware handlers and finally call the application handler. It is important to understand the control flow of middleware handlers when you chain with other middleware handlers. Let's write a couple of middleware handlers and wrap this into application handlers.

Listing 6-5 illustrates the control flow of middleware handlers.

Listing 6-5. Control Flow of Middleware Handlers

```go
package main

import (
    "fmt"
    "log"
    "net/http"
)

func middlewareFirst(next http.Handler) http.Handler {
    return http.HandlerFunc(func(w http.ResponseWriter, r *http.Request) {
        log.Println("MiddlewareFirst - Before Handler")
        next.ServeHTTP(w, r)
        log.Println("MiddlewareFirst - After Handler")
    })
}
```

```go
func middlewareSecond(next http.Handler) http.Handler {
    return http.HandlerFunc(func(w http.ResponseWriter, r *http.Request) {
        log.Println("MiddlewareSecond - Before Handler")
        if r.URL.Path == "/message" {
            if r.URL.Query().Get("password") == "pass123" {
                log.Println("Authorized to the system")
                next.ServeHTTP(w, r)
            } else {
                log.Println("Failed to authorize to the system")
                return
            }
        } else {
            next.ServeHTTP(w, r)
        }

        log.Println("MiddlewareSecond - After Handler")
    })
}

func index(w http.ResponseWriter, r *http.Request) {
    log.Println("Executing index Handler")
    fmt.Fprintf(w, "Welcome")
}
func message(w http.ResponseWriter, r *http.Request) {
    log.Println("Executing message Handler")
    fmt.Fprintf(w, "HTTP Middleware is awesome")
}

func iconHandler(w http.ResponseWriter, r *http.Request) {
}
func main() {

    http.HandleFunc("/favicon.ico", iconHandler)
    http.Handle("/", middlewareFirst(middlewareSecond(http.HandlerFunc(index))))
    http.Handle("/message", middlewareFirst(middlewareSecond(http.HandlerFunc(message))))
    server := &http.Server{
        Addr: ":8080",
    }
    log.Println("Listening...")
    server.ListenAndServe()
}
```

Run this program and make a request to "http://localhost:8080/". You should get the following output:

```
2015/04/30 11:10:53 MiddlewareFirst - Before Handler

2015/04/30 11:10:53 MiddlewareSecond - Before Handler

2015/04/30 11:10:53 Executing index Handler

2015/04/30 11:10:53 MiddlewareSecond - After Handler

2015/04/30 11:10:53 MiddlewareFirst - After Handler
```

When you make a request for "http://localhost:8080/message" by providing the wrong value for the querystring variable password (let's say you provide "http://localhost:8080/message?password= wrongpass"), you should get the following output:

```
2015/04/30 11:11:06 MiddlewareFirst - Before Handler

2015/04/30 11:11:06 MiddlewareSecond - Before Handler

2015/04/30 11:11:06 Failed to authorize to the system

2015/04/30 11:11:06 MiddlewareFirst - After Handler
```

When you make a request for "http://localhost:8080/message" by providing the correct value for the querystring variable password ("http://localhost:8080/message?password=pass123"), you should get the following output:

```
2015/04/30 11:11:35 MiddlewareFirst - Before Handler

2015/04/30 11:11:35 MiddlewareSecond - Before Handler

2015/04/30 11:11:35 Authorized to the system

2015/04/30 11:11:35 Executing message Handler

2015/04/30 11:11:35 MiddlewareSecond - After Handler

2015/04/30 11:11:35 MiddlewareFirst - After Handler
```

You can easily understand the control flow of middleware handlers by looking at the log messages generated by the program. Here middlewareFirst and middlewareSecond are called as the wrapper handlers; you can apply this into the application handler. In the middleware function middlewareSecond, the value of the querystring variable password is validated if the request URL path is "/message".

Here is the control flow that happens when the program is run and you make requests to the "/" and "/message" routes:

1. The control flow goes to the middlewareFirst middleware function.

2. After a log message is written (before executing the next handler) in the middlewareFirst function, the control flow goes to the middlewareSecond middleware function when next.ServeHTTP(w, r) is called.

3. After a log message is written (before executing the next handler) in the middlewareSecond function, the control flow goes to the application handler when next.ServeHTTP(w, r) is called:

    a. If the request URL path is "/", the index application handler is invoked without any authorization.

    b. If the request URL path is "/message", the middleware function validates the request with the querystring variable password. If you do not provide the value "pass123" for the querystring variable password, the control flow returns from the middleware function and goes back to the middlewareFirst function, invokes the logic after the next.ServeHTTP(w, r) code block, and then returns from the request-handling cycle without executing the application handler. If the request gets validated, the control flow goes to the application handler message when next.ServeHTTP(w, r) is called.

4. After invoking the application handler from the middlewareSecond function (if the request gets validated), the control flow goes back to the middlewareSecond function and invokes the logic after the next.ServeHTTP(w, r) code block.

5. After returning from the middlewareSecond handler, the control flow goes back to the middlewareFirst function and invokes the logic after the next.ServeHTTP(w, r) code block.

You can exit from middleware handler chains at any time, as the middlewareSecond handler does if the request is not valid. In this context, the control flow goes back to the previous handler if there is any handler in the request-handling cycle. When "/message" is requested without any valid querystring value, the application handler will not be invoked when you return from the middleware handler. The most important thing is that you can execute some logic before or after invoking a middleware handler function.

Using Third-Party Middleware

Using middleware is a great way to implement a reusable piece of code across applications. Many third-party libraries provide different kinds of reusable middleware components that can be used for many common functionalities such as authentication, logging, compressing responses, and so on. When you develop web applications in Go, you can leverage these third-party libraries to implement many of the common functionalities into your applications.

Using Gorilla Handlers

The Gorilla web toolkit (www.gorillatoolkit.org/) provides a collection of handlers for use with Go's net/http package. Let's write a program to use Gorilla's LoggingHandler and CompressHandler for logging HTTP requests and compressing HTTP responses.

Installing Gorilla Handlers

To install Gorilla handlers, run the following command in the terminal:

```
$ go get github.com/gorilla/handlers
```

Working with Gorilla Handlers

To work with Gorilla handlers, you must add github.com/gorilla/handlers to the import list:

```
import "github.com/gorilla/handlers"
```

Listing 6-6 shows Gorilla's logging and compression handlers.

Listing 6-6. Using Gorilla's Logging and Compression Handlers

```go
package main

import (
    "fmt"
    "log"
    "net/http"
    "os"

    "github.com/gorilla/handlers"
)

func index(w http.ResponseWriter, r *http.Request) {
    log.Println("Executing index handler")
    fmt.Fprintf(w, "Welcome!")
}
func about(w http.ResponseWriter, r *http.Request) {
    log.Println("Executing about handler")
    fmt.Fprintf(w, "Go Middleware")
}
func iconHandler(w http.ResponseWriter, r *http.Request) {
}
func main() {
    http.HandleFunc("/favicon.ico", iconHandler)
    indexHandler := http.HandlerFunc(index)
    aboutHandler := http.HandlerFunc(about)
    logFile, err := os.OpenFile("server.log", os.O_WRONLY|os.O_CREATE|os.O_APPEND, 0666)
    if err != nil {
        panic(err)
    }
    http.Handle("/", handlers.LoggingHandler(logFile, handlers.CompressHandler(indexHandler)))
    http.Handle("/about", handlers.LoggingHandler(logFile, handlers.CompressHandler(
    aboutHandler)))
    server := &http.Server{
        Addr: ":8080",
    }
    log.Println("Listening...")
    server.ListenAndServe()
}
```

Similar to Listing 6-5, handler chaining is done with LoggingHandler and CompressHandler, and then wraps into application handlers. This program does the logging for requests and compresses the responses using gzip or Deflate. The log file is provided as "server.log", so you can see the logging in this file. Run the program and make requests to "/" and "/about". You should get the following log in the "server.log" file:

> **::1 - - [26/Apr/2015:16:42:41 +0530] "GET / HTTP/1.1" 200 32**

> **::1 - - [26/Apr/2015:16:42:45 +0530] "GET /about HTTP/1.1" 200 37**

You can see the log messages that include HTTP status code as well.

Middleware Chaining with the Alice Package

The third-party Alice library package (https://github.com/justinas/alice) provides a convenient way to chain HTTP middleware functions and the application handler. The program shown in Listing 6-5 chained HTTP middleware functions as follows:

```
http.Handle("/", middlewareFirst(middlewareSecond(http.HandlerFunc(index))))
```

By using the Alice package, you can transform the preceding handler chains to the following:

```
http.Handle("/",alice.New(middlewareFirst, middlewareSecond).ThenFunc(http.HandlerFunc(index)))
```

This process is an elegant way to chain middleware functions and decorate them with application handlers.

Installing Alice

To install Alice, run the following command in the terminal:

$ go get github.com/justinas/alice

Working with Alice

To work with the Alice package, github.com/justinas/alice must be added to the import list:

import "github.com/ justinas/alice"

Let's rewrite the program shown in Listing 6-6 with the Alice package (see Listing 6-7).

Listing 6-7. Chaining Middleware Functions with the Alice Package

```
package main

import (
    "io"
    "log"
    "net/http"
    "os"

    "github.com/gorilla/handlers"
    "github.com/justinas/alice"
)

func loggingHandler(next http.Handler) http.Handler {
    logFile, err := os.OpenFile("server.log", os.O_WRONLY|os.O_CREATE|os.O_APPEND, 0777)
    if err != nil {
        panic(err)
    }
    return handlers.LoggingHandler(logFile, next)
}
```

```go
func index(w http.ResponseWriter, r *http.Request) {

    w.Header().Set(
        "Content-Type",
        "text/html",
    )
    io.WriteString(
        w,
        `<doctype html>
    <html>
        <head>
            <title>Index</title>
        </head>
        <body>
            Hello Gopher!
        </body>
    </html>`,
    )

}
func about(w http.ResponseWriter, r *http.Request) {
    w.Header().Set(
        "Content-Type",
        "text/html",
    )
    io.WriteString(
        w,
        `<doctype html>
    <html>
        <head>
            <title>About</title>
        </head>
        <body>
            Go Web development with HTTP Middleware
        </body>
    </html>`,
    )
}
func iconHandler(w http.ResponseWriter, r *http.Request) {
    http.ServeFile(w, r, "./favicon.ico")
}
func main() {
    http.HandleFunc("/favicon.ico", iconHandler)
    indexHandler := http.HandlerFunc(index)
    aboutHandler := http.HandlerFunc(about)
    commonHandlers := alice.New(loggingHandler, handlers.CompressHandler)
    http.Handle("/", commonHandlers.ThenFunc(indexHandler))
    http.Handle("/about", commonHandlers.ThenFunc(aboutHandler))
    server := &http.Server{
        Addr: ":8080",
    }
```

```
    log.Println("Listening...")
    server.ListenAndServe()
}
```

In this program, two Gorilla handlers are used for logging requests and compressing responses: LoggingHandler and CompressHandler. The HTML string is provided in the responses to verify the compression impact of the HTTP responses. Run the program, make requests to "/" and "/about", and watch the log file and HTTP responses.

Figure 6-1 shows the screenshot in Fiddler: an HTTP debugging tool showing that the web responses are compressing with gzip encoding.

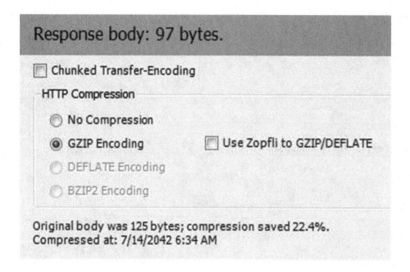

Figure 6-1. *Compressing HTTP responses with a Gorilla handler*

Chaining middleware functions can be done in an elegant way using the Alice package, which makes it easy to understand code blocks. Gorilla's LoggingHandler does not have the signature func (http.Handler) http.Handler, and it takes a log file as a function parameter along with the http.Handler. So by working properly with the Alice package and using this handler in multiple places, you can write a middleware function for logging, in which the Gorilla LoggingHandler is called by providing the log file as the parameter. This is a good approach whenever a middleware function is needed with multiple function parameters:

```
func loggingHandler(next http.Handler) http.Handler {
    logFile, err := os.OpenFile("server.log", os.O_WRONLY|os.O_CREATE|os.O_APPEND, 0777)
    if err != nil {
        panic(err)
    }
    return handlers.LoggingHandler(logFile, next)
}
```

The loggingHandler middleware function can be used with Alice, which calls the Gorilla LoggingHandler function with necessary arguments. When you use middleware handlers, you might need to decorate multiple middleware handlers into several application handlers. In this context, you can create common handlers with Alice by combining with multiple middleware handlers, and it can apply to multiple application handlers.

Here commonHandlers is defined as the common handlers for use with multiple application handlers:

```
indexHandler := http.HandlerFunc(index)
aboutHandler := http.HandlerFunc(about)
commonHandlers := alice.New(loggingHandler, handlers.CompressHandler)
http.Handle("/", commonHandlers.ThenFunc(indexHandler))
http.Handle("/about", commonHandlers.ThenFunc(aboutHandler))
```

The Alice package provides a fluent API for working with middleware functions that allows you to chain middleware functions in an elegant way. The Alice package is a very lightweight library that has fewer than 100 lines of code.

Using Middleware with the Negroni Package

When you work directly with the net/http package to build web applications, the Negroni third-party library is a great companion for you. Negroni is a library that is designed to be compatible with the net/http package. Negroni provides an idiomatic approach to using HTTP middleware in Go. It encourages you to use net/http handlers while providing a way to handle HTTP middleware functions.

The previous section discussed the Alice package, which is great for chaining middleware handlers. Negroni provides a different approach for handling HTTP middleware functions in a simple and nonintrusive way. If you prefer to use Alice for handling middleware functions, you can stick with it because both Alice and Negroni solve the same problems in a slightly different way. Negroni provides a full-fledged library for working with middleware functions, which also comes with some common middleware functions for logging requests and compressing responses, providing static file server and recovery from panics.

Negroni allows you to configure middleware functions at a global level to be used with all application handlers. You can also configure middleware functions for working with specific handlers. When you use middleware functions with all application handlers, you don't need to configure it for every application handler. Instead, you can just configure the middleware function with Negroni, which will wrap the configured middleware functions into all application handlers. You can also configure some middleware functions to be executed with some specific application handlers.

Getting Started with Negroni

Negroni provides a simple programming model for working with middleware handlers. When you work with it, you can also use its default middleware functions. Let's install and write a simple program to get started with the Negroni package.

Installing Negroni

To install Negroni, run the following command in the terminal:

```
$ go get github.com/codegangsta/negroni
```

To work with the Negroni package, the github.com/codegangsta/negroni package must be added to the import list:

```
import "github.com/codegangsta/negroni"
```

Listing 6-8 is an example program using Negroni:

Listing 6-8. Simple HTTP Server with Negroni

```
package main

import (
    "fmt"
    "net/http"

    "github.com/codegangsta/negroni"
)

func index(w http.ResponseWriter, req *http.Request) {
    fmt.Fprintf(w, "Welcome!")
}
func main() {
    mux := http.NewServeMux()
    mux.HandleFunc("/", index)
    n := negroni.Classic()
    n.UseHandler(mux)
    n.Run(":8080")
}
```

In this program, you don't use your own middleware functions; you simply run an HTTP server with the Negroni default middleware functions. A Negroni instance is created by calling the negroni.Classic function.

When a Negroni instance is created with the Classic function, it provides the following built-in middleware functions, which are useful for most web applications:

- negroni.Recovery: Panic recovery middleware

- negroni.Logging: Request/response logging middleware

- negroni.Static: Static file serving under the "public" directory

Negroni instances can also be created by calling the negroni.New function, which returns a new Negroni instance without any middleware preconfigured:

n := negroni.New()

The Run method of a Negroni instance is a convenience function that runs the Negroni stack as an HTTP server. The address string takes the same format as http.ListenAndServe:

n.Run(":8080")

Routing with Negroni

The UseHandler method of a Negroni instance allows you to provide your own http.Handler onto the middleware stack.

Listing 6-9 is an example program that uses Gorilla mux as the request multiplexer with the Negroni package.

Listing 6-9. Simple HTTP Server with Negroni and Gorilla mux

```
package main

import (
    "fmt"
    "net/http"

    "github.com/codegangsta/negroni"
    "github.com/gorilla/mux"
)

func index(w http.ResponseWriter, req *http.Request) {
    fmt.Fprintf(w, "Welcome!")
}
func main() {
    router := mux.NewRouter()
    router.HandleFunc("/", index)
    n := negroni.Classic()
    n.UseHandler(router)
    n.Run(":8080")
}
```

The Gorilla Mux.Router object is provided as the handler to be used with Negroni. You can provide any object of the http.Handler interface to the UseHandler method of the Negroni instance.

Registering Middleware

Negroni manages middleware flow through the negroni.Handler interface.

Listing 6-10 shows the definition of the negroni.Handler interface:

Listing 6-10. negroni.Handler Interface

```
type Handler interface {
  ServeHTTP(rw http.ResponseWriter, r *http.Request, next http.HandlerFunc)
}
```

Listing 6-11 provides the pattern for writing middleware handler functions for Negroni to work with the negroni.Handler interface.

Listing 6-11. negroni.Handler Interface

```
func myMiddleware(w http.ResponseWriter, r *http.Request, next http.HandlerFunc) {
    // logic before executing the next handler
    next(w, r)
    // logic after running next the handler

}
```

The function signature of a Negroni-compatible middleware function is different from the functions written in the previous sections. The Negroni middleware stack uses the following signature to write middleware functions:

```
func myMiddleware(w http.ResponseWriter, r *http.Request, next http.HandlerFunc)
```

Here you can call the next handler in the middleware stack by invoking the http.HandlerFunc object by passing the values of the http.ResponseWriter object and the *http.Request object:

```
// logic before executing the next handler
  next(w, r)
  // logic after running next the handler
```

You can map the middleware function to the Negroni handler chain with the Use function, which takes an argument of negroni.Handler. The Use function adds a negroni.Handler into the middleware stack (see Listing 6-12). Handlers are invoked in the order in which they are added to a Negroni instance.

Listing 6-12. Registering a Middleware Function with Negroni

```
n := negroni.New()
n.Use(negroni.HandlerFunc(myMiddleware))
```

The middleware function is converted into a negroni.HandlerFunc type and added to the Negroni middleware stack. HandlerFunc is an adapter that allows ordinary functions to be used as Negroni handlers.

Registering Middleware for Specific Routes

When middleware functions such as logging are used, they might be decorated with across-the-application handlers. But you may need to use middleware functions for some specific routes; for example, you might want to apply some middleware functions to be executed with some specific application handlers that will be accessible to an administrator user account. In this context, you can create a new Negroni instance and use it as your route handler.

Listing 6-13 is the code block that applies middleware functions to be used with some specific routes.

Listing 6-13. Registering Middleware Handlers for Specific Routes

```
router := mux.NewRouter()
adminRoutes := mux.NewRouter()
// add admin routes here

// Create a new negroni for the admin middleware
router.Handle("/admin", negroni.New(
  Middleware1,
  Middleware2,
  negroni.Wrap(adminRoutes),
))
```

Working with a Negroni Middleware Stack

Listing 6-5 showed the control flow of middleware functions in which two middleware functions have been decorated into application handlers. Let's rewrite the program to show how to write custom middleware functions with Negroni (see Listing 6-14).

Listing 6-14. Illustrating Middleware Control Flow with Negroni

```go
package main

import (
    "fmt"
    "log"
    "net/http"

    "github.com/codegangsta/negroni"
)

func middlewareFirst(w http.ResponseWriter, r *http.Request, next http.HandlerFunc) {
    log.Println("MiddlewareFirst - Before Handler")
    next(w, r)
    log.Println("MiddlewareFirst - After Handler")
}

func middlewareSecond(w http.ResponseWriter, r *http.Request, next http.HandlerFunc) {
    log.Println("MiddlewareSecond - Before Handler")
    if r.URL.Path == "/message" {
        if r.URL.Query().Get("password") == "pass123" {
            log.Println("Authorized to the system")
            next(w, r)
        } else {
            log.Println("Failed to authorize to the system")
            return
        }
    } else {
        next(w, r)
    }
    log.Println("MiddlewareSecond - After Handler")
}

func index(w http.ResponseWriter, r *http.Request) {
    log.Println("Executing index Handler")
    fmt.Fprintf(w, "Welcome")
}
func message(w http.ResponseWriter, r *http.Request) {
    log.Println("Executing message Handler")
    fmt.Fprintf(w, "HTTP Middleware is awesome")
}

func iconHandler(w http.ResponseWriter, r *http.Request) {
}
```

```go
func main() {
    mux := http.NewServeMux()
    mux.HandleFunc("/favicon.ico", iconHandler)
    mux.HandleFunc("/", index)
    mux.HandleFunc("/message", message)
    n := negroni.Classic()
    n.Use(negroni.HandlerFunc(middlewareFirst))
    n.Use(negroni.HandlerFunc(middlewareSecond))
    n.UseHandler(mux)
    n.Run(":8080")
}
```

Run the program and make requests to "/", and make requests to "/message" by providing the wrong value to the querystring variable password and providing the value "pass123" to the querystring variable password, respectively. You should get log messages similar to these:

> **[negroni] listening on :8080**
>
> **[negroni] Started GET /**
>
> **2015/04/30 14:45:44 MiddlewareFirst - Before Handler**
>
> **2015/04/30 14:45:44 MiddlewareSecond - Before Handler**
>
> **2015/04/30 14:45:44 Executing index Handler**
>
> **2015/04/30 14:45:44 MiddlewareSecond - After Handler**
>
> **2015/04/30 14:45:44 MiddlewareFirst - After Handler**
>
> **[negroni] Completed 200 OK in 1.0008ms**
>
> **[negroni] Started GET /message**
>
> **2015/04/30 14:45:52 MiddlewareFirst - Before Handler**
>
> **2015/04/30 14:45:52 MiddlewareSecond - Before Handler**
>
> **2015/04/30 14:45:52 Failed to authorize to the system**
>
> **2015/04/30 14:45:52 MiddlewareFirst - After Handler**
>
> **[negroni] Completed 0 in 1.0008ms**
>
> **[negroni] Started GET /message**
>
> **2015/04/30 14:46:00 MiddlewareFirst - Before Handler**
>
> **2015/04/30 14:46:00 MiddlewareSecond - Before Handler**
>
> **2015/04/30 14:46:00 Authorized to the system**
>
> **2015/04/30 14:46:00 Executing message Handler**
>
> **2015/04/30 14:46:00 MiddlewareSecond - After Handler**
>
> **2015/04/30 14:46:00 MiddlewareFirst - After Handler**
>
> **[negroni] Completed 200 OK in 1.0071ms**

You can easily understand the control flow of handler functions by looking at these log messages.

To rewrite an existing program to work with Negroni, the middleware handler functions must be modified to be compatible with the negroni.Handler interface:

```go
func middlewareFirst(w http.ResponseWriter, r *http.Request, next http.HandlerFunc) {
        //logic before next handler
        next(w, r)
        //logic after next handler
}

func middlewareSecond(w http.ResponseWriter, r *http.Request, next http.HandlerFunc) {
        //logic before next handler
        next(w, r)
        //logic after next handler
}
```

After the middleware handler functions are compatible with the negroni.Handler interface, they need to be added to the Negroni middleware stack by using the Use function of the Negroni instance. Handlers are invoked in the order in which are added to a Negroni middleware stack:

```go
n := negroni.Classic()
n.Use(negroni.HandlerFunc(middlewareFirst))
n.Use(negroni.HandlerFunc(middlewareSecond))
```

As the Negroni instance is created with the Classic function, the following built-in middleware functions will be available on the middleware stack:

- negroni.Recovery

- negroni.Logging

- negroni.Static

You can also add middleware functions when you create Negroni instances by using the New function:

```go
n := negroni.New(
        negroni.NewRecovery(),
        negroni.HandlerFunc(middlewareFirst),
        negroni.HandlerFunc(middlewareSecond),
        negroni.NewLogger(),
        negroni.NewStatic(http.Dir("public")),
)
```

Negroni provides a very simple and elegant library to work with HTTP middleware functions. This is a very tiny library, but really helpful when you build real-world web applications and RESTful services in Go. One of the major advantages of Negroni is that it is fully compatible with the net/http library. If you don't like to use full-fledged web development frameworks to build web applications in Go, making and using HTTP middleware with Negroni is a good choice for building efficient web applications, which helps you to achieve better reusability and maintainability.

Sharing Values Among Middleware

In the previous sections, you learned how to make and use HTTP middleware in Go. The example middleware was running independently without depending on any data from other middleware handlers and application handlers. In some cases, however, you may need to provide values to the next middleware or share values between middleware handlers and application handlers. For example, when you authorize to an application through a middleware handler function, it may need to provide some user-specific values to the next handler in the request-handling cycle.

Using Gorilla context

Many third-party packages are available for store values to be shared during a request lifetime. The `context` package from the Gorilla web toolkit is a great choice that can be used for sharing values during a request lifetime.

To install `context`, run the following command in the terminal:

```
$ go get github.com/gorilla/context
```

To work with the `context` package, the `github.com/gorilla/context` package must be added to the import list:

```
import "github.com/gorilla/context"
```

Setting and Getting Values with Gorilla context

To set values to a `context` object, use the `Set` function (see Listing 6-15).

Listing 6-15. Setting Values in Gorilla context

```
context.Set(r, "user", "shijuvar")
```

Here `r` is the `*http.Request` object in your handler functions. To get values from the `context` object, use `Get` or the `GetOk` function (see Listing 6-16).

Listing 6-16. Getting Values from Gorilla context

```
// val is "shijuvar"
val := context.Get(r, "user")
// returns ("shijuvar", true)
val, ok := context.GetOk(r, foo.MyKey)
```

Listing 6-17 is an example program in which a value from a middleware handler function is passed to an application handler.

Listing 6-17. Middleware Function Passing a Value to an App Handler

```
package main

import (
    "fmt"
    "log"
    "net/http"

    "github.com/codegangsta/negroni"
    "github.com/gorilla/context"
)

func Authorize(w http.ResponseWriter, r *http.Request, next http.HandlerFunc) {
    token := r.Header.Get("X-AppToken")
    if token == "bXlVc2VybmFtZTpteVBhc3N3b3Jk" {
        log.Printf("Authorized to the system")
        context.Set(r, "user", "Shiju Varghese")
        next(w, r)
    } else {
        http.Error(w, "Not Authorized", 401)
    }
}

func index(w http.ResponseWriter, r *http.Request) {
    user := context.Get(r, "user")
    fmt.Fprintf(w, "Welcome %s!", user)
}

func main() {
    mux := http.NewServeMux()
    mux.HandleFunc("/", index)
    n := negroni.Classic()
    n.Use(negroni.HandlerFunc(Authorize))
    n.UseHandler(mux)
    n.Run(":8080")
}
```

A middleware handler function is created to authorize HTTP requests. The HTTP header value "X-AppToken" is read from the request object and validates the security token. This is one of the ways to validate RESTful APIs in which HTTP clients must send the security token through an HTTP header. Some APIs validate the token and provide an access token to access the application for a specific session.

In this program, you want to pass the username into the next handler: the application handler. So you set the user value to the context object from the authorized middleware handler, which will be accessible in the HTTP request lifecycle. Here the value of the context object is accessed from the index application handler.

By leveraging the Gorilla context package to share values between middleware handlers, or share values with middleware handlers and application handlers, you can build useful middleware handler functions to build real-world applications.

Summary

Using HTTP middleware is an important practical approach for building real-world applications in Go. Middleware is a pluggable and self-contained piece of code that wraps application handlers, which can be used for implementing shared behaviors into across-the-application handlers or into some specific application handlers.

HTTP middleware allows you to build applications with pluggable logic that obtains a greater level of reusability maintainability. Using HTTP middleware, you can execute some logic before or after HTTP request handlers. Because HTTP middleware are pluggable components, you can add or remove them at any time.

The Alice third-party package allows you to implement chaining of middleware handlers with an elegant syntax using its fluent interface. The Negroni third-party package is a great library for handling middleware functions, which also come with some default middleware functions. Negroni provides an idiomatic approach to using HTTP middleware in Go.

When you build real-world applications, you may need to share values among various middleware handlers and application handlers. The third-party context package from the Gorilla web toolkit can be used for sharing values during a request lifetime. It is a great web development stack in Go to use net/http as the fundamental programming block for web development, Negroni as the handler for working with HTTP middleware, Gorilla mux as the router, and Gorilla context as the mechanism for sharing values during the request lifetime. With this web development stack, you don't need a full-fledged web development framework.

CHAPTER 7

■ ■ ■

Authentication to Web Apps

Security is one of the most important factors to consider when building a successful web application or web API. If you can't protect your applications from unauthorized access, the entire application won't make any sense, regardless of its functionality. You might have developed a brilliant user experience for your applications, but all your implementations will fail if you can't secure your applications. Authentication and authorization enable applications to be protected from unauthorized access to their protected resources.

This chapter shows you how to protect web-based systems using various authentication approaches. It focuses more on modern authentication approaches for securing applications, which are useful when you build web applications and mobile applications by using a web API as the server-side implementation.

Authentication and Authorization

Authentication is the process of identifying clients of applications and services that will gain access to protected resources. These clients will be end users or other applications and services. Typically, a database stores user credentials such as usernames and passwords, and end users enter valid usernames and passwords to gain access to applications.

Authorization is the process of granting permission to do certain actions or access resources, which is permitted for authenticated clients. Authorization works with the authentication process, in which you can attach authorization roles with user credentials. When you store user credentials in a database, you can associate authorization roles and permissions along with the user information. When you build applications, you can differentiate access permissions by defining multiple authorization roles. For example, if you want to provide administrator functionalities to certain authenticated users, you can define an authorization role for administrator users along with the access permissions, so you can differentiate the access permissions from other authenticated users. Some applications may not have any authorization roles because all authenticated users will have the same privileges to the applications.

A proper strategy for authentication and authorization is the most important factor when you design web applications. If you design your applications with proper authentication and authorization, you avoid lots of security challenges, which are very critical for a successful application.

Authentication Approaches

There are various approaches available for implementing authentication into applications. Typically, user credentials are stored in a database of an application. The web server takes the username and password through an HTML form and then validates these credentials with the credentials stored in the database. But in modern applications, people also use social identity providers such as Facebook, Twitter, LinkedIn, and Google as social identities for authentication, which helps applications avoid maintaining separate user identity systems for each individual application. End users don't need to remember their user ID and password for individual applications; they can use their existing social identities to authenticate to applications.

121

Modern web development is moving toward an API-based approach in this mobility era, in which these APIs are being consumed from both mobile clients and web clients. More-reliable security systems must be provided to modern web applications. APIs are developed based on a stateless design, which should be considered when authentication systems for APIs are designed. So you can't use the same approach for APIs, which you have been using for traditional web applications.

Once users have been logged in to the system, they must be able to access web server resources in subsequent HTTP requests without providing user credentials for each HTTP request. There are two kinds of approaches available for keeping the user as a "logged-in" user for subsequent HTTP requests. A conventional approach is to use an HTTP session and cookies, and a modern approach is to use an access token generated by the web server. A token-based approach is a convenient solution for web APIs; an HTTP session and cookies are appropriate for traditional web applications.

Cookie-Based Authentication

A cookie-based approach is the most widely used method of implementing authentication into web applications. In this approach, HTTP cookies are used to authenticate users on every HTTP request after they have logged in to the system with user credentials.

Figure 7-1 illustrates the cookie-based authentication workflow.

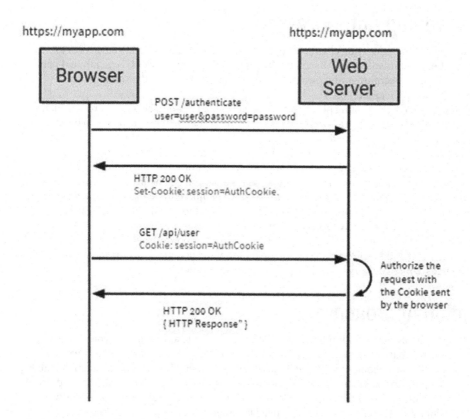

Figure 7-1. *Cookie-based authentication workflow*

In cookie-based authentication, the web server first validates the username and password, which are sent through an HTML form. Once the user credentials are validated with the credentials stored in the database, the HTTP server sets a session cookie that typically contains the user information. For each subsequent HTTP request, the web server can validate the HTTP request based on the value contained in the cookie. Some server-side technologies provide a very rich infrastructure for implementing this kind of authentication, in which you can easily implement cookie-based authentication by simply calling its API methods. In other server-side technologies and frameworks, you can manually write some code for writing cookies and storing values into session storage to implement the authentication.

A cookie-based approach that combines with sessions is a good fit for traditional web applications in which you implement everything at the server side, including the logic for UI rendering. The web application is accessed from normal desktop browsers.

In Go, you can use packages such as `sessions` (www.gorillatoolkit.org/pkg/sessions), which is provided by the Gorilla web toolkit, to implement authentication using cookie-based sessions.

Using a cookie-based approach to implement authentication into a web API is not a good idea for several reasons. When you build APIs, a stateless design is an ideal design choice. If you use a cookie-based approach, you need to maintain a session store for your API, which violates the design choice of being a stateless API. The cookie-based approach also doesn't work well when web server resources are accessed from different domains due to cross-origin resource sharing (CORS) constraints.

Token-Based Authentication

Methods of developing web applications have changed in the past few years. The era of mobile application development has also changed the way web-based systems are developed. Modern web development is moving toward an API-driven approach in which a web API (often a RESTful API) is provided on the server side, and web applications and mobile applications are built by consuming the web API.

A token-based approach is a modern approach for implementing authentication into web applications and web APIs. In a token-based approach (see Figure 7-2), an access token ID used for authentication on every HTTP request. In this approach, you can also use usernames and passwords to log in to the system. If the user gets access to the system, the authentication system generates an access token for the subsequent HTTP requests to get authentication into the web server. These access tokens are a securely signed string that can be used for accessing HTTP resources on every HTTP request. Typically, the access tokens are sent with an HTTP `Authorization` header as a bearer token that can be validated at the web server.

Token-Based Authentication

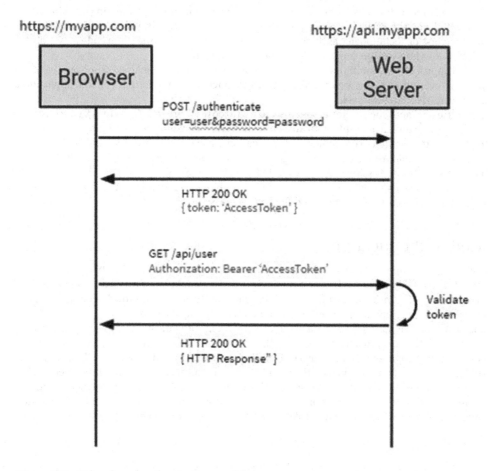

Figure 7-2. Token-based authentication workflow

Sometimes, you can use a third-party identity provider or a third-party API for authentication. In this context, a client ID and a secret key for getting logged in to the authentication system are used instead of a username and password.

Here is the token-based authentication process:

1. Authenticate into the system by providing a username and password, or by providing a client ID and a secret key.

2. If the authentication request is successful, the authentication system generates a securely signed string as an access token for subsequent HTTP requests.

3. The client application receives the token from the web server and uses it to access web server resources.

4. The client application provides the access token on every HTTP request into the web server. An HTTP header is used to transmit the access token into the web server.

5. The web server validates the access token provided by the client application and then provides the web server resources if the access token is valid.

A token-based approach is very convenient when you build mobile applications for which you don't need to leverage cookies on the client. When you use APIs as your server-side implementation, you don't need to maintain session stores that allow you to build stateless APIs on the server side, which can be easily consumed from variety of client applications without any hurdles. Another benefit of using a token-based approach is that you can easily make AJAX calls to any web server, regardless of domains, because you use an HTTP header to make the HTTP requests.

A token-based approach is an ideal solution for providing security to RESTful APIs. On the web technology space, Go is primarily used for building back-end APIs (often RESTful APIs), so the focus of this chapter is primarily on the token-based approach.

Authentication with OAuth 2

A token-based approach actually comes from an OAuth specification that is defined for solving problems with authentication, for enabling applications to access each other's data with an open authentication model. Let's have a brief look at OAuth before diving into an example authentication program using an OAuth 2 service provider.

Understanding OAuth 2

OAuth 2 is an open specification for authentication. The OAuth 2.0 authorization framework enables a third-party application to obtain limited access to an HTTP service such as Facebook, Twitter, GitHub, and Google. The most important thing is that OAuth 2 is a specification for authentication flow.

OAuth 2 provides the authorization flow for web applications, desktop applications, and mobile applications. When you build applications, you can delegate user authentication to the social identity providers such as Facebook, Twitter, GitHub, and Google. You can register your applications into an identity provider to authorize the application to access the user account. When you register your application into the identity provider, typically it gives you a client ID and a client secret key to obtain access to the user account of the identity provider. Once you are logged in with client ID and client secret key, the authentication server gives you an access token that can be used for accessing protected resources of the web server.

Section 7.2.2 discussed the token-based approach workflow for authentication. The use of a bearer token is a specification defined in the OAuth 2 authorization framework, which defines how to use bearer tokens in HTTP requests to access protected resources in OAuth 2.

Several OAuth 2 service providers are available for authentication. Because OAuth 2 is an open standard for authorization, you can implement these standards for your web APIs as an authentication mechanism for various client applications, including mobile and web applications.

■ **Note** OAuth 2.0 is the next evolution of the OAuth protocol that was originally created in 2006. OAuth 2.0 focuses on client developer simplicity while providing specific authorization flows for web applications, desktop applications, and mobile applications. The final version of the OAuth 2 specification can be found at http://tools.ietf.org/html/rfc6749.

Authentication with OAuth 2 using the Goth Package

The Go ecosystem provides various packages for working on the OAuth 2 authentication protocol. The Goth third-party package and its Gothic subpackage allow you to work with OAuth 2 providers. Goth supports OAuth 2 service providers such as LinkedIn, Facebook, Twitter, Google, and GitHub. The Goth package provides various providers to work with each service provider. For example, it provides the github.com/markbates/goth/providers/twitter package for working with the Twitter identity provider.

To install the Goth package, run the following command in the terminal:

```
go get github.com/markbates/goth
```

To work with the Goth package, you must add github.com/markbates/goth to the import list:

```
import "github.com/markbates/goth"
```

Listing 7-1 is an example program that uses Twitter and Facebook as identity providers. In this program, Twitter and Facebook login credentials are used to authenticate into an example application.

Listing 7-1. Authentication with OAuth 2 Service Providers

```go
package main

import (
    "encoding/json"
    "fmt"
    "html/template"
    "log"
    "net/http"
    "os"

    "github.com/gorilla/pat"
    "github.com/markbates/goth"
    "github.com/markbates/goth/gothic"
    "github.com/markbates/goth/providers/facebook"
    "github.com/markbates/goth/providers/twitter"
)

//Struct for parsing JSON configuration
type Configuration struct {
    TwitterKey     string
    TwitterSecret  string
    FacebookKey    string
    FacebookSecret string
}

var config Configuration

//Read configuration values from config.json
func init() {
    file, _ := os.Open("config.json")
    decoder := json.NewDecoder(file)
    config = Configuration{}
    err := decoder.Decode(&config)
```

```go
    if err != nil {
        log.Fatal(err)
    }
}
func callbackAuthHandler(res http.ResponseWriter, req *http.Request) {
    user, err := gothic.CompleteUserAuth(res, req)
    if err != nil {
        fmt.Fprintln(res, err)
        return
    }
    t, _ := template.New("userinfo").Parse(userTemplate)
    t.Execute(res, user)
}
func indexHandler(res http.ResponseWriter, req *http.Request) {
    t, _ := template.New("index").Parse(indexTemplate)
    t.Execute(res, nil)
}
func main() {
    //Register providers with Goth
    goth.UseProviders(
        twitter.New(config.TwitterKey, config.TwitterSecret, "http://localhost:8080/auth/
        twitter/callback"),
        facebook.New(config.FacebookKey, config.FacebookSecret, "http://localhost:8080/auth/
        facebook/callback"),
    )
    //Routing using Pat package
    r := pat.New()
    r.Get("/auth/{provider}/callback", callbackAuthHandler)
    r.Get("/auth/{provider}", gothic.BeginAuthHandler)
    r.Get("/", indexHandler)

    server := &http.Server{
        Addr:    ":8080",
        Handler: r,
    }
    log.Println("Listening...")
    server.ListenAndServe()

}

//View templates

var indexTemplate = `
<p><a href="/auth/twitter">Log in with Twitter</a></p>
<p><a href="/auth/facebook">Log in with Facebook</a></p>
`

var userTemplate = `
<p>Name: {{.Name}}</p>
<p>Email: {{.Email}}</p>
<p>NickName: {{.NickName}}</p>
```

```
<p>Location: {{.Location}}</p>
<p>AvatarURL: {{.AvatarURL}} <img src="{{.AvatarURL}}"></p>
<p>Description: {{.Description}}</p>
<p>UserID: {{.UserID}}</p>
<p>AccessToken: {{.AccessToken}}</p>
`
```

Twitter and Facebook are used to log in to the example application. To do this, register the application with the corresponding identity provider. When you register an application with an identity provider, you get a client ID and secret key. Twitter and Facebook providers are registered with the Goth package by providing a client ID, client secret key, and callback URL.

After a successful login with an OAuth2 service provider, the server redirects to the callback URL:

```
//Register OAuth2 providers with Goth
    goth.UseProviders(
        twitter.New(config.TwitterKey, config.TwitterSecret, "http://localhost:8080/auth/
        twitter/callback"),
        facebook.New(config.FacebookKey, config.FacebookSecret, "http://localhost:8080/auth/
        facebook/callback"),
    )
```

The client ID and client secret key are read from a configuration file in the init function.

Run the program and navigate to http://localhost:8080/. Figure 7-3 shows the home page of the application, which provides authentication with Twitter and Facebook.

Figure 7-3. *Index page of the example program*

Let's choose Twitter to obtain access to the identity provider. It asks to authorize the application with Twitter account credentials, as shown in Figure 7-4.

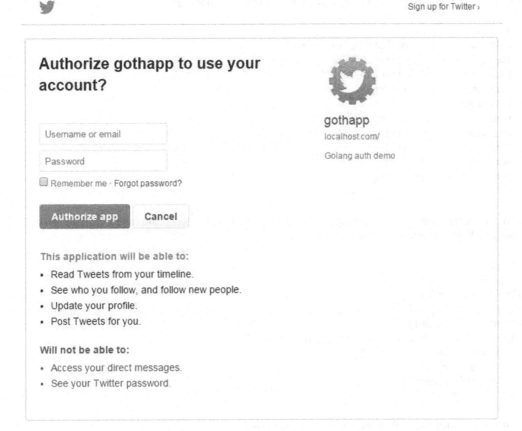

Figure 7-4. *Logging in with Twitter credentials*

After a successful login with a social identity provider, the application is authorized to obtain access to the authentication server and gives user information to the application, including an access token and redirect to the callback URL that was provided when the social identity provider was registered with the Goth package.

Here is the application handler for the callback URL:

```
func callbackAuthHandler(res http.ResponseWriter, req *http.Request) {
    user, err := gothic.CompleteUserAuth(res, req)
    if err != nil {
        fmt.Fprintln(res, err)
        return
    }
    t, _ := template.New("userinfo").Parse(userTemplate)
    t.Execute(res, user)
}
```

When the CompleteUserAuth function of the Goth package is called, it returns a User struct of the Goth package. The User struct contains the information common to most OAuth and OAuth2 providers. All the "raw" data from the provider can be found in the RawData field.

Here is the definition of User struct from the source of the Goth package:

```
type User struct {
        RawData              map[string]interface{}
        Email                string
        Name                 string
        NickName             string
        Description          string
        UserID               string
        AvatarURL            string
        Location             string
        AccessToken          string
        AccessTokenSecret    string
}
```

Finally, the view template is rendered by providing the User struct. Here is the view template used to render the UI to display user information:

```
var userTemplate = `
<p>Name: {{.Name}}</p>
<p>Email: {{.Email}}</p>
<p>NickName: {{.NickName}}</p>
<p>Location: {{.Location}}</p>
<p>AvatarURL: {{.AvatarURL}} <img src="{{.AvatarURL}}"></p>
<p>Description: {{.Description}}</p>
<p>UserID: {{.UserID}}</p>
<p>AccessToken: {{.AccessToken}}</p>
`
```

Figure 7-5 shows the user information obtained from Twitter.

← → C ⌂ 🗋 localhost:8080/auth/twitter/callback?oauth_token=p7aStxHLkyYLRDeVmGq2VUMKzLzSC›

Name: Shiju Varghese

Email:

NickName: shijucv

Location: Kochi, India

AvatarURL: http://pbs.twimg.com/profile_images/527027737848840192/x0yJcc0D_normal.png

Description: Architect focused on Cloud with an interest in APIs, Microservices, Containerization and Distributed apps.

UserID: 12009152

AccessToken: 12009152-6BUUQxk33AspnRWDqISYLDMdi4jb6wV9wt8oNKRul

---

Figure 7-5. *User information page obtained from Twitter*

Authentication with JSON Web Token

Section 7.2.2 discussed a token-based approach for authentication in which a bearer token is used to access the protected resources of a web server. JSON Web Token (JWT) is an open standard for generating and using bearer tokens for authentication between two parties. JWT is a compact, URL-safe way of representing claims to be transferred between two parties. The claims in a JWT are encoded as a JSON object that is digitally signed using JSON Web Signature (JWS). Like OAuth 2, JWT is an open standard for token-based authentication. (The pronunciation of JWT is the same as for the English word *jot*.)

JWT is a signed JSON object that can be used as a bearer token in OAuth 2 for authentication. A JWT token is made of three parts, separated by a . (period). The first part is called the Header, which is a JSON object that has been base64url-encoded. The second part, called the Claims, is also a JSON object that contains the claims conveyed by the JWT. The last part, called the Signature, is verified with the information provided by the Header.

■ **Note** The draft of the JWT specification is available here: http://self-issued.info/docs/draft-ietf-oauth-json-web-token.html

---

Working with JWT Using the jwt-go Package

The third-party Go package jwt-go provides various utility functions for working with JWT. It provides the following utilities:

- Generates and signs JWT tokens

- Parses and verifies JWT tokens

The jwt-go library supports the signing algorithms of RSA256 and HMAC SHA256.
To install the jwt-go package, enter the following command in the terminal:

```
go get github.com/dgrijalva/jwt-go
```

To work with the jwt-go package, you must add github.com/dgrijalva/jwt-go to the import list:

```
import "github.com/dgrijalva/jwt-go"
```

Let's write an example API to work with JWT tokens using the jwt-go package. Steps of the authentication flow in the example program are the following:

1. The API server validates the user credentials (username and password) provided by the client application.

2. If the login credentials are valid, the API server generates a JWT token and sends it to the client application as an access token.

3. The client applications can store the JWT token in client storage. HTML 5 local storage is generally used for storing JWT tokens.

4. To obtain access to protected resources of the API server, the client application sends an access token as a bearer token in the HTTP header Authorization (Authorization: Bearer "Access_Token") on every HTTP request.

Before starting the example program, let's generate RSA keys for the application to use to sign the tokens. The RSA keys can be generated by using the openssl command-line tool.

Run the following commands:

```
openssl genrsa -out app.rsa 1024
openssl rsa -in app.rsa -pubout > app.rsa.pub
```

These commands generate a private and public key. 1024 is the size of the key that was generated. Listing 7-2 shows the example program.

Listing 7-2. JWT Token-based Authentication with the jwt-go Package

```go
package main

import (
    "encoding/json"
    "fmt"
    "io/ioutil"
    "log"
    "net/http"
    "time"

    jwt "github.com/dgrijalva/jwt-go"
    "github.com/gorilla/mux"
)

// using asymmetric crypto/RSA keys
// location of the files used for signing and verification
const (
    privKeyPath = "keys/app.rsa"      // openssl genrsa -out app.rsa 1024
    pubKeyPath  = "keys/app.rsa.pub"  // openssl rsa -in app.rsa -pubout > app.rsa.pub
)

// verify key and sign key
var (
    verifyKey, signKey []byte
)

//struct User for parsing login credentials
type User struct {
    UserName string `json:"username"`
    Password string `json:"password"`
}

// read the key files before starting http handlers
func init() {
    var err error

    signKey, err = ioutil.ReadFile(privKeyPath)
    if err != nil {
        log.Fatal("Error reading private key")
        return
    }
```

```go
    verifyKey, err = ioutil.ReadFile(pubKeyPath)
    if err != nil {
        log.Fatal("Error reading private key")
        return
    }
}


// reads the login credentials, checks them and creates JWT the token
func loginHandler(w http.ResponseWriter, r *http.Request) {
    var user User
    //decode into User struct
    err := json.NewDecoder(r.Body).Decode(&user)
    if err != nil {
        w.WriteHeader(http.StatusInternalServerError)
        fmt.Fprintln(w, "Error in request body")
        return
    }
    // validate user credentials
    if user.UserName != "shijuvar" && user.Password != "pass" {
        w.WriteHeader(http.StatusForbidden)
        fmt.Fprintln(w, "Wrong info")
        return
    }

    // create a signer for rsa 256
    t := jwt.New(jwt.GetSigningMethod("RS256"))

    // set our claims
    t.Claims["iss"] = "admin"
    t.Claims["CustomUserInfo"] = struct {
        Name string
        Role string
    }{user.UserName, "Member"}

    // set the expire time
    t.Claims["exp"] = time.Now().Add(time.Minute * 20).Unix()
    tokenString, err := t.SignedString(signKey)
    if err != nil {
        w.WriteHeader(http.StatusInternalServerError)
        fmt.Fprintln(w, "Sorry, error while Signing Token!")
        log.Printf("Token Signing error: %v\n", err)
        return
    }
    response := Token{tokenString}
    jsonResponse(response, w)
}
```

133

```go
// only accessible with a valid token
func authHandler(w http.ResponseWriter, r *http.Request) {
    // validate the token
    token, err := jwt.ParseFromRequest(r, func(token *jwt.Token) (interface{}, error) {
        // since we only use one private key to sign the tokens,
        // we also only use its public counter part to verify
        return verifyKey, nil
    })

    if err != nil {
        switch err.(type) {

        case *jwt.ValidationError: // something was wrong during the validation
            vErr := err.(*jwt.ValidationError)

            switch vErr.Errors {
            case jwt.ValidationErrorExpired:
                w.WriteHeader(http.StatusUnauthorized)
                fmt.Fprintln(w, "Token Expired, get a new one.")
                return

            default:
                w.WriteHeader(http.StatusInternalServerError)
                fmt.Fprintln(w, "Error while Parsing Token!")
                log.Printf("ValidationError error: %+v\n", vErr.Errors)
                return
            }

        default: // something else went wrong
            w.WriteHeader(http.StatusInternalServerError)
            fmt.Fprintln(w, "Error while Parsing Token!")
            log.Printf("Token parse error: %v\n", err)
            return
        }

    }
    if token.Valid {
        response := Response{"Authorized to the system"}
        jsonResponse(response, w)
    } else {
        response := Response{"Invalid token"}
        jsonResponse(response, w)
    }

}

type Response struct {
    Text string `json:"text"`
}
type Token struct {
    Token string `json:"token"`
}
```

```go
func jsonResponse(response interface{}, w http.ResponseWriter) {
    json, err := json.Marshal(response)
    if err != nil {
        http.Error(w, err.Error(), http.StatusInternalServerError)
        return
    }

    w.WriteHeader(http.StatusOK)
    w.Header().Set("Content-Type", "application/json")
    w.Write(json)
}

//Entry point of the program
func main() {

    r := mux.NewRouter()
    r.HandleFunc("/login", loginHandler).Methods("POST")
    r.HandleFunc("/auth", authHandler).Methods("POST")

    server := &http.Server{
        Addr:    ":8080",
        Handler: r,
    }
    log.Println("Listening...")
    server.ListenAndServe()
}
```

Generating the JWT Token

If the login is successful, the API server generates the JWT token by using the jwt-go library:

```go
// create a signer for rsa 256
    t := jwt.New(jwt.GetSigningMethod("RS256"))

    // set our claims
    t.Claims["iss"] = "admin"
    t.Claims["CustomUserInfo"] = struct {
        Name string
        Role string
    }{user.UserName, "Member"}

    // set the expire time
    t.Claims["exp"] = time.Now().Add(time.Minute * 20).Unix()
    tokenString, err := t.SignedString(signKey)
```

In the code block, a signer with "RS256" was created. Claims were set, including an expiration (with the predefined claim "exp") for the JWT token. Finally, a JWT token was created using the RSA key (private key) that was generated in the beginning step. The tokenString variable contains the JWT token that is sent to the client applications.

Validating the JWT Token

Because there is only one private key ("app.rsa") to sign the tokens, only its public counterpart ("app.rsa.pub") is used to verify the access token.

Here is the authentication handler that validates the access token. It automatically looks at the Bearer token from the HTTP Authorization header of the HTTP request object.

```
func authHandler(w http.ResponseWriter, r *http.Request) {
    // validate the token
    token, err := jwt.ParseFromRequest(r, func(token *jwt.Token) (interface{}, error) {
        // since we only use one private key to sign the tokens,
        // we also only use its public counter part to verify
        return verifyKey, nil
    })

    if err != nil {
        switch err.(type) {

        case *jwt.ValidationError: // something was wrong during the validation
            vErr := err.(*jwt.ValidationError)

            switch vErr.Errors {
            case jwt.ValidationErrorExpired:
                w.WriteHeader(http.StatusUnauthorized)
                fmt.Fprintln(w, "Token Expired, get a new one.")
                return

            default:
                w.WriteHeader(http.StatusInternalServerError)
                fmt.Fprintln(w, "Error while Parsing Token!")
                log.Printf("ValidationError error: %+v\n", vErr.Errors)
                return
            }

        default: // something else went wrong
            w.WriteHeader(http.StatusInternalServerError)
            fmt.Fprintln(w, "Error while Parsing Token!")
            log.Printf("Token parse error: %v\n", err)
            return
        }

    }
    if token.Valid {
        response := Response{"Authorized to the system"}
        jsonResponse(response, w)
    } else {
        response := Response{"Invalid token"}
        jsonResponse(response, w)
    }

}
```

The ParseFromRequest function automatically looks at the HTTP header for the access token and validates the string with a corresponding verification key. By checking the error, you can see whether the token has expired. The jwt-go package is very helpful when you work with JWT tokens.

Running and Testing the API Server

Let's run the program and call the API endpoints using the REST client tool. To log in to the API server, send HTTP Post to "/login" by providing a username and password, as shown in Figure 7-6.

Figure 7-6. HTTP Post to "/login"

Figure 7-7 shows the response of the HTTP Post to "/login".

Figure 7-7. API server sends JWT access token as the response

If the login is valid, the API server sends a JWT token to the client as an access token for subsequent HTTP requests.

Let's authorize into the API server with the access token received from the HTTP Post to "/login".

Let's send a request to "/auth" by providing the access token in the HTTP Authorization header as shown in the following format (see Figure 7-8):

Authorization: Bearer "JWT Access Token"

Figure 7-8. *Authenticating into the API server with a JWT access token*

Figure 7-9 displays the response that shows a successful authentication into the system.

Figure 7-9. *Successful authentication into the API server*

When you build web APIs as the back end for mobile applications and web applications, a token-based approach is the preferred solution when you provide your own authentication and authorization infrastructure. This approach is good for mobile clients and SPAs to consume API resources. After logging in to the system using a username and a password, a client application can obtain an access token to access protected resources in subsequent HTTP requests. Once the client applications obtain the access token (JWT token) from an API server, the token can be persisted into a local storage of client applications. Whenever HTTP requests are sent to access the protected resources of the API server, they then can be taken from local storage.

Using HTTP Middleware to Validate JWT Tokens

When you work with JWT tokens as an authentication model for accessing the protected resources of a server, you have to validate the tokens on every HTTP request. It would be a tedious job to implement the validation logic in each HTTP request, so HTTP middleware is a great approach for implementing authentication and authorization logic in web applications in which you can decorate the authentication middleware into the routes (which is required for authentication). You write authentication logic in one place that can be applied into multiple routes in which you want to implement authorization for accessing its protected resources.

Listing 7-3 is an authentication middleware that can be used for decorating into multiple application handlers to perform authorization.

Listing 7-3. Authentication Middleware for Validating JWT Tokens

```
func authMiddleware(w http.ResponseWriter, r *http.Request, next http.HandlerFunc) {
    // validate the token
    token, err := jwt.ParseFromRequest(r, func(token *jwt.Token) (interface{}, error) {
        return verifyKey, nil
    })
    if(err==nil && token.Valid) {
        next(w,r)
    } else {
        w.WriteHeader(http.StatusUnauthorized)
        fmt.Fprint(w, "Authentication failed")
    }
}
```

If the token is valid, the next handler in the middleware stack is called.

Here is the code block that decorates an authentication middleware into an application handler for a protected resource:

```
r.HandleFunc("/login", loginHandler).Methods("POST")
r.Handle("/admin", negroni.New(
            negroni.HandlerFunc(authMiddleware),
            negroni.Wrap(http.HandlerFunc(adminHandler)),
        ))
```

The Negroni package for the middleware stack is used. For the protected resource "/admin", the authMiddleware middleware handler is decorated into the adminHandler application handler.

Summary

When you build web applications and RESTful APIs, security is one of the most important factors for a successful application. If you can't protect your application from unauthorized access, the entire application doesn't make any sense, despite providing a good user experience.

You usually use two kinds of authentication models for authorizing HTTP requests to access the protected resources of a server: cookie-based authentication and token-based authentication. A cookie-based authentication is the conventional approach that works well for traditional and stand-alone web applications in which server-side implementation provides everything, including UI rendering.

A token-based approach is great for adding authentication into RESTful APIs that can be easily accessed from various client applications, including mobile and web applications. A token-based approach is a very convenient model for mobile applications because tokens can be sent through an HTTP header as bearer tokens. When a token-based approach is used, Ajax requests can be sent to any API server, regardless of domain constrains, thus avoiding CORS issues.

OAuth 2 is an open standard for authentication that allows applications to delegate authentication to various OAuth 2 service providers such as LinkedIn, GitHub, Twitter, Facebook, and Google. Several OAuth 2 service providers are available as identity providers. The Go third-party package Goth allows you to implement authentication with various OAuth 2 service providers. In the OAuth 2 authentication flow, an access token is used to obtain access to protected resources.

JSON Web Token (JWT) is an open standard for generating and using bearer tokens for authentication between two parties. JWT is a compact, URL-safe way to represent claims to be transferred between two parties. The third-party Go package jwt-go provides various utility functions for working with JWT tokens. It allows you to easily generate JWT tokens and verify tokens for authentication. When you use token-based authentication, you might have to apply authentication logic into multiple application handlers. In this context, you can use HTTP middleware to implement authentication logic, which can decorate into multiple application handlers.

■ ■ ■

## CHAPTER 8

Persistence with MongoDB

When you build web applications, persistence of application data is very important. You can define the data model of your Go applications using structs, in which you can program against the structs for working with application data, but you need persistent storage for your application data.

This chapter shows you how to persist application data into MongoDB, which is a popular NoSQL database. This chapter covers the following:

- Introduction to MongoDB

- The mgo package

- Working with MongoDB using mgo

- Persistence with MongoDB

Introduction to MongoDB

MongoDB is a popular NoSQL database that has been widely used for modern web applications. MongoDB is an open-source document database that provides high performance, high availability, and automatic scaling. MongoDB is a nonrelational database that stores data as documents in a binary representation called BSON Binary JSON (BSON). In short, MongoDB is the data store for BSON documents. Go structs can be easily serialized into BSON documents.

For more details on MongoDB and to get instructions for download and install, check out the MongoDB web site here: www.mongodb.org/.

■ **Note**   A NoSQL (often interpreted as Not Only SQL) database provides a mechanism for data storage and retrieval. It provides an alternative approach to the tabular relations used in relational databases to design data models. A NoSQL database is designed to cope with modern application development challenges such as dealing with large volumes of data with easier scalability and performance. When compared with relational databases, the NoSQL database can provide high performance, better scalability, and cheaper storage. NoSQL databases are available in different types: document databases, graph stores, key-value stores, and wide-column stores. MongoDB is a popular document database.

A MongoDB database holds a set of collections that consists of documents. A document comprises one or more fields in which you store data as a set of key-value pairs. In MongoDB, you persist documents into collections, which are analogous to tables in a relational database. Documents are analogous to rows, and fields within a document are analogous to columns.

Unlike relational databases, MongoDB provides a greater level of flexibility for the schema of documents, which enables you to change the document schema whenever the data model is evolving. When you work on MongoDB with Go, your Go structs can become the schema of your documents; you can change the schema any time you want to alter the structure of application data. Documents in a collection don't need to have the same set of fields or schema, and common fields in a collection's documents can hold different types of data. This dynamic schema feature is very useful when you build applications in an evolving way with many development iterations.

Getting Started Using MongoDB

Once you have installed MongoDB, you can start working with it from Go applications using a Go driver for MongoDB. (Keep in mind that you have to start the MongoDB process before running applications.) You can start MongoDB from a command line by entering the mongod command with the appropriate command-line options.

In this chapter, you learn how to persist data and process it with MongoDB using the third-party package mgo, which is a popular Go driver for MongoDB.

Introduction to mgo Driver for MongoDB

mgo (pronounced *mango*) is a MongoDB driver for Go that supports the major features of MongoDB. The mgo package allows you to easily work with MongoDB from Go applications using its simple API that follows Go idioms. mgo is a mature package that was created in 2010 and sponsored by MongoDB Inc. since 2011. It is a battle-tested library that is used for larger production scenarios such as Facebook's Parse.com, a popular mobile back end as a service (MBaaS) platform written in Go.

Installing mgo

To install the mgo package, run the following command in the terminal:

```
go get gopkg.in/mgo.v2
```

To work with mgo, you must add gopkg.in/mgo.v2 and its subpackage gopkg.in/mgo.v2/bson to the import list:

```
import (
    "gopkg.in/mgo.v2"
    "gopkg.in/mgo.v2/bson"
)
```

Connecting to MongoDB

To get started working with MongoDB, you have to obtain a MongoDB Session using the Dial function (see Listing 8-1). The Dial function establishes the connection with the MongoDB server defined by the url parameter.

Listing 8-1. Connecting to MongoDB Server and Obtaining a Session

```
session, err := mgo.Dial("localhost")
```

The Dial function can also be used to connect with a cluster of servers (see Listing 8-2). This is useful when you scale a MongoDB database into a cluster of servers.

Listing 8-2. Connecting to a Cluster of MongoDB Servers and Obtaining a Session

```
session, err := mgo.Dial("server1.mongolab.com,server2.mongolab.com")
```

You can also use the DialWithInfo function to establish connection to one server or a cluster of servers (see Listing 8-3). The difference from the Dial function is that you can provide extra information to the cluster by using the value of the DialInfo type. DialWithInfo establishes a new Session to the cluster of MongoDB servers identified by the DialInfo type. The DialWithInfo function lets you customize values when you establish a connection to a server. When you establish a connection using the Dial function, the default timeout value is 10 seconds, so it times out after 10 seconds if Dial can't reach to a server. When you establish a connection using the DialWithInfo function, you can specify the value for the Timeout property.

Listing 8-3. Connecting to a Cluster of MongoDB Servers Using DialWithInfo

```
mongoDialInfo := &mgo.DialInfo{
        Addrs:    []string{"localhost"},
        Timeout:  60 * time.Second,
        Database: "taskdb",
        Username: "shijuvar",
        Password: "password@123",
    }

session, err := mgo.DialWithInfo(mongoDialInfo)
```

The mgo.Session object handles a pool of connections to MongoDB. Once you obtain a Session object, you can perform write and read operations with MongoDB. MongoDB servers are queried with multiple consistency rules. SetMode of the Session object changes the consistency mode for the session. Three types of consistency modes are available: Eventual, Monotonic, and Strong.

Listing 8-4 establishes a Session object and sets a consistency mode.

Listing 8-4. Establishing a Session Object and a Consistency Mode

```
session, err := mgo.Dial("localhost")
if err != nil {
    panic(err)
}
defer session.Close()

//Switch the session to a monotonic behavior.
session.SetMode(mgo.Monotonic, true)
```

It is important to close the Session object at the end of its lifetime by calling the Close method. In the previous listing, the Close method is called by using the defer function.

Accessing Collections

To perform CRUD operations into MongoDB, an object of *mgo.Collection is created, which represents the MongoDB collection. You can create an object of *mgo.Collection by calling method C of *mgo.Database. The mgo.Database type represents the named database that can be created by calling the DB method of *mgo.Session.

Listing 8-5 accesses the MongoDB collection named "categories".

Listing 8-5. Accessing a MongoDB Collection

```
c := session.DB("taskdb").C("categories")
```

The DB method returns a value representing a database named taskdb, which gets an instance of type Database. Method C of type Database returns a value representing a collection named "categories". The Collection object can be used for performing CRUD operations.

CRUD Operations with MongoDB

You now know how to establish a MongoDB Session object by using the Dial and DialWithInfo functions. Let's take a look at how to perform CRUD operations against the MongoDB database using the mgo package. In Go, you can persist structs, maps, and slices as BSON documents into a MongoDB database. When you persist your data as Go types such as structs, maps, and slices, the mgo driver automatically serializes it as BSON documents.

Inserting Documents

You can insert documents into MongoDB using the Insert method of mgo.Collection. The Insert method inserts one or more documents into the collection. Using this method, you can insert values of structs, maps, and document slices.

Inserting Struct Values

The struct type should be your choice when you define a data model for Go applications. So when you work with MongoDB, you primarily provide values of the struct type to insert BSON documents into a MongoDB collection. The mgo driver for MongoDB automatically serializes the struct values as BSON documents when the Insert method is used.

Listing 8-6 inserts three documents into a MongoDB collection.

Listing 8-6. Inserting Struct Values into MongoDB

```
package main

import (
    "fmt"
    "log"

    "gopkg.in/mgo.v2"
    "gopkg.in/mgo.v2/bson"
)
```

```go
type Category struct {
    Id          bson.ObjectId `bson:"_id,omitempty"`
    Name        string
    Description string
}

func main() {
    session, err := mgo.Dial("localhost")
    if err != nil {
        panic(err)
    }
    defer session.Close()

    // Optional. Switch the session to a monotonic behavior.
    // Reads may not be entirely up-to-date, but they will always see the
    // history of changes moving forward, the data read will be consistent
    // across sequential queries in the same session, and modifications made
    // within the session will be observed in following queries (read-your-writes).
    // http://godoc.org/labix.org/v2/mgo#Session.SetMode
    session.SetMode(mgo.Monotonic, true)

    //get collection
    c := session.DB("taskdb").C("categories")

    doc := Category{
        bson.NewObjectId(),
        "Open Source",
        "Tasks for open-source projects",
    }
    //insert a category object
    err = c.Insert(&doc)
    if err != nil {
        log.Fatal(err)
    }

    //insert two category objects
    err = c.Insert(&Category{bson.NewObjectId(), "R & D", "R & D Tasks"},
        &Category{bson.NewObjectId(), "Project", "Project Tasks"})

    var count int
    count, err = c.Count()
    if err != nil {
        log.Fatal(err)
    } else {
    fmt.Printf("%d records inserted", count)
  }
}
```

A struct named Category is created to define the data model and persist struct values into a MongoDB database. You can specify the type of _id field as bson.ObjectId. ObjectId is a 12-byte BSON type that holds uniquely identified values. BSON documents stored in a MongoDB collection require a unique _id field that acts as a primary key.

When you insert a new document, provide an _id field with a unique ObjectId. If an _id field isn't provided, MongoDB will add an _id field that holds an ObjectId. When you insert records into a MongoDB collection, you can call bson.NewObjectId() to generate a unique value for bson.ObjectId. Tag the _id field to be serialized as _id when the mgo driver serializes the values into a BSON document and also specifies the omitempty tag to omit values when serializing into BSON if the value is empty.

The Insert method of mgo.Collection is used for persisting values into MongoDB. The Collection object is created by specifying the name "categories" and inserting values into the "categories" collection by calling the Insert method. The Insert method inserts one or more documents into the collection. First, one document with the values of the Category struct is inserted and then two documents are inserted into the collection. The mgo driver automatically serializes the struct values into BSON representation and inserts them into the collection.

In this example program, three documents are inserted. The Count method of the Collection object is called to get the number of records in the collection and finally print the count.

When you run the program for the first time, you should get the following output:

```
3 records inserted
```

Inserting Map and Document SliceGo structs are an idiomatic way of defining a data model and persisting data into MongoDB. But in some contexts, you may need to persist values from maps and slices.

Listing 8-7 shows how to persist values of map objects and document slices (bson.D).

Listing 8-7. Inserting Values from Map and Document Slices (bson.D)

```go
package main

import (
    "log"

    "gopkg.in/mgo.v2"
    "gopkg.in/mgo.v2/bson"
)

func main() {
    session, err := mgo.Dial("localhost")
    if err != nil {
        panic(err)
    }
    defer session.Close()
    session.SetMode(mgo.Monotonic, true)

    //get collection
    c := session.DB("taskdb").C("categories")

    docM := map[string]string{
        "name": "Open Source",
        "description": "Tasks for open-source projects",
    }
```

```go
//insert a map object
err = c.Insert(docM)
if err != nil {
    log.Fatal(err)
}
docD := bson.D{
    {"name", "Project"},
    {"description", "Project Tasks"},

}

//insert a document slice
err = c.Insert(docD)
if err != nil {
    log.Fatal(err)
}

}
```

A document is inserted by using a map object and a document slice (bson.D). The bson.D type represents a BSON document containing ordered elements. Because the Insert method expects the interface{} type for parameter values, struct, map, and document slices can be provided.

Inserting Embedded Documents

The major difference between relational databases and document databases is that the latter doesn't support a relational approach for modeling a domain model. If you want to make a one-to-many relationship in a relational database, you can create a parent and a child table, in which each record in the parent table can be associated with multiple records in the child table. To enforce data integrity in this relational model, you can define a foreign key constraint in the child table that points to a primary key in the parent table.

MongoDB collections have flexible schema, so a data model can be defined in different ways to achieve the same objectives. You can choose the right strategy for defining a data model based on the context of the application. To make relationships among connected data, you can either embed the connected documents inside the main document or make references between two documents. For making relationships among connected data, the first strategy (embedding documents) is good in some scenarios; the latter is good for different scenarios.

■ **Note**   In Chapter 9, you will learn how to make relationships using a reference among documents. Check out the MongoDB documentation for more information on data model concepts: https://docs.mongodb.org/manual/data-modeling/

Listing 8-8 is an example that shows a data model that uses embedded documents to describe relationships among connected data. In this one-to-many relationship between Category and Tasks data, Category has multiple Task entities.

Listing 8-8. Inserting a Document with Embedded Documents

```go
package main

import (
    "log"
    "time"

    "gopkg.in/mgo.v2"
    "gopkg.in/mgo.v2/bson"
)

type Task struct {
    Description string
    Due        time.Time
}
type Category struct {
    Id          bson.ObjectId `bson:"_id,omitempty"`
    Name        string
    Description string
    Tasks       []Task
}

func main() {
    session, err := mgo.Dial("localhost")
    if err != nil {
        panic(err)
    }
    defer session.Close()
    session.SetMode(mgo.Monotonic, true)
    //get collection
    c := session.DB("taskdb").C("categories")
    //Embedding child collection
    doc := Category{
        bson.NewObjectId(),
        "Open-Source",
        "Tasks for open-source projects",
        []Task{
            Task{"Create project in mgo", time.Date(2015, time.August, 10, 0, 0, 0, 0,
                time.UTC)},
            Task{"Create REST API", time.Date(2015, time.August, 20, 0, 0, 0, 0, time.UTC)},
        },
    }
    //insert a Category object with embedded Tasks
    err = c.Insert(&doc)
    if err != nil {
        log.Fatal(err)
    }

}
```

A Category struct is created, in which a slice of the Task struct is specified for the Tasks field to embed child collection. Embedding documents enables you to get the parent document and associated child documents by using a single query (you don't need to execute another query to get the child details).

Reading Documents

The Find method of Collection allows you to query MongoDB collections. When you call the Find method, you can provide a document to filter the collection data. The Find method prepares a query using the provided document. To provide the document for querying the collection, you can provide a map or a struct value capable of being marshalled with BSON. You can use a generic map such as bson.M to provide the document for querying the data. To query all documents in the collection, you can use nil as the argument that is equivalent to an empty document such as bson.M{}. The Find method returns the value of the mgo. Query type, in which you can retrieve results using methods such as One, For, Iter, or Tail.

Retrieving All Records

Listing 8-9 retrieves all documents in a collection by providing nil as the parameter value for the Find method. This query executes against the data model defined in Listing 8-8.

Listing 8-9. Querying All Documents in a Collection

```
iter := c.Find(nil).Iter()
    result := Category{}
    for iter.Next(&result) {
        fmt.Printf("Category:%s, Description:%s\n", result.Name, result.Description)
        tasks := result.Tasks
        for _, v := range tasks {
            fmt.Printf("Task:%s Due:%v\n", v.Description, v.Due)
        }
    }
if err = iter.Close(); err != nil {
        log.Fatal(err)
    }
```

The Iter method of the Query object is used to iterate over the documents. Iter executes the query and returns an iterator capable of iterating over all the results. When you use embedded documents to define a parent-child relationship, you can obtain the associated documents in a single query.

Sorting Records

Documents can be sorted using the Sort method provided by the Query type. The Sort method prepares the query to order returned documents according to the provided field names.

Listing 8-10 sorts the collection documents.

Listing 8-10. Ordering Documents Using the Sort Method

```
iter := c.Find(nil).Sort("name").Iter()
    result := Category{}
    for iter.Next(&result) {
        fmt.Printf("Category:%s, Description:%s\n", result.Name, result.Description)
        tasks := result.Tasks
```

```
        for _, v := range tasks {
            fmt.Printf("Task:%s Due:%v\n", v.Description, v.Due)
        }
    }
    if err = iter.Close(); err != nil {
        log.Fatal(err)
    }
```

You can sort the value in reverse order by providing a field name prefixed by a – (minus sign), as shown in Listing 8-11.

Listing 8-11. Sorting Documents in Reverse Order

```
iter := c.Find(nil).Sort("-name").Iter()
```

Retrieving a Single Record

Listing 8-12 retrieves a single record from a collection by providing a map object to make the query.

Listing 8-12. Querying a Single Record from a Collection

```
result := Category{}
err := c.Find(bson.M{"name": "Open-Source"}).One(&result)
if err != nil {
    log.Fatal(err)
}
fmt.Printf("Category:%s, Description:%s\n", result.Name, result.Description)
tasks := result.Tasks
for _, v := range tasks {
    fmt.Printf("Task:%s Due:%v\n", v.Description, v.Due)
}
```

The bson.M map type is provided to query the data. Here, it queries the collection with the value provided for the Name field. The One method of the Query type executes the query and unmarshals the first obtained document into the result argument.

The Collection type provides the method FindId that is a convenience helper equivalent to the following:

```
query := c.Find(bson.M{"_id": id})
```

The FindId method allows you to query the collection with a document _id field.

Listing 8-13 queries the collection with the FindId method.

Listing 8-13. Querying a Single Record Using FindId

```
result = Category{}
err = c.FindId(obj_id).One(&result)
```

Updating Documents

The Update method of the Collection type allows you to update existing documents.

Here is the method signature of the Update method:

```
func (c *Collection) Update(selector interface{}, update interface{}) error
```

The Update method finds a single document from the collection, matches it with the provided selector document, and modifies it based on the provided update document. A partial update can be done by using the keyword "$set" in the update document.

Listing 8-14 updates an existing document.

Listing 8-14. Updating a Document

```
err := c.Update(bson.M{"_id": id},
        bson.M{"$set": bson.M{
            "description": "Create open-source projects",
            "tasks": []Task{
                Task{"Evaluate Negroni Project", time.Date(2015, time.August, 15, 0, 0, 0,
                    0, time.UTC)},
                Task{"Explore mgo Project", time.Date(2015, time.August, 10, 0, 0, 0, 0,
                    time.UTC)},
                Task{"Explore Gorilla Toolkit", time.Date(2015, time.August, 10, 0, 0, 0, 0,
                    time.UTC)},
            },
        }})
```

A partial update is performed for the fields' descriptions and tasks. The Update method finds the document with the provided _id value and modifies the fields based on the provided document.

Deleting Documents

The Remove method of the Collection type allows you to remove a single document.

Here is the method signature of the Remove method:

```
func (c *Collection) Remove(selector interface{}) error
```

Remove finds a single document from the collection, matches it with the provided selector document, and removes it from the database.

Listing 8-15 removes a single document from the collection.

Listing 8-15. Deleting a Single Document

```
err := c.Remove(bson.M{"_id": id})
```

The single document matching the _id field is removed.

The RemoveAll method of the Collection type allows you to remove multiple documents.

Here is the method signature of the RemoveAll method:

```
func (c *Collection) RemoveAll(selector interface{}) (info *ChangeInfo, err error)
```

RemoveAll finds all documents from the collection, matches the provided selector document, and removes all documents from the database. If you want to remove all documents from a collection, pass the selector document as a `nil` value.

Listing 8-16 removes all documents from a collection.

Listing 8-16. Removing All Documents from a Collection

```
c.RemoveAll(nil)
```

Indexes in MongoDB

MongoDB databases can provide high performance on read operations as compared with relational databases. In addition to the default performance behavior of MongoDB, you can further improve performance by adding indexes to MongoDB collections. Indexes in collections provide high performance on read operations for frequently used queries. MongoDB defines indexes at the collection level and supports indexes on any field or subfield of the documents in a MongoDB collection.

All MongoDB collections have an index on the _id field that exists by default. If you don't provide an _id field, the MongoDB process (mongod) creates an _id field with a unique ObjectId value. The _id index is unique (you can think of it as a primary key). In addition to the default index on the _id field, you can add an index to any field.

If you frequently query collections by filtering with a specific field, you should apply an index to ensure better performance for read operations. The mgo driver provides support for creating indexes using the EnsureIndex method of Collection, in which you can add the mgo.Index type as the argument.

Listing 8-17 applies a unique index to the field name and later queries with the Name field.

Listing 8-17. Creating an Index in a MongoDB Collection

```go
package main

import (
    "fmt"
    "log"

    "gopkg.in/mgo.v2"
    "gopkg.in/mgo.v2/bson"
)

type Category struct {
    Id          bson.ObjectId `bson:"_id,omitempty"`
    Name        string
    Description string
}

func main() {
    session, err := mgo.Dial("localhost")
    if err != nil {
        panic(err)
    }
    defer session.Close()
```

```
    session.SetMode(mgo.Monotonic, true)

    c := session.DB("taskdb").C("categories")
    c.RemoveAll(nil)
    // Index
    index := mgo.Index{
        Key:        []string{"name"},
        Unique:     true,
        DropDups:   true,
        Background: true,
        Sparse:     true,
    }
    //Create Index
    err = c.EnsureIndex(index)
    if err != nil {
        panic(err)
    }

    //insert three category objects
    err = c.Insert(
        &Category{bson.NewObjectId(), "Open-Source", "Tasks for open-source projects"},
        &Category{bson.NewObjectId(), "R & D", "R & D Tasks"},
        &Category{bson.NewObjectId(), "Project", "Project Tasks"},
    )
    if err != nil {
        panic(err)
    }

    result := Category{}
    err = c.Find(bson.M{"name": "Open-Source"}).One(&result)
    if err != nil {
        log.Fatal(err)
    } else {
        fmt.Println("Description:", result.Description)
    }
}
```

An instance of mgo.Index type is created, and the EnsureIndex function is called by providing an Index type instance as the argument:

```
index := mgo.Index{
    Key:        []string{"name"},
    Unique:     true,
    DropDups:   true,
    Background: true,
    Sparse:     true,
}
err = c.EnsureIndex(index)
if err != nil {
    panic(err)
}
```

The Key property of the Index type allows you to specify a slice of field names to be applied as indexes on the collections. Here, the field name is specified as an index. Because field names are provided as a slice, you can provide multiple fields along with a single instance of the Index type. The Unique property of the Index type prevents two documents from having the same index key.

By default, the index is in ascending order. To create an index in descending order, the field name should be specified with a prefix dash (-) as shown here:

```
Key:    []string{"-name"}
```

Managing Sessions

The Dial method of the mgo package establishes a connection to the cluster of MongoDB servers, which returns an mgo.Session object. You can manage all CRUD operations using the Session object, which manages the pool of connections to the MongoDB servers. A connection pool is a cache of database connections, so connections can be reused when new connections to the database are required. When you develop web applications, using a single global Session object for all CRUD operations is a really bad practice.

A recommended process for managing the Session object in web applications is shown here:

1. Obtain a Session object using the Dial method.

2. Create a new Session object during the lifetime of an individual HTTP request by using the New, Copy, or Clone methods on the Session object obtained from the Dial method. This approach enables the Session object to use the connection pool appropriately.

3. Use the newly obtained Session object to perform all CRUD operations during the lifetime of an HTTP request.

The New method creates a new Session with the same parameters as the original Session. The Copy method works just like New, but the copied Session preserves the exact authentication information from the original Session. The Clone method works just like Copy, but it also reuses the same socket (connection to the server) as the original Session.

Listing 8-18 is an example HTTP server that uses a copied Session object during the lifetime of an HTTP request. In this example, a struct type is created to hold the Session object for easily managing database operations from the application handlers.

Listing 8-18. HTTP Server Using a New Session for Each HTTP Request

```go
package main

import (
    "encoding/json"
    "log"
    "net/http"

    "github.com/gorilla/mux"
    "gopkg.in/mgo.v2"
    "gopkg.in/mgo.v2/bson"
)

var session *mgo.Session
```

```go
type (
    Category struct {
        Id          bson.ObjectId `bson:"_id,omitempty"`
        Name        string
        Description string
    }
    DataStore struct {
        session *mgo.Session
    }
)

//Close mgo.Session
func (d *DataStore) Close() {
    d.session.Close()
}

//Returns a collection from the database.
func (d *DataStore) C(name string) *mgo.Collection {
    return d.session.DB("taskdb").C(name)
}

//Create a new DataStore object for each HTTP request
func NewDataStore() *DataStore {
    ds := &DataStore{
        session: session.Copy(),
    }
    return ds
}

//Insert a record
func PostCategory(w http.ResponseWriter, r *http.Request) {
    var category Category
    // Decode the incoming Category json
    err := json.NewDecoder(r.Body).Decode(&category)
    if err != nil {
        panic(err)
    }
    ds := NewDataStore()
    defer ds.Close()
    //Getting the mgo.Collection
    c := ds.C("categories")
    //Insert record
    err = c.Insert(&category)
    if err != nil {
        panic(err)
    }
    w.WriteHeader(http.StatusCreated)
}
```

```go
//Read all records
func GetCategories(w http.ResponseWriter, r *http.Request) {

    var categories []Category
    ds := NewDataStore()
    defer ds.Close()
    //Getting the mgo.Collection
    c := ds.C("categories")
    iter := c.Find(nil).Iter()
    result := Category{}
    for iter.Next(&result) {
        categories = append(categories, result)
    }
    w.Header().Set("Content-Type", "application/json")
    j, err := json.Marshal(categories)
    if err != nil {
        panic(err)
    }
    w.WriteHeader(http.StatusOK)
    w.Write(j)
}

func main() {
    var err error
    session, err = mgo.Dial("localhost")
    if err != nil {
        panic(err)
    }
    r := mux.NewRouter()
    r.HandleFunc("/api/categories", GetCategories).Methods("GET")
    r.HandleFunc("/api/categories", PostCategory).Methods("POST")

    server := &http.Server{
        Addr:    ":8080",
        Handler: r,
    }
    log.Println("Listening...")
    server.ListenAndServe()

}
```

A DataStore struct type is defined to easily manage mgo.Session. Two methods are added to the DataStore type: Close and C. The Close method releases the resources of the newly created Session object by calling the Close method of the Session object. This method is invoked by using the defer function after the lifetime of an HTTP request. The C method returns the Collection object with the given name:

```go
type DataStore struct {
        session *mgo.Session
 }
```

```
//Close mgo.Session
func (d *DataStore) Close() {
    d.session.Close()
}

//Returns a collection from the database.
func (d *DataStore) C(name string) *mgo.Collection {
    return d.session.DB("taskdb").C(name)
}
```

The NewDataStore function creates a new DataStore object by providing a new Session object using the Copy method of the Session obtained from the Dial method:

```
func NewDataStore() *DataStore {
    ds := &DataStore{
        session: session.Copy(),
    }
    return ds
}
```

The NewDataStore function is called to create a DataStore object for providing a copied Session object being used in the lifetime of an HTTP request. For each handler for a route, a new Session object is used through the DataStore type. In short, using a global Session object is not a good practice; it is recommended to use a copied Session object for the lifetime of each HTTP request. This approach allows you to having multiple Session objects if required.

Summary

When working with web applications, it is important that you persist application data into persistence storage. In this chapter, you learned how to persist data into MongoDB using the mgo package, which is a MongoDB driver for Go.

MongoDB is an open-source document database that provides high performance, high availability, and automatic scaling. MongoDB is the most popular NoSQL database; it has been widely used by modern web applications. The mgo driver provides a simple API that follows the Go idioms.

You can add indexes to fields of MongoDB collections, which provide high performance on read operations. When developing web applications in Go, using a global mgo.Session object is not a good practice. The right approach for managing Session is to create a new Session object by calling Copy, Clone, or New on the obtained Session object, which was obtained by the Dial method of the mgo package.

The next chapter will show you more about working with the MongoDB database using the mgo package.

CHAPTER 9

■ ■ ■

Building RESTful Services

The last few chapters discussed various aspects of building web-based systems, including the fundamentals of Go web programming using the http package, the html/template package for rendering the UI, various approaches for authentication, HTTP middleware, and data persistence with MongoDB.

This chapter will implement a full-fledged RESTful API application named TaskManager by using the concepts discussed in previous chapters. This application will also have new features, such as the capability to manage dependencies for external packages and deploy an HTTP server with Docker.

RESTful APIs: the Backbone of Digital Transformation

Representational State Transfer (REST) is an architectural style for building scalable web services. RESTful systems typically communicate over the Hypertext Transfer Protocol (HTTP) by using HTTP verbs. The REST architectural style was first described by Roy Fielding in his doctoral dissertation, in which he described six constraints applied to the REST architecture.

Here are the six constraints described by Roy Fielding:

- Uniform interface

- Stateless

- Cacheable

- Client-server

- Layered system

- Code on demand (optional)

■ **Note**   For a better understanding of the REST architectural style, read Roy Fielding's doctoral dissertation at http://www.ics.uci.edu/~fielding/pubs/dissertation/rest_arch_style.htm.

The greatest advantages of REST architecture is that it uses the basic components of web programming. If you have basic knowledge of HTTP programming, you can easily adopt the REST architecture style for your applications. It uses HTTP as a transport system to communicate with remote servers. You can use XML and JSON as the data format to communicate among clients and servers. Resource is a key concept in RESTful systems, as described by Fielding in his dissertation:

> *The key abstraction of information in REST is a resource. Any information that can be named can be a resource: a document or image, a temporal service (e.g. "today's weather in Los Angeles"), a collection of other resources, a non-virtual object (e.g. a person), and so on. In other words, any concept that might be the target of an author's hypertext reference must fit within the definition of a resource. A resource is a conceptual mapping to a set of entities, not the entity that corresponds to the mapping at any particular point in time.*

By using uniform resource identifiers (URIs) and HTTP verbs, you can perform actions against the resources. Let's say you define the resource "/api/employees". Now you can retrieve the information about an employee resource using the HTTP verb Get, create a new employee resource using the HTTP verb Post, update an existing employee resource using the HTTP verb Put, and delete an employee resource using the HTTP verb Delete.

Web service APIs that follow the REST architecture style are known as RESTful APIs. When you build RESTful APIs, you use XML and JSON as the data format for exchanging data among client applications and API servers. Some APIs support both XML and JSON formats; others support a single data format: either XML or JSON. When you build APIs targeted for mobile applications, the most commonly used data format is JSON because it is lightweight and easier to consume than it compared to XML. In this chapter, you will build a JSON-based RESTful API.

API-Driven Development with RESTful APIs

APIs, often RESTful APIs, are becoming the backbone of modern applications by enabling digital transformation in enterprises. RESTful APIs enable better integration among applications, regardless of technology, platforms, and devices. They are very important components in many application development scenarios, including Big Data, the Internet of Things (IoT), Microservice architecture, web applications, and mobile applications.

The importance of API-based development has increased a lot in the era of mobility. When you build mobile applications, RESTful APIs can be used as the back end and for building web front-end applications. In enterprise mobility, the biggest challenge is not about building mobile front-end applications, but to expose enterprise data into mobile devices. These data might be spans in multiple systems, technologies, and platforms. RESTful APIs allow you to expose your enterprise data into mobile devices. A RESTful services layer is an important part of implementation in most enterprise mobility scenarios.

In the past, web applications were developed by implemented everything on the server side, including user interface rendering logic using server-side templates. Today's APIs are becoming the central point of web applications and mobile applications: developers are building RESTful services on the server side and then building the front-end applications for both web and mobile by leveraging these RESTful services as the back end.

Go: the Great Stack for RESTful Services

I believe that Go may not be a great choice for building conventional web applications in which everything, including UI rendering, is implemented on the server side. I am not saying that Go is not good for building traditional web applications; you can build conventional web applications by simply using Go standard library packages. Go web development frameworks such as Beego and Revel are great for building web applications, but I strongly believe that Go is a good choice for building highly scalable RESTful API systems to power the back end for modern applications. Among the technology stacks available for building RESTful APIs, I highly recommended Go, which gives high performance, greater concurrency support, and simplicity for building scalable back-end systems. Go's simplicity and package ecosystem are excellent for writing loosely coupled, maintainable RESTful services.

The standard library package http provides a great foundation for building scalable web systems. It comes with built-in concurrency support that executes each HTTP request in a separate goroutine. The http package comes with a greater number of extensibility points that work well with third-party package ecosystems. If you want to extend or replace any functionality of the http package, you can easily build your own package without destroying the design goals of the package. Several useful third-party packages extend the functionality of the http package, enabling you to build highly scalable web applications and RESTful APIs using Go.

When you build web-based systems, the ecosystem is very important, and there are many mature database driver packages available for Go. Chapter 8 discussed how to work with MongoDB using the mgo package. Database driver packages are available for major relational databases and NoSQL databases. If your back-end systems need to work with middleware messaging systems, you can find client library packages to work with those systems. NSQ, a real-time distributed messaging platform, is built with Go. In short, the Go ecosystem, including third-party packages and tools, provides everything required for building scalable RESTful APIs and other web-based, back-end systems using Go.

Go: the Great Stack for Microservice Architecture

Software development practices have been continuously evolving to cater to solving new challenges. As a programming language, Go is a great example of language as a solution for solving today's challenges of building larger applications. The evolution is happening in software architectures as well. *Microservice architecture* is the hottest buzzword in software architectures, which is a fundamental shift in software development for building larger distributed applications.

In the past, many applications used a monolithic architecture pattern in which all components of the application, including presentation components, business logic, database access logic, and applications integration logic, were put in a single deployable unit. When the scope and functionalities of these applications were evolving, they were maintained as a single application unit by adding new functionalities and software components. Scaling and maintaining monolithic applications are always a big challenge because of the complex nature of maintaining everything as a single deployable unit. Microservice architecture is an alternative architecture pattern that addresses the limitations and challenges of monolithic architecture.

Microservice architecture is a paradigm shift in software development that focuses on building independently deployable and individual pieces of software. Instead of developing larger monolithic applications, Microservice architecture recommends building loosely coupled, small pieces of software services that can be deployed independently of other services. Unlike monolithic architecture, each service in the Microservice architecture is developed and deployed independently so that you can easily scale development and deployment. You can even use different technology stacks for developing individual services because they are deploying and updating independently of other services.

RESTful Services in Microservice Architecture

In Microservice architecture, loosely coupled software services are developed, and the application is built by composing these services. In this architecture approach, each microservice needs to communicate with other microservices; RESTful APIs can be used to communicate among these microservices. RESTful APIs are very important components in the Microservice architecture.

Go is a great technology stack for building applications with the Microservice pattern and its design philosophy intersects with the Microservice architecture pattern. The idiomatic approach of Go programming is to develop small pieces of software components as packages and then build applications by composing these packages.

Building RESTful APIs

Let's build a simple RESTful API application by using the knowledge you have gained from previous chapters. This RESTful API application provides the back end for building a simple "TaskManager" application that can be used to manage tasks and give updates and notes about each task. The application will be persisted into a MongoDB database. This TaskManager RESTful API will be a JSON-based API in which the JSON data format will be used for sending and receiving messages among client applications and the RESTful API server.

Third-Party Packages

The following third-party packages will be used for building the TaskManager application:

- `gopkg.in/mgo.v2`: The `mgo` package provides a MongoDB driver for Go.

- `gopkg.in/mgo.v2/bson`: A subpackage of `mgo`, it provides implementation of the BSON specification for Go.

- `github.com/gorilla/mux`: The `mux` package implements a request router and dispatcher.

- `github.com/dgrijalva/jwt-go`: The `jwt-go` package implements helper functions for working with JSON Web Tokens (JWT).

- `github.com/codegangsta/negroni`: The `Negroni` package provides an idiomatic approach to HTTP middleware.

Application Structure

Figure 9-1 illustrates the high-level folder structure of the RESTful API application.

Figure 9-1. Application folder structure

Figure 9-2 illustrates the folder structure and associated files of the completed version of the RESTful API application.

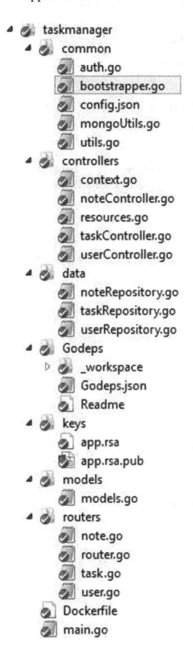

Figure 9-2. Folders and associated files of the completed application

Besides the keys and Godeps folders, all other folders represent Go packages. The keys folder, which contains cryptographic keys for signing JWT and its verification, is used for the authentication of APIs with JWT. The Godeps folder is used to manage external dependencies of the application using the godep third-party tool.

The RESTful API application has been divided into the following packages:

- common: Implements some utility functions and provides initialization logic for the application

- controllers: Implements the application's application handlers

- data: Implements the persistence logic with the MongoDB database

- models: Describes the data model of the application

- routers: Implements the HTTP request routers for the RESTful API

Data Model

The application provides the API for managing tasks. A user can add tasks and can provide updates and notes against the individual task. Let's define the data model for this application to be used with the MongoDB database.

Listing 9-1 defines the data model for the RESTful API application.

Listing 9-1. Data Model for the Application in models.go

```go
package models

import (
    "time"

    "gopkg.in/mgo.v2/bson"
)

type (
    User struct {
        Id           bson.ObjectId `bson:"_id,omitempty" json:"id"`
        FirstName    string        `json:"firstname"`
        LastName     string        `json:"lastname"`
        Email        string        `json:"email"`
        Password     string        `json:"password,omitempty"`
        HashPassword []byte        `json:"hashpassword,omitempty "`
    }
    Task struct {
        Id           bson.ObjectId `bson:"_id,omitempty" json:"id"`
        CreatedBy    string        `json:"createdby"`
        Name         string        `json:"name"`
        Description  string        `json:"description"`
        CreatedOn    time.Time     `json:"createdon,omitempty"`
        Due          time.Time     `json:"due,omitempty"`
        Status       string        `json:"status,omitempty"`
        Tags         []string      `json:"tags,omitempty"`
    }
    TaskNote struct {
        Id           bson.ObjectId `bson:"_id,omitempty" json:"id"`
        TaskId       bson.ObjectId `json:"taskid"`
        Description  string        `json:"description"`
        CreatedOn    time.Time     `json:"createdon,omitempty"`
    }
)
```

Three structs are created: User, Task, and TaskNote. The User struct represents users of the application. A user should register at the application to create tasks. An authenticated user can add tasks, which will be represented with the Task struct. A user can add notes against each task, which will be represented with the TaskNote struct. The TaskNote entity holds the child details of its parent entity: Task.

Chapter 8 showed how to make a parent–child relationship by embedding child documents into the parent document. That approach is good for some scenarios, but document references are also appropriate in other contexts. Here, the parent-child relationships are made with document references. Whenever a TaskNote object is created, a reference is put to the parent Task document by specifying the TaskId in the TaskNote object. In this approach, you have to execute separate queries into the MongoDB database to get the documents of the Task object and TaskNote object. When you follow embedded documents to make a one-to-many relationship, you can retrieve the information for both parent and child entities by executing a single query because child documents are embedded into the parent entity.

Resource Modeling for RESTful APIs

When you design RESTful APIs, resource modeling is a very important concept; it is the foundational layer for designing RESTful APIs. Let's define the resources of the RESTful API by leveraging URIs as resource identifiers and HTTP verbs.

Table 9-1 shows the resources identified for the RESTful API.

Table 9-1. *Resources Identified for the RESTful API*

URI	HTTP Verb	Functionality
/users/register	Post	Creates a new user.
/users/login	Post	User logs in to the system, which returns a JWT if the login is successful.
/tasks	Post	Creates a new task.
/tasks/{id}	Put	Updates an existing task.
/tasks	Get	Gets all tasks.
/tasks/{id}	Get	Gets a single task for a given ID. The value of the ID comes from the route parameter.
/tasks/users/{id}	Get	Gets all tasks associated with a user. The value of the user ID comes from the route parameter.
/tasks/{id}	Delete	Deletes an existing task for a given ID. The value of the ID comes from the route parameter.
/notes	Post	Creates a new note against an existing task.
/notes/{id}	Put	Updates an existing task note.
/notes	Get	Gets all task notes.
/notes/{id}	Get	Gets a single note for a given ID. The value of the ID comes from the route parameter.
/notes/tasks/{id}	Get	Gets all task notes for a given task ID. The value of the ID comes from the route parameter.
/notes/{id}	Delete	Deletes an existing note for a given ID. The value of the ID comes from the route parameter.

Mapping Resources with Application Routes

You have to map the resource identifiers with the HTTP server's application routes to execute appropriate application handlers for the HTTP requests to RESTful API resources. All routes are organized in the routers package, in which separate Go source files are written to specify the routes for each resource path. In this RESTful API application, three entities are used: User, Task, and TaskNote. These entities are mapped with three resources: "/users", "/tasks", and "/notes".

Figure 9-3 illustrates the structure of the routers package directory:

Figure 9-3. *Structure of routers package*

Routes for the Users Resource

Let's define the routes for the Users resource (see Listing 9-2).

Listing 9-2. Routes for the Users Resource in user.go

```
package routers

import (
    "github.com/gorilla/mux"
    "github.com/shijuvar/go-web/taskmanager/controllers"
)

func SetUserRoutes(router *mux.Router) *mux.Router {
    router.HandleFunc("/users/register", controllers.Register).Methods("POST")
    router.HandleFunc("/users/login", controllers.Login).Methods("POST")
    return router
}
```

The SetUserRoutes function receives a pointer to the Gorilla mux router object (mux.Router) as an argument and returns the pointer of the mux.Router object. Two routes are specified: for registering a new user and for user login to the system. Application handler functions are called from the controllers package, which is discussed later in the chapter.

Routes for the Tasks Resource

A user must log in to the system to access the resources of Task and TaskNote. When users log in using a username and password, the system gives them a JWT that can be used as authorization to access the resources of the Task and TaskNote entities. The server validates the JWT of HTTP requests in the Task and TaskNote resources by using an HTTP middleware that wraps the application handlers and ensures that HTTP requests have a valid bearer token as a JWT.

The third-party package Negroni is used for handling HTTP middleware (refer to Chapter 6). A middleware handler function named Authorize is in the common package and used to authorize HTTP requests with the JWT. In the RESTful API application, it isn't necessary to use the authorization middleware across the routes of the application; when the resources of User - Register and Login are accessed, the middleware function should not be invoked. The authentication middleware function is applied into the Task and TaskNote entities. Here, the resources of the Task entity are mapped with the URI "/tasks", so the authorization middleware has to be added to work with the "/tasks" URL path. The Negroni package allows you to add middleware to route specific URL paths.

Listing 9-3 provides the routes specified for the Tasks resource.

Listing 9-3. Routes for the Tasks Resource in task.go

```
package routers

import (
    "github.com/codegangsta/negroni"
    "github.com/gorilla/mux"
    "github.com/shijuvar/go-web/taskmanager/common"
    "github.com/shijuvar/go-web/taskmanager/controllers"
)

func SetTaskRoutes(router *mux.Router) *mux.Router {
    taskRouter := mux.NewRouter()
    taskRouter.HandleFunc("/tasks", controllers.CreateTask).Methods("POST")
    taskRouter.HandleFunc("/tasks/{id}", controllers.UpdateTask).Methods("PUT")
    taskRouter.HandleFunc("/tasks", controllers.GetTasks).Methods("GET")
    taskRouter.HandleFunc("/tasks/{id}", controllers.GetTaskById).Methods("GET")
    taskRouter.HandleFunc("/tasks/users/{id}", controllers.GetTasksByUser).Methods("GET")
    taskRouter.HandleFunc("/tasks/{id}", controllers.DeleteTask).Methods("DELETE")
    router.PathPrefix("/tasks").Handler(negroni.New(
        negroni.HandlerFunc(common.Authorize),
        negroni.Wrap(taskRouter),
    ))
    return router
}
```

Adding Route-Specific Middleware

You can add the authorization middleware for the route path "/tasks" to restrict access only to authenticated users. In the SetTaskRoutes function, a new router instance of mux router is created, the routes for the "/tasks" resource are specified, and the authorization middleware is wrapped into the handler functions of the routes path "/tasks":

```
router.PathPrefix("/tasks").Handler(negroni.New(
    negroni.HandlerFunc(common.Authorize),
    negroni.Wrap(taskRouter),
))
```

Routes for the TaskNote Resource

The TaskNote entity is wrapped with the URI "/notes". Like the "/tasks" resources, authorization middleware has to be added to the "/notes" resource.

Listing 9-4 provides the routes specified for the TaskNote resource.

Listing 9-4. Routes for the TaskNote Resource in note.go

```
package routers

import (
    "github.com/codegangsta/negroni"
    "github.com/gorilla/mux"
    "github.com/shijuvar/go-web/taskmanager/common"
    "github.com/shijuvar/go-web/taskmanager/controllers"
)

func SetNoteRoutes(router *mux.Router) *mux.Router {
    noteRouter := mux.NewRouter()
    noteRouter.HandleFunc("/notes", controllers.CreateNote).Methods("POST")
    noteRouter.HandleFunc("/notes/{id}", controllers.UpdateNote).Methods("PUT")
    noteRouter.HandleFunc("/notes/{id}", controllers.GetNoteById).Methods("GET")
    noteRouter.HandleFunc("/notes", controllers.GetNotes).Methods("GET")
    noteRouter.HandleFunc("/notes/tasks/{id}", controllers.GetNotesByTask).Methods("GET")
    noteRouter.HandleFunc("/notes/{id}", controllers.DeleteNote).Methods("DELETE")
    router.PathPrefix("/notes").Handler(negroni.New(
        negroni.HandlerFunc(common.Authorize),
        negroni. Wrap(noteRouter),
    ))
    return router
}
```

Initializing Routes for a RESTful API

All routes are now specified for the RESTful API application. Let's write the code to initialize all routes specified in the previous steps.

Listing 9-5 initializes all routes for the RESTful API.

Listing 9-5. Initializing Routes in router.go

```
package routers

import (
    "github.com/gorilla/mux"
)

func InitRoutes() *mux.Router {
    router := mux.NewRouter().StrictSlash(false)
    // Routes for the User entity
    router = SetUserRoutes(router)
    // Routes for the Task entity
```

```
    router = SetTaskRoutes(router)
    // Routes for the TaskNote entity
    router = SetNoteRoutes(router)
    return router
}
```

The InitRoutes function in main.go is called when the HTTP server starts, as discussed in a later section of the chapter.

Setting up the RESTful API Application

The resource modeling for the RESTful API application is complete. This section focuses on setting up the application and starting the HTTP server after executing some essential initialization logic.

Before starting the HTTP server, follow these steps:

1. Initialize the AppConfig identifier of the common package by reading configuration values from config.json. The AppConfig identifier provides the configuration values such as the host URI of HTTP server and MongoDB, name of the MongoDB database, and authentication credentials to access the MongoDB database.

2. Initialize asymmetric cryptographic keys for signing the JWT and verifying the tokens.

3. Create a MongoDB Session object using the mgo package.

4. Add indexes into MongoDB collections.

These are one-time activities that are invoked before starting the HTTP server. These functionalities are implemented in the common package. Let's take a look at the bootstrapping logic implemented in the common package (discussed in the following sections).

Figure 9-4 illustrates the source files contained in the common package.

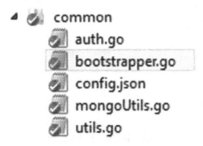

Figure 9-4. *Source files of the common package*

Initializing Configuration Values

Configuration values are put in a file named config.json, which stores values such as host URIs of the HTTP server and MongoDB server, authentication credentials to connect MongoDB, and so on. This helps you avoid using hard-coded strings in an application. The config.json file is read and decodes the JSON values into a variable AppConfig. Configuration values are read from this package variable to start the HTTP server and connect to the MongoDB database.

Listing 9-6 decodes the JSON string from config.json and puts the values into AppConfig.

Listing 9-6. Initializing AppConfig in utils.go

```
package common

import (
        "encoding/json"
        "log"
        "os"
)
type configuration struct {
        Server, MongoDBHost, DBUser, DBPwd, Database string
}
// AppConfig holds the configuration values from config.json file
var AppConfig configuration

// Initialize AppConfig
func initConfig() {
        loadAppConfig()
}

// Reads config.json and decode into AppConfig
func loadAppConfig() {
        file, err := os.Open("common/config.json")
        defer file.Close()
        if err != nil {
                log.Fatalf("[loadConfig]: %s\n", err)
        }
        decoder := json.NewDecoder(file)
        AppConfig = configuration{}
        err = decoder.Decode(&AppConfig)
        if err != nil {
                log.Fatalf("[loadAppConfig]: %s\n", err)
        }
}
```

Loading Private/Public RSA Keys

RSA keys are loaded into two variables for representing private and public keys, which are used for the authorization infrastructure of the application. The private/public keys are used to generate JWT and verify the token in HTTP requests to authorize access to protected resources of the application. The private/public keys are loaded into two variables before the HTTP server starts so they can be used for a login handler and for authorizing HTTP requests in authorization middleware.

The command-line tool OpenSSL is used to generate the keys. To generate the private key, run the following command on the command-line window:

```
openssl genrsa -out app.rsa 1024
```

This command generates a 1024-bit key named app.rsa. To generate a counterpart public key for the private key, run the following command on the command-line window:

```
openssl rsa -in app.rsa -pubout > app.rsa.pub
```

This code generates a counterpart public key named app.rsa.pub. The RSA keys are stored in the directory keys.

Listing 9-7 loads the private/public RSA keys from the keys folder and stores them into two variables.

Listing 9-7. Initializing Private/Public Keys in auth.go

```go
package common

import (
        "io/ioutil"
)

// using asymmetric crypto/RSA keys
const (
    // openssl genrsa -out app.rsa 1024
    privKeyPath = "keys/app.rsa"
    // openssl rsa -in app.rsa -pubout > app.rsa.pub
    pubKeyPath  = "keys/app.rsa.pub"
)

// private key for signing and public key for verification
var (
    verifyKey, signKey []byte
)

// Read the key files before starting http handlers
func initKeys() {
        var err error

        signKey, err = ioutil.ReadFile(privKeyPath)
        if err != nil {
                log.Fatalf("[initKeys]: %s\n", err)
        }

        verifyKey, err = ioutil.ReadFile(pubKeyPath)
        if err != nil {
                log.Fatalf("[initKeys]: %s\n", err)
                panic(err)
        }
}
```

The private key is used for signing the JWT; the public key verifies the JWT in HTTP requests to access the resources of the RESTful API. You can use the OpenSSL tool to generate the RSA keys.

Creating a MongoDB Session Object

A MongoDB Session object is created before the HTTP server starts. The createDbSession function in mongoUtils.go creates a mgo.Session object by calling the DialWithInfo function of the mgo package. The DialWithInfo function establishes a new Session to the cluster of MongoDB servers provided by the instance of DialInfo type. The URI of MongoDB is read from the AppConfig variable. The Session object will be accessed through the GetSession function. Whenever CRUD operations are performed, the GetSession function is called, and the Session object is copied using the Copy method of mgo.Session. A copied Session object will be used for all CRUD operations.

Listing 9-8 provides the implementation of createDbSession and GetSession to use with the Session object.

Listing 9-8. MongoDB Session in mongoUtils.go

```
package common

import (
    "gopkg.in/mgo.v2"
)

var session *mgo.Session

func GetSession() *mgo.Session {
        if session == nil {
                var err error
                session, err = mgo.DialWithInfo(&mgo.DialInfo{
                        Addrs:    []string{AppConfig.MongoDBHost},
                        Username: AppConfig.DBUser,
                        Password: AppConfig.DBPwd,
                        Timeout:  60 * time.Second,
                })
                if err != nil {
                        log.Fatalf("[GetSession]: %s\n", err)
                }
        }
        return session
}
func createDbSession() {
        var err error
        session, err = mgo.DialWithInfo(&mgo.DialInfo{
                Addrs:    []string{AppConfig.MongoDBHost},
                Username: AppConfig.DBUser,
                Password: AppConfig.DBPwd,
                Timeout:  60 * time.Second,
        })
        if err != nil {
                log. Fatalf("[createDbSession]: %s\n", err)
        }
}
```

Adding Indexes into MongoDB

Indexes provide improved performance for executing queries in MongoDB. Because the User collection is frequently queried with the email field, the Task collection with the createdby field, and the TaskNote collection with the taskid field, indexes are added for these fields. The addIndexes function adds indexes into MongoDB collections.

Listing 9-9 adds indexes into MongoDB.

Listing 9-9. Adding Indexes in MongoDB in mongoUtils.go

```go
// Add indexes into MongoDB
func addIndexes() {
    var err error
    userIndex := mgo.Index{
        Key:        []string{"email"},
        Unique:     true,
        Background: true,
        Sparse:     true,
    }
    taskIndex := mgo.Index{
        Key:        []string{"createdby"},
        Unique:     false,
        Background: true,
        Sparse:     true,
    }
    noteIndex := mgo.Index{
        Key:        []string{"taskid"},
        Unique:     false,
        Background: true,
        Sparse:     true,
    }
    // Add indexes into MongoDB
    session := GetSession().Copy()
    defer session.Close()
    userCol := session.DB(AppConfig.Database).C("users")
    taskCol := session.DB(AppConfig.Database).C("tasks")
    noteCol := session.DB(AppConfig.Database).C("notes")
    err = userCol.EnsureIndex(userIndex)
    if err != nil {
        log.Fatalf("[addIndexes]: %s\n", err)
    }
    err = taskCol.EnsureIndex(taskIndex)
    if err != nil {
        log.Fatalf("[addIndexes]: %s\n", err)
    }
    err = noteCol.EnsureIndex(noteIndex)
    if err != nil {
        log.Fatalf("[addIndexes]: %s\n", err)
    }
}
```

Initialization Logic in the common Package

The bootstrapper.go source file in the common package provides a StartUp function that calls the necessary initialization logic before the HTTP server starts. The StartUp function of the common package is called from main.go.

Listing 9-10 provides the implementation of the StartUp function that calls the initialization logic, which is required before running the HTTP server.

Listing 9-10. StartUp Function in bootstrapper.go

```go
package common

func StartUp() {
    // Initialize AppConfig variable
    initConfig()
    // Initialize private/public keys for JWT authentication
    initKeys()
    // Start a MongoDB session
    createDbSession()
    // Add indexes into MongoDB
    addIndexes()
}
```

Starting the HTTP Server

The HTTP server is created in main.go.
Listing 9-11 provides the implementation of main.go.

Listing 9-11. Entry Point of the Program in main.go

```go
package main

import (
    "log"
    "net/http"

    "github.com/codegangsta/negroni"
    "github.com/shijuvar/go-web/taskmanager/common"
    "github.com/shijuvar/go-web/taskmanager/routers"
)

//Entry point of the program
func main() {

    // Calls startup logic
    common.StartUp()
    // Get the mux router object
    router := routers.InitRoutes()
    // Create a negroni instance
    n := negroni.Classic()
    n.UseHandler(router)
```

```
server := &http.Server{
    Addr:    common.AppConfig.Server,
    Handler: n,
}
log.Println("Listening...")
server.ListenAndServe()
}
```

The HTTP server is created in main.go, in which the StartUp function of the common package is called to execute initialization logic for the RESTful API application. The InitRoutes function of the routers package is then called to get the *mux.Router, which is used for creating the Negroni handler. The http.Server object is created by providing the Negroni handler and finally starting the HTTP server. The host URI of the HTTP server is read from common.AppConfig.

Authentication

Here is the authentication workflow defined in the application:

1. Users register into the system by sending HTTP requests to the resource "/users/register".

2. Registered users can log in to the system by sending HTTP requests to the resource "/users/login". The server validates the login credential and generates a JWT as an access token for accessing the protected resources of the RESTful API server.

3. Users can use the JWT to access the protected resources of the RESTful API. Users must send this token as a bearer token with the "Authorization" HTTP header.

The authentication workflow is described in more detail in the following sections.

Generating and Verifying JWT

JWT is used to authorize HTTP requests to access RESTful API resources. The third-party package jwt-go is used for working with JWT (refer to Chapter 7). The auth.go source file in the common package provides the functionalities for generating JWT and verifying the token using a middleware handler function. The third-party package jwt-go is used for generating and verifying the JWT, and the private key is used for signing the JWT. It will be invoked from the application handler for the request "/users/login" if the login user is successfully authenticated into the system.

Listing 9-12 shows the helper functions for generating JWT and verifying it in a HTTP middleware handler.

Listing 9-12. Helper Functions for JWT Authentication in auth.go

```
package common

import (
        "io/ioutil"
        "log"
        "net/http"
        "time"

        jwt "github.com/dgrijalva/jwt-go"
)
```

```go
// using asymmetric crypto/RSA keys
// location of private/public key files
const (
        // openssl genrsa -out app.rsa 1024
        privKeyPath = "keys/app.rsa"
        // openssl rsa -in app.rsa -pubout > app.rsa.pub
        pubKeyPath  = "keys/app.rsa.pub"
)

// Private key for signing and public key for verification
var (
        verifyKey, signKey []byte
)

// Read the key files before starting http handlers
func initKeys() {
        var err error

        signKey, err = ioutil.ReadFile(privKeyPath)
        if err != nil {
                log.Fatalf("[initKeys]: %s\n", err)
        }

        verifyKey, err = ioutil.ReadFile(pubKeyPath)
        if err != nil {
                log.Fatalf("[initKeys]: %s\n", err)
                panic(err)
        }
}

// Generate JWT token
func GenerateJWT(name, role string) (string, error) {
    // create a signer for rsa 256
    t := jwt.New(jwt.GetSigningMethod("RS256"))

    // set claims for JWT token
    t.Claims["iss"] = "admin"
    t.Claims["UserInfo"] = struct {
        Name string
        Role string
    }{name, role}

    // set the expire time for JWT token
    t.Claims["exp"] = time.Now().Add(time.Minute * 20).Unix()
    tokenString, err := t.SignedString(signKey)
    if err != nil {
        return "", err
    }
    return tokenString, nil
}
```

```go
// Middleware for validating JWT tokens
func Authorize(w http.ResponseWriter, r *http.Request, next http.HandlerFunc) {
    // validate the token
    token, err := jwt.ParseFromRequest(r, func(token *jwt.Token) (interface{}, error) {

        // Verify the token with public key, which is the counter part of private key
        return verifyKey, nil
    })

    if err != nil {
        switch err.(type) {

        case *jwt.ValidationError: // JWT validation error
            vErr := err.(*jwt.ValidationError)

            switch vErr.Errors {
            case jwt.ValidationErrorExpired: //JWT expired
                DisplayAppError(
                    w,
                    err,
                    "Access Token is expired, get a new Token",
                    401,
                )
                return

            default:
                DisplayAppError(w,
                    err,
                    "Error while parsing the Access Token!",
                    500,
                )
                return
            }

        default:
            DisplayAppError(w,
                err,
                "Error while parsing Access Token!",
                500)
            return
        }

    }
    if token. Valid {
        next(w, r)
    } else {
        DisplayAppError(w,
            err,
            "Invalid Access Token",
            401,
        )
    }
}
```

Generating JWT

The GenerateJWT function generates the JWT by using the private key. Various claims are set onto the JWT, including expiration information for the token. The go-jwt package is used for signing the encoded security token. The GenerateJWT function is invoked from the application handler for the request "/users/login" and is called only if the login process is successful.

When a user logs in to the system, the server sends back a JSON response, as shown here:

```
{"data":
{"user":{"id":"55b9f7e13f06221910000001","firstname":"Shiju","lastname":"Varghese",
"email":"shijuvar@gmail.com"},
"token":"eyJhbGciOiJSUzI1NiIsInR5cCI6IkpXVCJ9.eyJVc2VySW5mbyI6eyJOYW1lIjoic2hpanVAZ21haWwu
Y29tIiwiUm9sZSI6Im1lbWJlciJ9LCJleHAiOjE0MzgyNTI5MzgsImlzcyI6ImFkbWluIn0.WtdM55KEOcNlj5c2
VYwtIUQS8L6UI_ViLiwe0wH_0cpDj0dKkMTMtZ6LSHoIxtZyt92z19WX5gQCi3z-7Mly4kPe5Yvp3IXuDNdgJvB
kQvEd_xg0-Vx9bhm_ztf0Hb2CInsVgux49EIxgjFoinwdzrxmM9ZbY7msBYSKutcRKLU"}
}
```

From the JSON response, users can take the JWT from the JSON field "token", which can be used for authorizing the HTTP requests to access protected resources of the RESTful API.

JWT has three parts, separated by a . (period):

- Header

- Payload

- Signature

JWT is a JSON-based security encoding that can be decoded to get JSON representation of these parts. Figure 9-5 shows the decoded representation of the Header and Payload sections.

Encoded PASTE A TOKEN HERE

```
eyJhbGciOiJSUzI1NiIsInR5cCI6IkpXVCJ9.eyJVc2
VySW5mbyI6eyJOYW1lIjoic2hpanVAZ21haWwuY29tI
iwiUm9sZSI6Im1lbWJlciJ9LCJleHAiOjE0MzgyNTI5
MzgsImlzcyI6ImFkbWluIn0.WtdM55KE0cNlj5c2VYw
tIUQS8L6UI_ViLiwe0wH_0cpDj0dKkMTMtZ6LSHoIxt
Zyt92z19WX5gQCi3z-
7Mly4kPe5Yvp3IXuDNdgJvBkQvEd_xg0-
Vx9bhm_ztf0Hb2CInsVgux49EIxgjFoinwdzrxmM9Zb
Y7msBYSKutcRKLU
```

Decoded EDIT THE PAYLOAD AND SECRET !

HEADER: ALGORITHM & TOKEN TYPE

```
{
  "alg": "RS256",
  "typ": "JWT"
}
```

PAYLOAD: DATA

```
{
  "UserInfo": {
    "Name": "shiju@gmail.com",
    "Role": "member"
  },
  "exp": 1438252938,
  "iss": "admin"
}
```

Figure 9-5. *Decoded JSON representation of JWT*

The Header section contains the algorithm used for generating the token, which is RS256, and the type, which is JWT. Payload carries the JWT claims in which you can provide user information, expiration, and other information about the JWT.

Sending JWT to the Server

When users successfully log in to the system, they provide a JWT as the access token to authorize the subsequent HTTP requests to the API server. So whenever HTTP requests are sent to access protected resources, the JWT must be provided in the HTTP request to get authorization to the API server. Once the login process is successfully completed, the returned token string can be put into any kind of client storage to be easily accessed whenever HTTP requests are sent to access the resources of the RESTful API.

In front-end web applications, you can use HTML5 Web Storage (localStorage/sessionStorage) or web cookies to persist the JWT. But you should consider the security aspects when you put JWT into various kinds of client application storage.

When you send HTTP requests to access RESTful API resources, you must provide a bearer token in the HTTP request header "Authorization".

Here is the format for sending a JWT string with the "Authorization" header:

```
"Authorization": "Bearer token_string"
```

Here is an example that provides a JWT as a bearer token with the "Authorization" header:

```
"Authorization":"Bearer eyJhbGciOiJIUzI1NiIsInR5cCI6IkpXVCJ9.eyJzdWIiOiIxMjMwNTY3ODkw
IiwibmFtZSI6IkpvaG4gRG9lIiwiYWRtaW4iOnRydWV9.TJVA95OrM7E2cBab3ORMHrHDcEfxjoYZgeFONFh7HgQ"
```

Authorizing JWT

The Authorize middleware handler function authorizes HTTP requests, which validate whether the HTTP request has a valid JWT in the "Authorization" header as a bearer token. The ParseFromRequest helper function of the go-jwt package is used to verify the token with a public key. In this application, one private key is used to sign the tokens, so its public counterpart is also used to verify the token:

```
token, err := jwt.ParseFromRequest(r, func(token *jwt.Token) (interface{}, error) {
    return verifyKey, nil
})
```

If the request has a valid token, the middleware function calls the next handler in the middleware stack. If the token is invalid, the DisplayAppError helper function is called to display HTTP errors in JSON format. When the DisplayAppError function is called, the error value is provided a custom message for the error and an HTTP status code. The HTTP status code 401 represents the HTTP status "Unauthorized":

```
if token.Valid {
        next(w, r)
    } else {
        w.WriteHeader(http.StatusUnauthorized)
        DisplayAppError(
            w,
            err,
            "Invalid Access Token",
            401,
        )
    }
```

When next(w,r) is called, it calls the next handler function. The Negroni package is called for the middleware stack and uses the signature func (http.ResponseWriter, *http.Request, http. HandlerFunc) to write middleware handler functions to be used with Negroni. All HTTP requests to the URL "/tasks" and "/notes" paths must be authorized with a valid access token. So the middleware function Authorize is added into the Negroni middleware stack.

Here is the code block in task.go of the routers package to add authentication middleware function to the "/tasks" path:

```go
func SetTaskRoutes(router *mux.Router) *mux.Router {
    taskRouter := mux.NewRouter()
    taskRouter.HandleFunc("/tasks", controllers.CreateTask).Methods("POST")
    taskRouter.HandleFunc("/tasks/{id}", controllers.UpdateTask).Methods("PUT")
    taskRouter.HandleFunc("/tasks", controllers.GetTasks).Methods("GET")
    taskRouter.HandleFunc("/tasks/{id}", controllers.GetTaskById).Methods("GET")
    taskRouter.HandleFunc("/tasks/users/{id}", controllers.GetTasksByUser).Methods("GET")
    taskRouter.HandleFunc("/tasks/{id}", controllers.DeleteTask).Methods("DELETE")
    router.PathPrefix("/tasks").Handler(negroni.New(
        negroni.HandlerFunc(common.Authorize),
        negroni.Wrap(taskRouter),
    ))
    return router
}
```

You can add middleware functions to specific routes by using the PathPrefix function of the router instance.

Here is the code block in note.go of the routers package to add authentication middleware function to the "/notes" path:

```go
func SetNoteRoutes(router *mux.Router) *mux.Router {
    noteRouter := mux.NewRouter()
    noteRouter.HandleFunc("/notes", controllers.CreateNote).Methods("POST")
    noteRouter.HandleFunc("/notes/{id}", controllers.UpdateNote).Methods("PUT")
    noteRouter.HandleFunc("/notes/{id}", controllers.GetNoteById).Methods("GET")
    noteRouter.HandleFunc("/notes", controllers.GetNotes).Methods("GET")
    noteRouter.HandleFunc("/notes/tasks/{id}", controllers.GetNotesByTask).Methods("GET")
    noteRouter.HandleFunc("/notes/{id}", controllers.DeleteNote).Methods("DELETE")
    router.PathPrefix("/notes").Handler(negroni.New(
        negroni.HandlerFunc(common.Authorize),
        negroni.Wrap(noteRouter),
    ))
    return router
}
```

Middleware functions are great for implementing shared functionalities across application handlers. Middleware functions can also be applied to specific routes, as was done for URL paths "/tasks" and "/notes".

Application Handlers

Previous sections looked at application data models, RESTful API resource modeling and mapping it with an application's HTTP routes, setting up the HTTP server with essential initialization logic, and authentication of RESTful APIs. Let's now take a look at application handlers for serving HTTP requests against each route.

Application handlers are organized in the `controllers` package. Figure 9-6 shows the source files contained in the `controllers` package.

Figure 9-6. *Source files of the controllers package*

Helper for Displaying HTTP Errors

Error handling in Go is different from most mainstream programming languages because it provides a simple and minimalistic approach for handling exceptions using a built-in `error` type. The values of the `error` type are used to indicate an abnormal state in the applications. When you look at the standard library packages, you see that most of the functions return multiple values, including an `error` type value to indicate an abnormal state.

You can check the value of the `error` type to see whether any exception occurred during the function execution:

```
file, err := os.Open("common/config.json")
    if err != nil {
        log.Fatalf("[loadConfig]: %s\n", err)
    }
```

The `Fatalf` function of the `log` package is called if the error variable contains any value. The `Fatalf` function aborts the program after writing the log message. In HTTP handlers of the RESTful API application, the program doesn't abort for any kind of abnormal state. Instead, a JSON response is provided as the HTTP response with the appropriate HTTP status code. A helper function is written in a `common` package to display HTTP errors in JSON format so that client applications can understand anything wrong with their HTTP requests.

Listing 9-13 provides a helper function to display HTTP errors in JSON format, which includes appropriate HTTP status codes in the error response.

Listing 9-13. Helper Function for Displaying Errors in utils.go

```
package common

import (
        "encoding/json"
        "log"
        "net/http"
)
```

```go
type (
        appError struct {
                Error      string `json:"error"`
                Message    string `json:"message"`
                HttpStatus int    `json:"status"`
        }
        errorResource struct {
                Data appError `json:"data"`
        }
)

func DisplayAppError(w http.ResponseWriter, handlerError error, message string, code int) {
        errObj := appError{
                Error:      handlerError.Error(),
                Message:    message,
                HttpStatus: code,
        }
        log.Printf("AppError]: %s\n", handlerError)
        w.Header().Set("Content-Type", "application/json; charset=utf-8")
        w.WriteHeader(code)
        if j, err := json.Marshal(errorResource{Data: errObj}); err == nil {
                w.Write(j)
        }
}
```

A helper function named `DisplayAppError` is written to provide error messages in JSON as the HTTP response. Client applications can check the HTTP status code to verify whether the HTTP request is successful. A struct type named `appError` is used to create the model object for providing error messages. In the `appError` type, the `Error` property is used for holding the string value of the error object, the `Message` property is used for holding a custom message on the error, and the `HttpStatus` property is used for holding HTTP status code. An instance of the `errorResource` type is created by providing the value of `appError` to encode the response as JSON.

Figure 9-7 shows the error response of an invalid HTTP request that contains an expired access token.

Figure 9-7. HTTP response for error messages in JSON

The DisplayAppError function is a simple helper function to provide HTTP errors. You can also write the error-handling logic in HTTP middleware, which can be used to wrap application handlers and is a more elegant approach to implement error handling in Go web applications. If any error occurred in an application handler, you can return a model object for holding the error data, and within the middleware function you can check whether the error model contains any value. You can also provide the HTTP response for an error if one occurs. This approach is not discussed in this chapter, but you can try it when you build your own web applications.

Handling Data for an HTTP Request Lifecycle

Let's define a type for handling the data during the lifecycle of an HTTP request. Here, a Context struct type is defined, on which the MongoDB Session object is put as a property, exposing the DbCollection method for getting the MongoDB Collection object and the Close method for closing the MongoDB Session object.

Listing 9-14 provides the code block of the Context struct type that will be used with HTTP handler functions to hold the data during an HTTP request lifecycle.

Listing 9-14. Context Struct in context.go

```
package controllers

import (
        "gopkg.in/mgo.v2"

        "github.com/shijuvar/go-web/taskmanager/common"
)

// Struct used for maintaining HTTP Request Context
type Context struct {
        MongoSession *mgo.Session
}

// Close mgo.Session
func (c *Context) Close() {
        c.MongoSession.Close()
}

// Returns mgo.collection for the given name
func (c *Context) DbCollection(name string) *mgo.Collection {
        return c.MongoSession.DB(common.AppConfig.Database).C(name)
}

// Create a new Context object for each HTTP request
func NewContext() *Context {
        session := common.GetSession().Copy()
        context := &Context{
                MongoSession: session,
        }
        return context
}
```

This source file provides a NewContext function that returns an instance of Context type by providing a copied version of the MongoDB Session object. The GetSession function of the common package is called to get the Session object and take a copy from it. Within the application handlers, the NewContext function is called to get an instance of a Context type in which the MongoDB Session object of the Context type is used for performing CRUD operations against the MongoDB database.

In the Context type, you are simply storing the MongoDB Session object, but you can use any kind of data in the Context type to be used with the lifecycle of an HTTP request. In many use cases, you may need to share these data among various middleware handler functions and application handler functions. In short, you need to share data among different handler functions.

In this scenario, you can use a mechanism to store objects to work with the HTTP request context. The context package from the Gorilla web toolkit (www.gorillatoolkit.org/pkg/context) provides the functionality for putting data in the HTTP Context object for holding the data during the lifecycle of an HTTP request. You can put the data into HTTP context in one handler, which is accessible from other handlers. In the RESTful API example, you use the data in the application handler and don't need to share data among handlers. So you aren't putting the Context struct into the HTTP Context object.

Handlers for the Users Resource

Here are the routes specified for the Users resource:

```
router.HandleFunc("/users/register", controllers.Register).Methods("POST")
router.HandleFunc("/users/login", controllers.Login).Methods("POST")
```

Two routes are specified for the Users resource. The resource "/users/register" is used to register a user into the system, and "/users/login" is used to authenticate into the system for getting an access token to be used to authorize the HTTP requests to access RESTful API resources.

JSON Resource Models

The RESTful API is a JSON-based API in which the client applications need to send data in JSON format, and the server sends the responses in JSON as well. To work with JSON API standards (http://jsonapi.org), resource models are defined for sending and receiving data in formatted JSON. "data" is defined as the root element for all JSON representations.

Listing 9-15 shows the resource models to be used with the Users resource.

Listing 9-15. JSON Resources for Working with "/users" in resources.go

```
package controllers

import (
    "github.com/shijuvar/go-web/taskmanager/models"
)

type (
    //For Post - /user/register
    UserResource struct {
        Data models.User `json:"data"`
    }
```

```
    //For Post - /user/login
    LoginResource struct {
        Data LoginModel `json:"data"`
    }
    // Response for authorized user Post - /user/login
    AuthUserResource struct {
        Data AuthUserModel `json:"data"`
    }
    //Model for authentication
    LoginModel struct {
        Email    string `json:"email"`
        Password string `json:"password"`
    }
    //Model for authorized user with access token
    AuthUserModel struct {
        User  models.User `json:"user"`
        Token string      `json:"token"`
    }
)
```

Handlers for the Users Resource

Application handler functions for the Users resource are written in the userController.go source file, which is organized in the controllers package.

Listing 9-16 provides the implementation of handler functions for the Users resource.

Listing 9-16. Application Handler Functions in userController.go

```
package controllers

import (
    "encoding/json"
    "net/http"

    "github.com/shijuvar/go-web/taskmanager/common"
    "github.com/shijuvar/go-web/taskmanager/data"
    "github.com/shijuvar/go-web/taskmanager/models"
)

// Handler for HTTP Post - "/users/register"
// Add a new User document
func Register(w http.ResponseWriter, r *http.Request) {
    var dataResource UserResource
    // Decode the incoming User json
    err := json.NewDecoder(r.Body).Decode(&dataResource)
    if err != nil {
        common.DisplayAppError(
            w,
            err,
            "Invalid User data",
            500,
        )
```

```go
        return
    }
    user := &dataResource.Data
    context := NewContext()
    defer context.Close()
    c := context.DbCollection("users")
    repo := &data.UserRepository{c}
    // Insert User document
    repo.CreateUser(user)
    // Clean-up the hashpassword to eliminate it from response
    user.HashPassword = nil
    if j, err := json.Marshal(UserResource{Data: *user}); err != nil {
        common. DisplayAppError(
            w,
            err,
            "An unexpected error has occurred",
            500,
        )
        return
    } else {
        w.Header().Set("Content-Type", "application/json")
        w.WriteHeader(http.StatusCreated)
        w.Write(j)
    }

}

// Handler for HTTP Post - "/users/login"
// Authenticate with username and apssword
func Login(w http.ResponseWriter, r *http.Request) {
    var dataResource LoginResource
    var token string
    // Decode the incoming Login json
    err := json.NewDecoder(r.Body).Decode(&dataResource)
    if err != nil {
        common.DisplayAppError(
            w,
            err,
            "Invalid Login data",
            500,
        )
        return
    }
    loginModel := dataResource.Data
    loginUser := models.User{
        Email:    loginModel.Email,
        Password: loginModel.Password,
    }
    context := NewContext()
    defer context.Close()
    c := context.DbCollection("users")
    repo := &data.UserRepository{c}
```

```go
    // Authenticate the login user
    if user, err := repo.Login(loginUser); err != nil {
        common.DisplayAppError(
            w,
            err,
            "Invalid login credentials",
            401,
        )
        return
    } else { //if login is successful

        // Generate JWT token
        token, err = common.GenerateJWT(user.Email, "member")
        if err != nil {
            common.DisplayAppError(
                w,
                err,
                "Eror while generating the access token",
                500,
            )
            return
        }
        w.Header().Set("Content-Type", "application/json")
        user.HashPassword = nil
        authUser := AuthUserModel{
            User:  user,
            Token: token,
        }
        j, err := json.Marshal(AuthUserResource{Data: authUser})
        if err != nil {
            common.DisplayAppError(
                w,
                err,
                "An unexpected error has occurred",
                500,
            )
            return
        }
        w.WriteHeader(http.StatusOK)
        w.Write(j)
    }
}
```

Registering New Users

To register a new user, the client application should send an HTTP Post to the URI "/users/register". In the Register handler function, the incoming JSON string is decoded into the type UserResource and creates an instance of the models.User struct by accessing the Data property of the UserResource object.

The Context type is used to access the MongoDB Session object (mgo.Session) in application handlers. So an instance of Context type and the MongoDB Collection object (mgo.Collection) are created by calling the DbCollection method:

```
context := NewContext()
defer context.Close()
c := context.DbCollection("users")
```

The Close method of the Context type is added into the defer function to close the MongoDB Session object, which is a copied version of the Session object. In all HTTP handler functions, a copied version of the MongoDB Session object is created and will use the same instance in a single HTTP request lifecycle and release the resources using the defer function.

In the Register handler function, an instance of UserRepository is created by providing the MongoDB Collection object. The CreateUser method of the UserRepository struct is created to persist the User object into the MongoDB database. All data persistence logic is written in the data package:

```
repo := &data.UserRepository{c}
// Insert User document
repo.CreateUser(user)
```

UserRepository provides all CRUD operations against the User entity. (This topic is discussed in the next section of the chapter.) The Register handler function sends back a response as a JSON representation of the newly created User entity.

Let's test the functionality of the Users resource by using a RESTful API client tool "Postman" (www.getpostman.com/), which allows you to test your APIs (also very useful for testing RESTful APIs).

Figure 9-8 shows the HTTP Post request sent to the URI endpoint "users/register" using the RESTful API client tool "Postman".

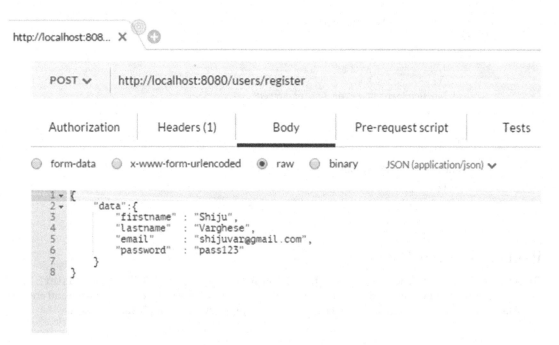

Figure 9-8. *HTTP Post to "/users/register"*

Figure 9-9 shows the response from the RESTful API server, indicating that a new resource has been created.

Figure 9-9. HTTP response from "/users/register"

Logging in to the System

Users of client applications must obtain a JWT to access the protected resources of the RESTful API. To get the token, a user must log in to the system with a username and password. If the user is getting authenticated, the server sends back a JWT that can be used for accessing the RESTful API resources.

The application handler Login is used for serving HTTP requests to the login resource. If the login is successful, the GenerateJWT function of the common package is called to generate JWT. The generated JWT is included in the JSON response:

```
if user, err := repo.Login(loginUser); err != nil {
        common.DisplayAppError(
            w,
            err,
            "Invalid login credentials",
            401,
        )
        return
    } else { //if login is successful

        // Generate JWT token
        token, err = common.GenerateJWT(user.Email, "member")
        if err != nil {
            common.DisplayAppError(
                w,
                err,
                "Eror while generating the access token",
                500,
            )
            return
        }
```

189

```
        w.Header().Set("Content-Type", "application/json")
        user.HashPassword = nil
        authUser := AuthUserModel{
            User:  user,
            Token: token,
        }
        j, err := json.Marshal(AuthUserResource{Data: authUser})
        if err != nil {
            common.DisplayAppError(
                w,
                err,
                "An unexpected error has occurred",
                500,
            )
            return
        }
        w.WriteHeader(http.StatusOK)
        w.Write(j)
    }
```

Figure 9-10 shows that login credentials were sent to the system by sending an HTTP Post to the URI endpoint "users/register" to get the JWT.

Figure 9-10. *HTTP Post to "/users/login"*

Figure 9-11 shows the HTTP response from the RESTful API server after the successful login to the system.

Body   Cookies   Headers (3)   Tests   Status   200 OK   Time   467 ms

Pretty   Raw   Preview   HTML ∨   ℐ   ⧉   Q

1   {"data":{"user":{"id":"55bc4bd5fd3092110c000001","firstname":"Shiju","lastname":"Varghese","email":"shijuvar@gmail
    .com"},"token":"eyJhbGciOiJSUzI1NiIsInR5cCI6IkpXVCJ9.eyJVc2VySW5mbyI6eyJOYW1lIjoic2hpanV2YXJAZ21haWwuY29tIiwiUm9sZSI6I
    m1lbWJlciI9LCJleHAiOjE0Mzg0MDUyNzcsImlzcyI6ImFkbWluIn0.g_lGC6wOQnlYpeL83ZBoN36EWQwb1J_92sKsmIBd_8JGpOdyx7tWqtSHPNo7hTB
    ZDOWuWSiYNF1PScMVF84MJx6JA2OjCNVdd-btBQ-1vFL8mFXl4d-9OruqiZuGwRG53Bd3ubuXBPXWATJBLqov7CY-OVAjD_qCfXyZSxhzy1w"}}

Figure 9-11. *HTTP Response from "/users/login"*

The server will send back the response to the client applications, which includes user information and JWT.

Data Persistence with MongoDB

Chapter 8 discussed how to perform CRUD operations with MongoDB. In the RESTful API application, the logic for data persistence is organized in the data package. Separate struct types are organized for handling CRUD operations against each data model of the application.

Figure 9-12 illustrates the source files contained in the data package.

Figure 9-12. *Source files in the data package*

Listing 9-17 provides the source of userRepository.go that implements the functionalities to insert a new user and log in with user credentials.

Listing 9-17. Data Persistence Logic for User Entity in userRepository.go

```
package data

import (
    "github.com/shijuvar/go-web/taskmanager/models"
    "golang.org/x/crypto/bcrypt"
    "gopkg.in/mgo.v2"
    "gopkg.in/mgo.v2/bson"
)

type UserRepository struct {
    C *mgo.Collection
}
```

```go
func (r *UserRepository) CreateUser(user *models.User) error {
    obj_id := bson.NewObjectId()
    user.Id = obj_id
    hpass, err := bcrypt.GenerateFromPassword([]byte(user.Password), bcrypt.DefaultCost)
    if err != nil {
        panic(err)
    }
    user.HashPassword = hpass
    //clear the incoming text password
    user.Password = ""
    err = r.C.Insert(&user)
    return err
}

func (r *UserRepository) Login(user models.User) (u models.User, err error) {

    err = r.C.Find(bson.M{"email": user.Email}).One(&u)
    if err != nil {
        return
    }
    // Validate password
    err = bcrypt.CompareHashAndPassword(u.HashPassword, []byte(user.Password))
    if err != nil {
        u = models.User{}
    }
    return
}
```

The UserRepository struct has a property C of type *mgo.Collection. The instance of the UserRepository struct is created from the userController.go source by providing the mgo.Collection object that will be created from the Context type. The bcrypt package is used for encrypting the password using a hashing algorithm and validating the password by using the CompareHashAndPassword method.

Handlers for the Tasks Resource

Here are the routes configured for the Tasks resource:

```go
taskRouter := mux.NewRouter()
    taskRouter.HandleFunc("/tasks", controllers.CreateTask).Methods("POST")
    taskRouter.HandleFunc("/tasks/{id}", controllers.UpdateTask).Methods("PUT")
    taskRouter.HandleFunc("/tasks", controllers.GetTasks).Methods("GET")
    taskRouter.HandleFunc("/tasks/{id}", controllers.GetTaskById).Methods("GET")
    taskRouter.HandleFunc("/tasks/users/{id}", controllers.GetTasksByUser).Methods("GET")
    taskRouter.HandleFunc("/tasks/{id}", controllers.DeleteTask).Methods("DELETE")
    router.PathPrefix("/tasks").Handler(negroni.New(
        negroni.HandlerFunc(common.Authorize),
        negroni.Wrap(taskRouter),
    ))
```

The requests to the URL path "/tasks" are decorated with an authorization middleware handler named Authorize, which is provided by the Negroni stack. Authenticated users can create Tasks by providing the JWT in the HTTP requests as an access token to the Server.

JSON Resource Models

The operations on the "/tasks" resource use the data model Task to persist the values of data objects.

Listing 9-18 provides the resource models for representing JSON data for sending and receiving messages with the Tasks resource.

Listing 9-18. JSON Resources for Working with "/tasks" in resources.go

```go
//Models for JSON resources
type (
    // For Post/Put - /tasks
    // For Get - /tasks/id
    TaskResource struct {
        Data models.Task `json:"data"`
    }
    // For Get - /tasks
    TasksResource struct {
        Data []models.Task `json:"data"`
    }

)
```

Handlers for the Tasks Resource

The application handler functions for the Tasks resource are written in the taskController.go source file, which is organized in the controllers package.

Listing 9-19 provides the handler functions for the Tasks resource.

Listing 9-19. Application Handler Functions in taskController.go

```go
package controllers

import (
    "encoding/json"
    "log"
    "net/http"

    "github.com/gorilla/mux"
    "github.com/shijuvar/go-web/taskmanager/data"
    "gopkg.in/mgo.v2"
    "gopkg.in/mgo.v2/bson"
)
```

```go
// Handler for HTTP Post - "/tasks"
// Insert a new Task document
func CreateTask(w http.ResponseWriter, r *http.Request) {
    var dataResource TaskResource
    // Decode the incoming Task json
    err := json.NewDecoder(r.Body).Decode(&dataResource)
    if err != nil {
        common.DisplayAppError(
            w,
            err,
            "Invalid Task data",
            500,
        )
        return
    }
    task := &dataResource.Data
    context := NewContext()
    defer context.Close()
    c := context.DbCollection("tasks")
    repo := &data.TaskRepository{c}
    // Insert a task document
    repo.Create(task)
    if j, err := json.Marshal(TaskResource{Data: *task}); err != nil {
        common.DisplayAppError(
            w,
            err,
            "An unexpected error has occurred",
            500,
        )
        return

    } else {
        w.Header().Set("Content-Type", "application/json")
        w.WriteHeader(http.StatusCreated)
        w.Write(j)
    }
}

// Handler for HTTP Get - "/tasks"
// Returns all Task documents
func GetTasks(w http.ResponseWriter, r *http.Request) {
    context := NewContext()
    defer context.Close()
    c := context.DbCollection("tasks")
    repo := &data.TaskRepository{c}
    tasks := repo.GetAll()
    j, err := json.Marshal(TasksResource{Data: tasks})
    if err != nil {
        common.DisplayAppError(
            w,
            err,
```

```
                "An unexpected error has occurred",
                500,
            )
            return
        }
    w.WriteHeader(http.StatusOK)
    w.Header().Set("Content-Type", "application/json")
    w.Write(j)
}

// Handler for HTTP Get - "/tasks/{id}"
// Returns a single Task document by id
func GetTaskById(w http.ResponseWriter, r *http.Request) {
    // Get id from the incoming url
    vars := mux.Vars(r)
    id := vars["id"]
    context := NewContext()
    defer context.Close()
    c := context.DbCollection("tasks")
    repo := &data.TaskRepository{c}
    task, err := repo.GetById(id)
    if err != nil {
        if err == mgo.ErrNotFound {
            w.WriteHeader(http.StatusNoContent)
            return
        } else {
            common.DisplayAppError(
                w,
                err,
                "An unexpected error has occurred",
                500,
            )
        return
        }
    }
    if j, err := json.Marshal(task); err != nil {
        common.DisplayAppError(
                w,
                err,
                "An unexpected error has occurred",
                500,
            )
        return
    } else {
        w.Header().Set("Content-Type", "application/json")
        w.WriteHeader(http.StatusOK)
        w.Write(j)
    }
}
```

```go
// Handler for HTTP Get - "/tasks/users/{id}"
// Returns all Tasks created by a User
func GetTasksByUser(w http.ResponseWriter, r *http.Request) {
    // Get id from the incoming url
    vars := mux.Vars(r)
    user := vars["id"]
    context := NewContext()
    defer context. Close()
    c := context.DbCollection("tasks")
    repo := &data.TaskRepository{c}
    tasks := repo.GetByUser(user)
    j, err := json.Marshal(TasksResource{Data: tasks})
    if err != nil {
        common.DisplayAppError(
            w,
            err,
            "An unexpected error has occurred",
            500,
        )
        return
    }
    w.WriteHeader(http.StatusOK)
    w.Header().Set("Content-Type", "application/json")
    w.Write(j)
}

// Handler for HTTP Put - "/tasks/{id}"
// Update an existing Task document
func UpdateTask(w http.ResponseWriter, r *http.Request) {
    // Get id from the incoming url
    vars := mux.Vars(r)
    id := bson.ObjectIdHex(vars["id"])
    var dataResource TaskResource
    // Decode the incoming Task json
    err := json.NewDecoder(r.Body).Decode(&dataResource)
    if err != nil {
        common.DisplayAppError(
            w,
            err,
            "Invalid Task data",
            500,
        )
        return
    }
    task := &dataResource.Data
    task.Id = id
    context := NewContext()
    defer context.Close()
    c := context.DbCollection("tasks")
    repo := &data.TaskRepository{c}
```

```go
    // Update an existing Task document
    if err := repo.Update(task); err != nil {
        common.DisplayAppError(
            w,
            err,
            "An unexpected error has occurred",
            500,
        )
        return
    } else {
        w.WriteHeader(http.StatusNoContent)
    }
}

// Handler for HTTP Delete - "/tasks/{id}"
// Delete an existing Task document
func DeleteTask(w http.ResponseWriter, r *http.Request) {
    vars := mux.Vars(r)
    id := vars["id"]
    context := NewContext()
    defer context.Close()
    c := context.DbCollection("tasks")
    repo := &data.TaskRepository{c}
    // Delete an existing Task document
    err := repo.Delete(id)
    if err != nil {
        common.DisplayAppError(
            w,
            err,
            "An unexpected error has occurred",
            500,
        )
        return
    }
    w.WriteHeader (http.StatusNoContent)
}
```

The handler functions in taskController.go use the package "data" for performing CRUD operations against the data model Task, which is implemented in the taskRepository struct.

Listing 9-20 provides the data persistence logic written in taskRepository.go.

Listing 9-20. Data Persistence Logic for the Task Entity in taskRepository.go

```go
package data

import (
    "time"

    "github.com/shijuvar/go-web/taskmanager/models"
    "gopkg.in/mgo.v2"
    "gopkg.in/mgo.v2/bson"
)
```

```go
type TaskRepository struct {
    C *mgo.Collection
}

func (r *TaskRepository) Create(task *models.Task) error {
    obj_id := bson.NewObjectId()
    task.Id = obj_id
    task.CreatedOn = time.Now()
    task.Status = "Created"
    err := r.C.Insert(&task)
    return err
}

func (r *TaskRepository) Update(task *models.Task) error {
    // partial update on MogoDB
    err := r.C.Update(bson.M{"_id": task.Id},
        bson.M{"$set": bson.M{
            "name":        task.Name,
            "description": task.Description,
            "due":         task.Due,
            "status":      task.Status,
            "tags":        task.Tags,
        }})
    return err
}
func (r *TaskRepository) Delete(id string) error {
    err := r.C. Remove(bson.M{"_id": bson.ObjectIdHex(id)})
    return err
}
func (r *TaskRepository) GetAll() []models.Task {
    var tasks []models.Task
    iter := r.C.Find(nil).Iter()
    result := models.Task{}
    for iter.Next(&result) {
        tasks = append(tasks, result)
    }
    return tasks
}
func (r *TaskRepository) GetById(id string) (task models.Task, err error) {
    err = r.C.FindId(bson.ObjectIdHex(id)).One(&task)
    return
}
func (r *TaskRepository) GetByUser(user string) []models.Task {
    var tasks []models.Task
    iter := r.C.Find(bson.M{"createdby": user}).Iter()
    result := models.Task{}
    for iter.Next(&result) {
        tasks = append(tasks, result)
    }
    return tasks
}
```

Testing API Operations for the Tasks Resource

Let's test the API operations of the Tasks resource by using a RESTful API client tool. To access the API operations of the Tasks resource, client applications must provide a JWT in the "Authorization" header as a bearer token. You get the JWT from the URI endpoint "/users/login".

Figure 9-13 shows the HTTP Post request to "/Tasks" for creating a new Task resource by providing the JSON data in the request body.

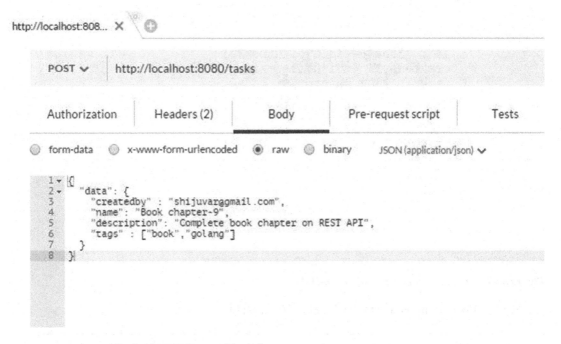

Figure 9-13. *Request body of HTTP Post to "/tasks"*

Figure 9-14 shows that the HTTP Post request to "/Tasks" provides a JWT in the "Authorization" header.

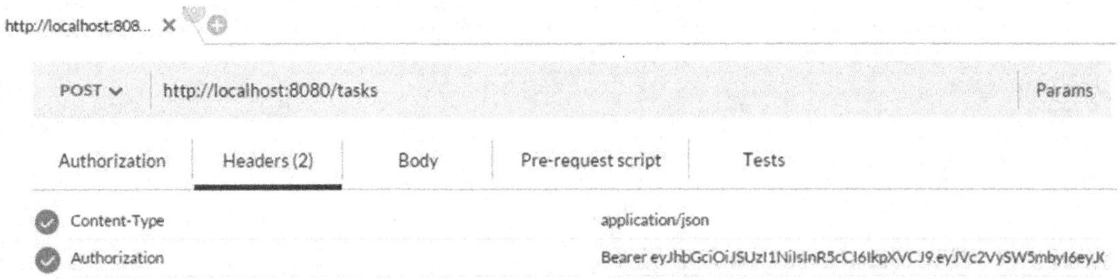

Figure 9-14. *Authorization headers of HTTP Post to "/tasks"*

Figure 9-15 shows the response from the RESTful API server for the HTTP Post to "/tasks".

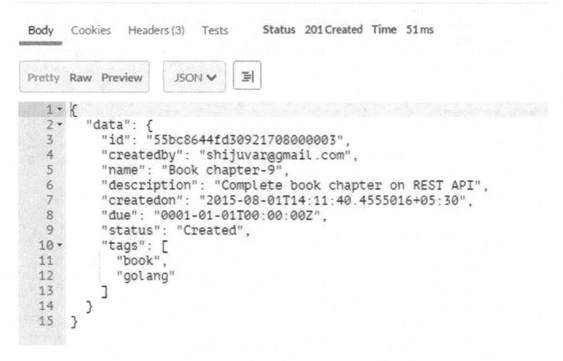

Figure 9-15. *Response from HTTP Post of "/tasks"*

Figure 9-16 shows the request for HTTP Get to "/tasks/{id}".

Figure 9-16 shows the request for HTTP Get to "/tasks/{id}".

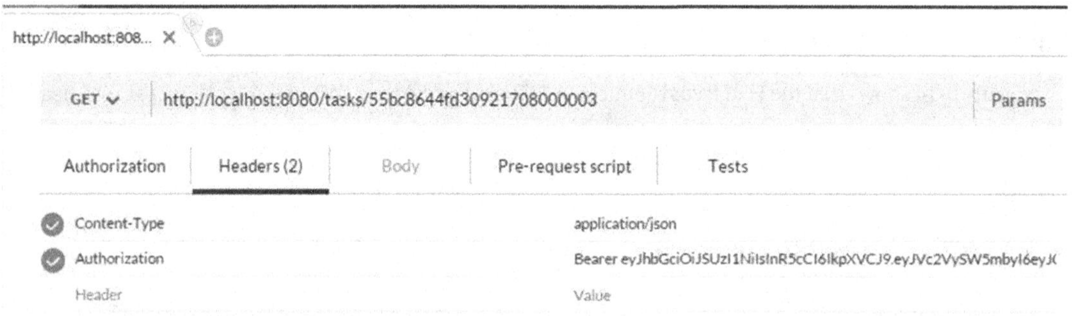

Figure 9-16. *HTTP request Get to "/tasks/{id}"*

Figure 9-17 shows the response from the RESTful API server for the HTTP Get to "/tasks{id}".

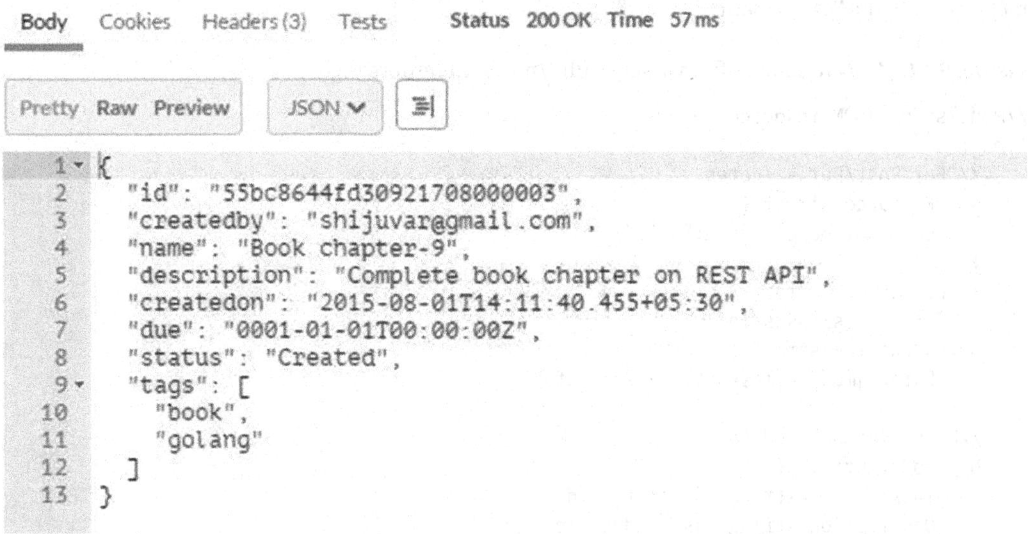

| Body | Cookies | Headers (3) | Tests | Status 200 OK Time 57 ms |

Pretty Raw Preview   JSON ✔   ≣|

```
 1▾ {
 2       "id": "55bc8644fd30921708000003",
 3       "createdby": "shijuvar@gmail.com",
 4       "name": "Book chapter-9",
 5       "description": "Complete book chapter on REST API",
 6       "createdon": "2015-08-01T14:11:40.455+05:30",
 7       "due": "0001-01-01T00:00:00Z",
 8       "status": "Created",
 9▾      "tags": [
10         "book",
11         "golang"
12       ]
13  }
```

Figure 9-17. *Response from HTTP Get of "/tasks{id}"*

Handlers for Notes Resource

The operations on the "/notes" resource uses the data model TaskNote for persisting the values of data objects.

Here is the route specified for the Notes resource:

```
noteRouter := mux.NewRouter()
    noteRouter.HandleFunc("/notes", controllers.CreateNote).Methods("POST")
    noteRouter.HandleFunc("/notes/{id}", controllers.UpdateNote).Methods("PUT")
    noteRouter.HandleFunc("/notes/{id}", controllers.GetNoteById).Methods("GET")
    noteRouter.HandleFunc("/notes", controllers.GetNotes).Methods("GET")
    noteRouter.HandleFunc("/notes/tasks/{id}", controllers.GetNotesByTask).Methods("GET")
    noteRouter.HandleFunc("/notes/{id}", controllers.DeleteNote).Methods("DELETE")
    router.PathPrefix("/notes").Handler(negroni.New(
        negroni.HandlerFunc(common.Authorize),
        negroni.Wrap (noteRouter),
    ))
```

JSON Resource Models

Listing 9-21 provides the resource models for representing the JSON data for sending and receiving messages with the Notes resource:

Listing 9-21. JSON Resources for Working with "/notes" in resources.go

```
//Models for JSON resources
type (
    // For Post/Put - /notes
    NoteResource struct {
        Data NoteModel `json:"data"`
    }
    // For Get - /notes
    // For /notes/tasks/id
    NotesResource struct {
        Data []models.TaskNote `json:"data"`
    }
    //Model for a TaskNote
    NoteModel struct {
        TaskId      string `json:"taskid"`
        Description string `json:"description"`
    }
)
```

The implementation of the Users and Tasks resources is complete. You can implement the API operations for the "/notes" resource as you did for "/tasks".

■ **Note**   The source code of the completed version of the TaskManager application is available at github.com/shijuvar/go-web/tree/master/taskmanager

---

Go Dependencies Using Godep

In previous sections, you completed the RESTful API application named TaskManager that uses a few third-party packages. Now let's focus on managing the dependencies of the application to reduce external build dependencies for productivity when building the application.

When you work on Go applications using many third-party packages, the dependency management is always a painful experience. Most software development teams work with version control systems to manage and distribute their source code. A proper dependency management tool is an essential component for speeding up the development process and build process.

Many technology stacks such as Ruby and Node.js provide a package management system with better dependency management. Those environments provide a centralized repository system to get external packages, so it is extremely easy to provide a dependency management system for those technology stacks. Go doesn't provide a centralized system for its package ecosystem, which is designed for simplicity like most of the Go features. This has some limitations for managing external dependencies while enabling simplicity for exposing and using third-party packages. By default, Go doesn't provide any mechanism for managing external dependencies.

The godep tool helps you build packages reproducibly by fixing their dependencies. This tool ensures a better experience for doing repeatable builds.

Installing the godep Tool

To install the godep tool, run the following command:

```
go get github.com/tools/godep
```

Using godep with TaskManager

Let's use godep with the RESTful API application to manage external dependencies. Run the following command:

```
godep save -r
```

The save command saves a list of the application's dependencies to the file Godeps.json inside the Godeps directory. The Godeps.json file contains the JSON representation of the application's dependencies and the Go version. It also copies the source code of the dependencies into the Godeps/_workspace directory, reflecting the structure of GOPATH.

Figure 9-18 illustrates the structure created by the godep save command to manage the application's dependencies.

Figure 9-18. *Godeps directory structure*

Listing 9-22 shows the Godeps.json file.

Listing 9-22. Godeps.json file for the TaskManager Application

```json
{
    "ImportPath": "github.com/shijuvar/go-web/taskmanager",
    "GoVersion": "go1.5.1",
    "Deps": [
        {
            "ImportPath": "github.com/codegangsta/negroni",
            "Comment": "v0.1-70-gc7477ad",
            "Rev": "c7477ad8e330bef55bf1ebe300cf8aa67c492d1b"
        },
        {
            "ImportPath": "github.com/dgrijalva/jwt-go",
            "Comment": "v2.2.0-23-g5ca8014",
            "Rev": "5ca80149b9d3f8b863af0e2bb6742e608603bd99"
        },
        {
            "ImportPath": "github.com/gorilla/context",
            "Rev": "215affda49addc4c8ef7e2534915df2c8c35c6cd"
        },
        {
            "ImportPath": "github.com/gorilla/mux",
            "Rev": "8a875a034c69b940914d83ea03d3f1299b4d094b"
        },
        {
            "ImportPath": "golang.org/x/crypto/bcrypt",
            "Rev": "02a186af8b62cb007f392270669b91be5527d39c"
        },
        {
            "ImportPath": "golang.org/x/crypto/blowfish",
            "Rev": "02a186af8b62cb007f392270669b91be5527d39c"
        },
        {
            "ImportPath": "gopkg.in/mgo.v2",
            "Comment": "r2015.10.05-1-g4d04138",
            "Rev": "4d04138ffef2791c479c0c8bbffc30b34081b8d9"
        }
    ]
}
```

You can run the godep save command any time you want to update the newly imported packages.

Restoring an Application's Dependencies

To restore an application's dependencies on a target machine, run the following command:

```
godep restore
```

The godep restore command installs the package versions specified in Godeps/Godeps.json to the $GOPATH, which modifies the state of the packages in the GOPATH location.

Deploying HTTP Servers with Docker

You have completed the TaskManager application and provided dependency management infrastructure using the godep tool. It is time to provide the deployment infrastructure for running the RESTful API application onto production servers. You can deploy HTTP servers with on-premise servers and Cloud computing environments. (In Chapter 11, you will learn how to deploy Go servers with Google Cloud Platform.)

Linux containers (https://linuxcontainers.org/) are gradually becoming a preferred approach for deploying and running applications regardless of on-premise servers and Cloud computing platforms. Docker is a technology that revolutionized the concept of using Linux containers for building, shipping, and running applications in a Linux container. You can use Docker for running applications in both on-premise servers and Cloud computing infrastructures.

In this section, a *Dockerfile* will be written for the TaskManager application to be used with Docker to deploy the application onto both on-premise servers and Cloud environments. A Dockerfile is a text document that is used to build and run applications with Docker. Before writing the Dockerfile, let's briefly discuss Docker.

Introduction to Docker

Docker is a platform for developers and SAs to develop, ship, and run applications in the container virtualization environment. An application container is a lightweight Linux environment that you can leverage to deploy and run an independently deployable unit of code. This chapter briefly discussed Microservice architecture, in which independently deployable service units are composed to build larger applications. A Docker container (application container) is a perfect fit for running a microservice in the Microservices architecture. Docker is not just a technology; it is an ecosystem that lets you quickly compose applications from components (analogous to a microservice in the Microservice architecture).

In traditional computing environments, you develop applications for virtual machines (VMs), in which you target an idealized hardware environment, including the OS, network infrastructure layers, and so on. The greatest advantage of using an application container is that it separates applications from the infrastructure and from where it runs, enabling great opportunities for application developers. With Docker, developers can now develop applications against an idealized OS — a static Linux environment — and ship their applications as quickly as possible.

Docker eliminates complexities and hurdles that can occur when applications are deployed and run. It also provides a great abstraction on the top of Linux container technology to easily work on container virtualization, which is becoming a big revolution in the IT industry, thanks to the Docker ecosystem.

Docker was developed with the Go language, which is becoming a language of choice for building many innovative systems. On the container ecosystem, the majority of systems are being developed with Go. Kubernetes is an example of a technology developed with Go that is used for clustering application containers. You can also use Kubernetes to cluster Docker applications.

Although Docker is a Linux technology, you can also run it in both Mac and Windows by using the Docker Toolbox (www.docker.com/docker-toolbox). To get more information about Docker, check out its documentation at https://docs.docker.com/.

The Docker ecosystem consists of the following:

- **Docker Engine**: A lightweight, powerful, open source, container virtualization technology combined with a workflow for building and containerizing applications

- **Docker Hub**: An SaaS portal (https://hub.docker.com/) for sharing and managing application stacks known as Docker images

In Docker, images and containers are important concepts. A *container* is a "stripped-to-basics" version of a Linux OS in which an image is loaded. A container is created from an *image*, which is an immutable file that provides a snapshot of a container. You can make changes to an existing image, but you persist it as a new image. Images are created with the docker build command. When these images run using the docker run command, a container is produced. Images are stored in Docker registry systems such as Docker Hub (provided by Docker) and private registry systems.

Writing Dockerfile

In this chapter, the objective will be to create a Dockerfile to automate the build process of the TaskManager application to run on Dockerized containers.

When you work with Docker, you create application containers by manually making changes into a base image or by building a Dockerfile, the text document that contains all instructions and commands to create a desired image automatically without manually running commands. A Dockerfile lets you automate your build to execute several command-line instructions. The docker build command builds an image from a Dockerfile and a build context.

You create a Dockerfile by naming a text file as a Dockerfile without a file extension. Typically, you put this file onto the root directory of your project repository.

Listing 9-23 provides a Dockerfile for the TaskManager application.

Listing 9-23. Dockerfile for the TaskManager Application

```
# golang image where workspace (GOPATH) configured at /go.
FROM golang

# Copy the local package files to the container's workspace.
ADD . /go/src/github.com/shijuvar/go-web/taskmanager

# Setting up working directory
WORKDIR /go/src/github.com/shijuvar/go-web/taskmanager

# Get godeps for managing and restoring dependencies
RUN go get github.com/tools/godep

# Restore godep dependencies
RUN godep restore

# Build the taskmanager command inside the container.
RUN go install github.com/shijuvar/go-web/taskmanager

# Run the taskmanager command when the container starts.
ENTRYPOINT /go/bin/taskmanager

# Service listens on port 8080.
EXPOSE 8080
```

Let's explore the commands used in the Dockerfile:

- The command FROM golang instructs Docker to start from an official golang Docker image, which is a Debian image with the latest version of Go installed, and a workspace (GOPATH) configured at /go.

- The Add command copies the local code to the container's workspace.

- The WORKDIR command sets the working directory in the container.

- The RUN command runs commands within the container. Using the RUN command, the godep tool is installed.

- The godep restore command restores dependencies into a container's GOPATH location.

- The taskmanager command runs inside the container's GOPATH/bin location (/go/bin) using the go install command.

- The ENTRYPOINT command instructs Docker to run the taskmanager command from the /go/bin location when the container is started.

- The EXPOSE command instructs Docker that the container listens on the specified network ports at runtime. It exposes port 8080. The EXPOSE command doesn't open up the ports of the container to the public. To do that, the publish flag (--publish) is used to open up the ports by mapping with external HTTP ports.

The Dockerfile for building and running the TaskManager API server in an application container using Docker is complete. Now let's build the image from the Dockerfile. Run the following command from the root directory of the TaskManager application:

```
docker build -t taskmanager
```

A local image is built by executing the instructions defined in the Dockerfile. The resulting image tags as taskmanager.

An image named taskmanager (the resulting image from the Docker build) is created. Use the following to run a container from this image:

```
docker run --publish 80:8080 --name taskmanager_api --rm taskmanager
```

Let's explore the flags used in the docker run command:

- The --publish flag instructs Docker to publish the container's exposed port 8080 on the external port 80.

- The --name flag gives a name to the container created from the taskmanager image. The name taskmanager_api is given to the container.

- The --rm flag instructs Docker to remove the container image when the container exits. Otherwise, the container image will be there even after the container exits.

The docker run command runs the container by exposing external port 80. You can access the server application by navigating to http://localhost:80.

The Dockerfile for the TaskManager application provides everything for running the HTTP server inside an application container. When you move the TaskManager application into production environments with Docker, the pending action is the implementation on MongoDB into an application container. The TaskManager application uses MongoDB as the persistence store, so you have to run the MongoDB database in another container. You can use one container for running the HTTP server and another for running the MongoDB database.

Containerized applications running on containers are referred as jailed services running in a jail. This kind of virtualization isolates containers from each other. But when you build real-world applications, you have to compose multiple containers to make them an application. In this case, you need to compose the containers from the HTTP server and MongoDB database.

In this scenario, you can use *Docker Compose* (https://docs.docker.com/compose/) to define and run multicontainer applications on the Docker platform. The design philosophy of Docker is to build independently deployable microservices into containers and compose these services to build larger applications.

Go Web Frameworks

In this chapter, you learned how to develop a RESTful API application from scratch without leveraging a Go web framework. In the Go web development stack, using a full-fledged web framework is not very popular within the Go developer community. Go developers prefer to use Go standard library packages as the foundation for building their web applications and web APIs. On top of standard library packages, developers do use a few third-party library packages for extending the functionality of standard library packages and getting some utility functions to speed up web development.

This chapter used the same approach: developing a full-fledged application using the net/http standard library package and a few third-party packages. In my opinion, a web framework is not necessary for developing RESTful APIs. You can build highly scalable RESTful APIs in Go without using any web framework. Having said that, using a web framework might be helpful in some contexts, especially when you develop conventional web applications.

Here are some Go web frameworks to use if you want a full-fledged web framework:

- **Beego** (http://beego.me/): A full-featured MVC framework that includes a built-in ORM

- **Martini** (https://github.com/go-martini/martini): A web framework inspired from Sinatra (a Ruby web framework)

- **Revel** (https://revel.github.io/): A full-stack web framework focused on high productivity

- **Goji** (https://goji.io/): A lightweight and minimalist web framework

- **Gin** (https://github.com/gin-gonic/gin): A web framework with Martini-like API that promises better performance

Summary

In this chapter, you learned how to build a production-ready RESTful API with Go. You used MongoDB as the data store for the RESTful API application, in which you organized the application logic into multiple packages to easily maintain the application. (Some business validations and best practices were ignored in the application due to the constraints of a book chapter, but a few best practices were included in the application.)

Negroni was used to handle the middleware stack, and middleware was added to specific routes. A struct type for holding the values during the lifecycle of an HTTP request was created. A MongoDB Session object was created before the HTTP server was started, and a copied version of the MongoDB Session object was taken and closed for each HTTP request after executing the application handler. Go is a great technology stack for building highly scalable RESTful APIs and is a perfect technology stack for developing applications with the Microservice architecture pattern.

Go doesn't provide a centralized repository for managing third-party packages, so managing external dependencies is bit difficult. The godep third-party tool was used to manage dependencies of the RESTful API application. It allows you to restore the dependencies into the GOPATH system location.

Docker is a revolutionary ecosystem for containerizing applications that enables developers and SAs to develop, ship, and run applications in the container virtualization environment. An application container is a lightweight Linux environment. A Dockerfile was created for the RESTful API application to automate the build process of the application with Docker.

You can build web-based, scalable back-end systems in Go without using any web framework. In this chapter, a production-ready RESTful API application was created by using the standard library package net/http and a few third-party libraries. When you build RESTful APIs, you might not need a web framework, but when you develop conventional web applications, using one might be helpful. Beego is a fully featured web framework that provides everything, including an ORM.

References

https://docs.docker.com/

https://github.com/tools/godep

■ ■ ■

## CHAPTER 10

Testing Go Applications

Automated testing is an important practice in software engineering that ensures the quality of your applications. If you are concerned about application quality, you should write automated tests to verify the behavior of the components of your applications. In your Go applications, automated tests can ensure that the Go packages behave the way they were designed to work. Go provides the fundamental testing capabilities through its standard library packages and tooling support. In this chapter, you will learn how to write unit tests using standard library packages and third-party packages.

Unit Testing

It isn't easy to develop reliable software systems and maintain them long term. When you develop applications, you must ensure that they work as intended every time. A good software system should be maintainable so you can modify the functionality of the applications at any time without breaking any parts of the application. When you modify some parts of an application, it should not destroy the functionality of other parts. So you need to adopt good software engineering practices to ensure the quality of your applications. Unit testing is an important software development practice that can be used for ensuring this quality.

Unit testing is a kind of automated testing process in which the smallest pieces of testable software in the application, called units, are individually and independently tested to determine whether they behave exactly as designed. When you write unit tests, it is important to isolate the units (the smallest testable parts) from the remaining parts of the code to individually and independently test the application code. When you write unit tests, you should identify the units to be tested.

In OOP, the smallest unit might be a method that belongs to a class. In procedural programming, the smallest unit might be a single function. In Go programs, a function or a method might be considered a unit. But it doesn't necessarily make a function as a unit because it is a situation in which the context of the application functionality and the software design will decide which part can be treated as a unit.

Test-Driven Development (TDD)

Test-driven development (TDD) is a software development process that follows test-first development in which unit tests are written before the production code. TDD is a design approach that encourages developers to think about their implementation before writing the code, which is similar to developing mock-up user interfaces. The mock-up design lets you learn what user interface you will develop for your application.

In TDD, you first write a unit test that defines a newly identified requirement or a desired improvement before writing the production code, which gives you an understanding about what you will develop. You write a unit test against a newly identified functional requirement, and the development process starts with the newly added unit test. A developer must clearly understand the functional requirement in order to write a new unit test. In a pure TDD approach, you run all unit tests along with the newly added test before writing the implementation and see the newly added test fail. After writing a unit test, you write just enough code to pass the test. Once your test is successful, you can fearlessly refactor the application code because it is covered by the unit tests.

The TDD approach is highly recommended by those who are using agile development methodologies for their software delivery. Agile methodologies emphasize developing software based on an evolutionary approach rather than following an upfront design. When you develop software based on an evolutionary design approach, TDD gives you lots of values as you continuously refactor application code for a newly identified requirement or desired improvement. Because your application code is covered by unit tests, you can run the suite of unit tests at any time to ensure that your application is working as you designed. Unit tests define the design of your application.

Here are the steps involved in TDD:

1. Add a unit test to define a new functional requirement.

2. Run all tests and see whether the new unit test gets a fail.

3. Write some code to pass the tests.

4. Run the tests.

5. Refactor the code.

These steps will continue for the entire evolution of the software development process.

This chapter doesn't use the test-first approach or TDD as the design approach for the examples. It focuses more on writing automated unit tests. TDD is an advanced technique of using automated unit tests, so you can easily practice TDD if you know how to write automated unit tests.

Unit Testing with Go

Go provides the core functionality to write automated unit tests through its testing standard library package. The testing package provides all the essential functionality to write automated unit tests, which is intended to be used with the go test command. So you can write unit tests with the testing package, and these unit tests can then be run with the go test command. Like the net/http package that performs the fundamental block to web programming available for extensibility, the testing package does the same for unit testing.

The testing package lacks some advanced features required for writing unit tests, but there are many third-party packages built on top of the package that provide additional functionalities that are required for writing automated unit tests for several advanced scenarios. Besides the testing package, the Go standard library provides two more packages: httptest (net/http/httptest) provides utilities for HTTP testing, and quick (testing/quick) provides utility functions to help with black box testing.

The testing package is intended to be used with the go test command. To perform it, some naming conventions and patterns are used for writing the test functions to be used with this command.

The go test command looks for the following conventions for identifying test functions:

```
func TestXxx(*testing.T)
```

Here, Xxx can be any alphanumeric string that starts with an uppercase letter.

The following conventions are used to write a new test suite:

- Create a source file with a name ending in _test.go.

- Within the test suite (the source file ends with _test.go), write functions with signature func TestXxx(*testing.T).

You can put the test suite files in the same package that is being tested. These test files are excluded when you build the packages, but are included when you run the go test command, which recompiles each package along with any files with names matching the file pattern "*_test.go".

To get help with go test, run the following command:

```
go help test
```

To get help with the various flags used by the go test command, run the following command:

```
go help testflag
```

Writing Unit Tests

Let's write some unit tests using the testing package (this chapter doesn't focus on the test-first development process). First, let's write a couple of string utility functions to demonstrate unit tests.

Listing 10-1 provides several string utility functions to change the case of a string parameter and reverse a string parameter.

Listing 10-1. String Utility Functions in utils.go

```go
package stringutils

import (
    "bytes"
    "unicode"
)

// Swap the case of a string parameter
func SwapCase(str string) string {

    buf := &bytes.Buffer{}
    for _, r := range str {
        if unicode.IsUpper(r) {
            buf.WriteRune(unicode.ToLower(r))
        } else {
            buf.WriteRune(unicode.ToUpper(r))
        }
    }

    return buf.String()
}
```

```go
// Reverse the string parameter
func Reverse(s string) string {
    r := []rune(s)
    for i, j := 0, len(r)-1; i < len(r)/2; i, j = i+1, j-1 {
        r[i], r[j] = r[j], r[i]
    }
    return string(r)
}
```

There are two functions to be tested: SwapCase and Reverse. The SwapCase function swaps the case of a string parameter; the Reverse function reverses the string parameter.

Let's write the test cases for testing the SwapCase and Reverse functions.

Listing 10-2 provides the tests in the source file utils_test.go.

Listing 10-2. Unit Tests for the stringutils package in utils_test.go

```go
package stringutils

import (
    "testing"
)

// Test case for the SwapCase function
func TestSwapCase(t *testing.T) {
    input, expected := "Hello, World", "hELLO, wORLD"
    result := SwapCase(input)

    if result != expected {

        t.Errorf("SwapCase(%q) == %q, expected %q", input, result, expected)
    }

}

// Test case for the Reverse function
func TestReverse(t *testing.T) {
    input, expected := "Hello, World", "dlroW ,olleH"
    result := Reverse(input)

    if result != expected {

        t.Errorf("Reverse(%q) == %q, expected %q", input, result, expected)
    }

}
```

The test suite file utils_test.go is created in the stringutils package directory. Within the utils_test.go file, two test functions with the pattern func TestXxx(*testing.T) are written. The TestSwapCase function is written to verify the behavior of the SwapCase function, and TestReverse is written to verify the Reverse function.

If the test results don't match with the expected results, Error, Fail, or related functions can be called to signal failure of the test cases. The Error and Fail functions signal the failure of a test case, but it will continue the execution for the rest of the test cases. If you want to stop the execution when any test case fails, you can call the FailNow or Fatal functions. The FailNow function calls the Fail function and stops the execution. Fatal is equivalent to Log followed by FailNow. In these test cases, the Errorf function is called to signal their failure:

```
if result != expected {

    t.Errorf("SwapCase(%q) == %q, expected %q", input, result, expected)
}
```

Let's run the test cases. Navigate to the package directory and then run the following command on the command-line window:

```
go test
```

The go test command will execute all _test.go files in the package directory, and you should see output something like this:

```
PASS
ok      github.com/shijuvar/go-web/chapter-10/stringutils        0.524s
```

The output of the previous test result is not very descriptive. The verbose (-v) flag is provided to get descriptive information about the test cases. Let's run the go test command by providing the verbose flag:

```
go test -v
```

When you run go test with the verbose flag, you should see output something like this:

```
=== RUN   TestSwapCase
--- PASS: TestSwapCase (0.00s)
=== RUN   TestReverse
--- PASS: TestReverse (0.00s)
PASS
ok      github.com/shijuvar/go-web/chapter-10/stringutils        0.466s
```

This output shows descriptive information about each test case.

Getting Test Coverage

The coverage (-cover) flag helps to get coverage of the test case against the code. Let's take a look at the test coverage of the stringutil package.

Let's provide the coverage flag along with the verbose flag:

```
go test -v -cover
```

You should see output something like this:

```
=== RUN    TestSwapCase
--- PASS: TestSwapCase (0.00s)
=== RUN    TestReverse
--- PASS: TestReverse (0.00s)
PASS
coverage: 100.0% of statements
```

This output shows that there is 100% test coverage against the code written in the stringutils package. In the stringutils package, two utility functions that were covered in the utils_test.go test suite file are written.

For the sake of the demonstration, let's comment out the test function TestSwapCase and run the go test command with the coverage flag. You should see output something like this:

```
=== RUN    TestReverse
--- PASS: TestReverse (0.00s)
PASS
coverage: 40.0% of statements
ok       github.com/shijuvar/go-web/chapter-10/stringutils       0.371s
```

This output shows that the test coverage is 40% because the SwapCase function is not covered (the TestSwapCase function was commented out) in the test suite file.

Benchmark Unit Tests

Listing 10-2 showed a couple of test cases to verify the behavior of code using the testing package. These tests focused on verifying the code behavior and design of the application. In addition to writing these kind of tests, the testing package also provides the capability to benchmark your code, which allows you to analyze the performance of a unit of work.

Here is the convention for writing benchmark tests:

```
func BenchmarkXxx(*testing.B)
```

You write benchmark functions inside the _test.go files. The benchmark tests are executed by the go test command when its benchmark (-bench) flag is provided.

Let's write the benchmark tests inside the utils_test.go test suite file to benchmark the functions written in utils.go.

Listing 10-3 provides the benchmark tests for analyzing the functions written in utils.go: SwapCase and Reverse.

Listing 10-3. Benchmark Test Cases in utils_test.go

```
//Benchmark for SwapCase function
func BenchmarkSwapCase(b *testing.B) {
    for i := 0; i < b.N; i++ {
        SwapCase("Hello, World")
    }
}
```

```
//Benchmark for Reverse function
func BenchmarkReverse(b *testing.B) {
    for i := 0; i < b.N; i++ {
        Reverse("Hello, World")
    }
}
```

Two benchmark test cases are written to determine the performance of the SwapCase and Reverse functions. To reliably benchmark the test functions, it must run the target code for b.N times. The value of b.N will be adjusted during the execution of the benchmark functions. Test benchmarks give you a reliable response time per loop.

When the benchmark (-bench) flag is provided, you have to provide a regular expression to indicate the benchmarks to be tested. To run all benchmarks, use "-bench ." or "-bench=.".

Let's run the tests by providing "-bench .":

```
go test -v -cover -bench .
```

You should see output something like this:

```
=== RUN    TestSwapCase
--- PASS: TestSwapCase (0.00s)
=== RUN    TestReverse
--- PASS: TestReverse (0.00s)
PASS
BenchmarkSwapCase-4      3000000                 562 ns/op
BenchmarkReverse-4       3000000                 404 ns/op
coverage: 100.0% of statements
ok      github.com/shijuvar/go-web/chapter-10/stringutils       4.471s
```

This output shows that the loop within the BenchmarkSwapCase benchmark function ran 3,000,000 times at a speed of 562 ns per loop. The loop within the BenchmarkReverse function ran 3,000,000 times at a speed of 404 ns per loop. In the output, the BenchmarkReverse function performed a bit better than the BenchmarkSwapCase function.

Verifying Example Code

In addition to providing support for writing tests to verify behavior and writing benchmark tests, the testing package also provides support for running and verifying example code. Example code for packages, functions, types, and methods can be provided by using this capability.

Here are the naming conventions used to declare examples for the package, a function F, a type T, and a method M on type T:

```
func Example()    // Example test for package
func ExampleF()   // Example test for function F
func ExampleT()   // Example test for type T
func ExampleT_M() // Example test for M on type T
```

Within the example test functions is a concluding line comment that begins with "Output:" and is compared with the standard output of the function when the tests are run.

Listing 10-4 provides the example code for the Reverse and SwapCase functions.

Listing 10-4. Example code for Reverse and SwapCase Functions

```
//Example code for Reverse function
func ExampleReverse() {
    fmt.Println(Reverse("Hello, World"))
    // Output: dlroW ,olleH
}

//Example code for Reverse function
func ExampleSwapCase() {
    fmt.Println(SwapCase("Hello, World"))
    // Output: hELLO, wORLD
}
```

The example test function is written inside the `utils_test.go` file. In the example code, a concluding line comment that begins with "`Output:`" is included.

Let's run the tests with the `go test` command:

```
go test -v -cover
```

You should see output something like this:

```
=== RUN    TestSwapCase
--- PASS: TestSwapCase (0.00s)
=== RUN    TestReverse
--- PASS: TestReverse (0.00s)
=== RUN    ExampleReverse
--- PASS: ExampleReverse (0.00s)
=== RUN    ExampleSwapCase
--- PASS: ExampleSwapCase (0.00s)
PASS
coverage: 100.0% of statements
ok      github.com/shijuvar/go-web/chapter-10/stringutils        0.359s
```

This output shows that the example tests have successfully passed. In addition to verifying the example code, example tests are available as examples for package documentation. When documentation is generated with the godoc tool, the example code in the example test functions is available as an example in the documentation.

Figure 10-1 illustrates the documentation for the Reverse function, showing that the example is taken from the ExampleReverse function.

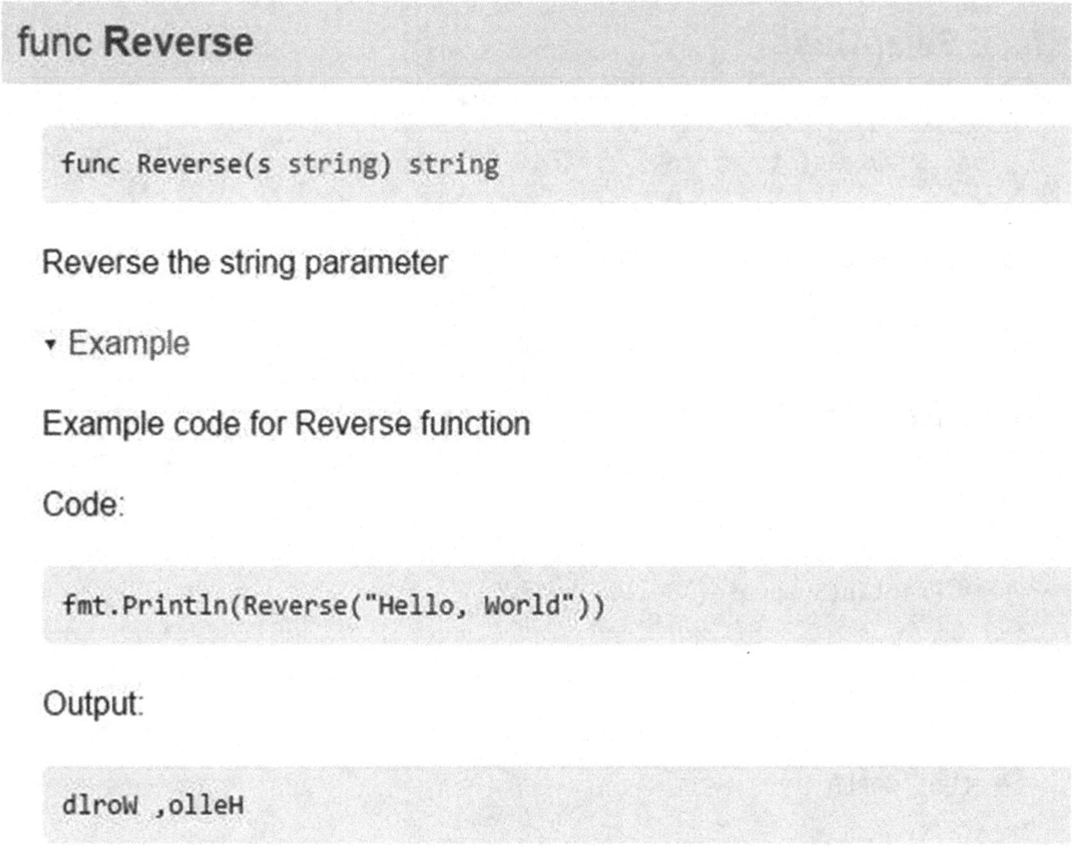

func **Reverse**

```
func Reverse(s string) string
```

Reverse the string parameter

▾ Example

Example code for Reverse function

Code:

```
fmt.Println(Reverse("Hello, World"))
```

Output:

```
dlroW ,olleH
```

Figure 10-1. *Documentation for the Reverse function generated by the godoc tool*

Figure 10-2 illustrates the documentation for the SwapCase function, showing that the example is taken from the ExampleSwapCase function.

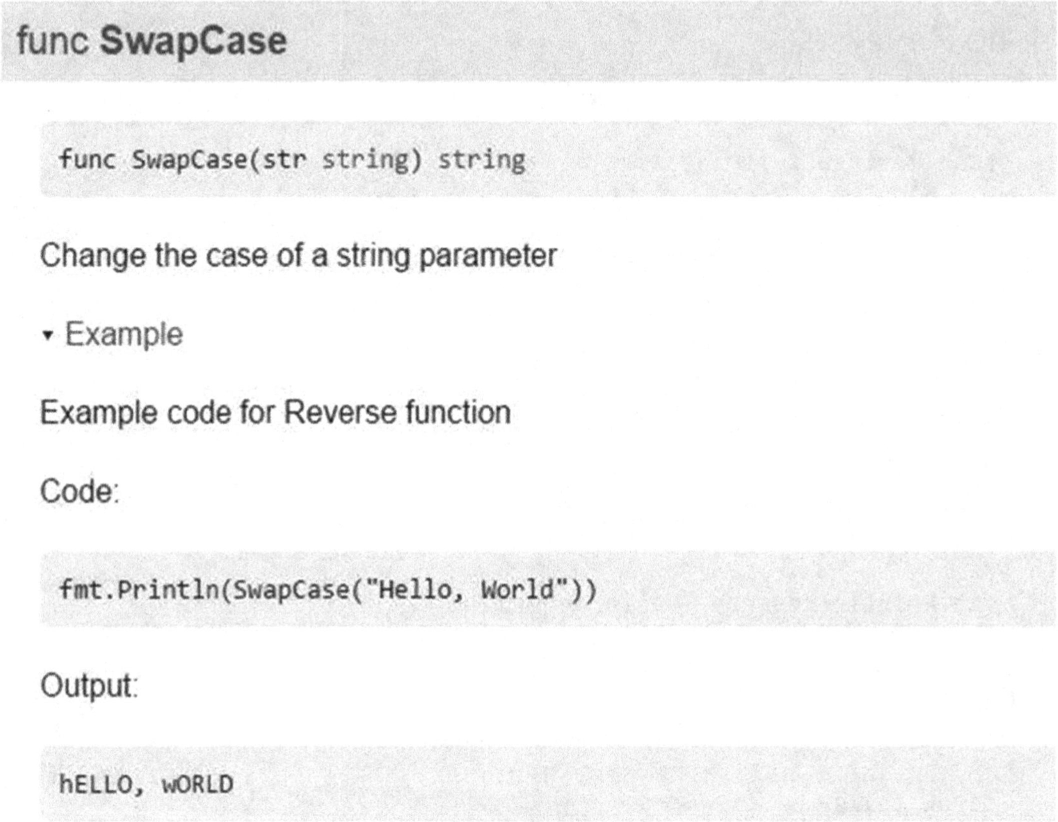

func **SwapCase**

```
func SwapCase(str string) string
```

Change the case of a string parameter

▾ Example

Example code for Reverse function

Code:

```
fmt.Println(SwapCase("Hello, World"))
```

Output:

```
hELLO, wORLD
```

Figure 10-2. *Documentation for the SwapCase function generated by the godoc tool*

Skipping Test Cases

When you run tests, you can skip some of the test cases by leveraging the Skip function provided by the testing package and providing the short (-short) flag to the go test command. This is useful in some specific scenarios. If you want to skip some time-consuming test cases when running the tests, you can leverage the capability of skipping test cases.

In another scenario, some test cases may require a dependency to resources such as a configuration file or an environment variable that should be provided for running those tests. If these resources are not available during the execution of those tests, you can simply skip those tests instead of letting them fail. The testing package provides a Skip method of testing.T type that allows you to skip test cases.

Listing 10-5 provides a test case in utils_test.go to illustrate skipping test cases.

Listing 10-5. Skipping Test Cases

```
func TestLongRun(t *testing.T) {
    // Checks whether the short flag is provided
    if testing.Short() {
        t.Skip("Skipping test in short mode")
    }
    // Long running implementation goes here
    time.Sleep(5 * time.Second)
}
```

Within the TestLongRun function, you see whether the short flag is provided by calling testing.Short(). If the short flag is provided, call the Skip method to skip the test case. Otherwise, the test case executes normally. When the test function TestLongRun executes normally, the execution is delayed by 5 seconds for the sake of the demonstration.

Let's run the tests without providing the short flag:

```
go test -v -cover
```

You should see output something like this:

```
=== RUN    TestSwapCase
--- PASS: TestSwapCase (0.00s)
=== RUN    TestReverse
--- PASS: TestReverse (0.00s)
=== RUN    TestLongRun
--- PASS: TestLongRun (5.00s)
=== RUN    ExampleReverse
--- PASS: ExampleReverse (0.00s)
=== RUN    ExampleSwapCase
--- PASS: ExampleSwapCase (0.00s)
PASS
coverage: 100.0% of statements
ok      github.com/shijuvar/go-web/chapter-10/stringutils      5.457s
```

Here, the tests are run normally without the short flag, so the test function ExampleSwapCase executes normally and takes 5 seconds to complete the execution. Now let's run the tests by providing the short flag:

```
go test -v -cover -short
```

You should see output something like this:

```
=== RUN   TestSwapCase
--- PASS: TestSwapCase (0.00s)
=== RUN   TestReverse
--- PASS: TestReverse (0.00s)
=== RUN   TestLongRun
--- SKIP: TestLongRun (0.00s)
        utils_test.go:61: Skipping test in short mode
=== RUN   ExampleReverse
--- PASS: ExampleReverse (0.00s)
=== RUN   ExampleSwapCase
--- PASS: ExampleSwapCase (0.00s)
PASS
coverage: 100.0% of statements
ok      github.com/shijuvar/go-web/chapter-10/stringutils        0.449s
```

This output shows that the test case TestLongRun skipped during the execution:

```
--- SKIP: TestLongRun (0.00s)
        utils_test.go:61: Skipping test in short mode
```

Running Tests Cases in Parallel

Although test cases are run sequentially, you can run test cases in parallel if you want to speed up the test execution. When you run a large set of sequential test cases, you can leverage the capability of running tests in parallel to speed up the execution. To run a test case in parallel, call the Parallel method of the testing.T type as the first statement in the test case.

Listing 10-6 provides couple of test cases inside the utils_test.go file to run test cases in parallel.

Listing 10-6. Test Cases to Run in Parallel

```
// Test case for the SwapCase function to execute in parallel
func TestSwapCaseInParallel(t *testing.T) {
    t.Parallel()
    // Delaying 1 second for the sake of demonstration
    time.Sleep(1 * time.Second)
    input, expected := "Hello, World", "hELLO, wORLD"
    result := SwapCase(input)

    if result != expected {

        t.Errorf("SwapCase(%q) == %q, expected %q", input, result, expected)
    }

}
```

```go
// Test case for the Reverse function to execute in parallel
func TestReverseInParallel(t *testing.T) {
    t.Parallel()
    // Delaying 2 seconds for the sake of demonstration
    time.Sleep(2 * time.Second)
    input, expected := "Hello, World", "dlroW ,olleH"
    result := Reverse(input)

    if result != expected {

        t.Errorf("Reverse(%q) == %q, expected %q", input, result, expected)
    }

}
```

A couple of test cases are written in which t.Parallel() is called to run test cases in parallel. The SwapCase and Reverse functions are run and tested to ensure that there is parallel execution.

Let's run the tests by providing the parallel (-parallel) flag:

```
go test -v -cover -short -parallel 2
```

With the parallel flag, you specify running two test cases at a time in parallel. If you don't specify the parallel flag, it defaults to runtime.GOMAXPROCS(0), which is 1, so the parallel tests will be run one at a time.

When you run the tests, you should see output something like this:

```
=== RUN    TestSwapCaseInParallel
=== RUN    TestReverseInParallel
=== RUN    TestSwapCase
--- PASS: TestSwapCase (0.00s)
=== RUN    TestReverse
--- PASS: TestReverse (0.00s)
=== RUN    TestLongRun
--- SKIP: TestLongRun (0.00s)
        utils_test.go:91: Skipping test in short mode
--- PASS: TestSwapCaseInParallel (1.00s)
--- PASS: TestReverseInParallel (2.00s)
=== RUN    ExampleReverse
--- PASS: ExampleReverse (0.00s)
=== RUN    ExampleSwapCase
--- PASS: ExampleSwapCase (0.00s)
PASS
coverage: 100.0% of statements
ok      github.com/shijuvar/go-web/chapter-10/stringutils        2.345s
```

This output shows that test cases TestSwapCaseInParallel and TestReverseInParallel ran in parallel:

```
=== RUN    TestSwapCaseInParallel
=== RUN    TestReverseInParallel
```

Within these functions, the execution time is delayed by using the time.Sleep function for the sake of this demonstration. Both tests complete in different order by taking 1 second for TestSwapCaseInParallel and 2 seconds for TestReverseInParallel:

```
--- PASS: TestSwapCaseInParallel (1.00s)
--- PASS: TestReverseInParallel (2.00s)
```

If you look at the logs generated by go test, you see that other test cases ran sequentially one by one after completing each test case:

```
=== RUN    TestSwapCase
--- PASS: TestSwapCase (0.00s)
=== RUN    TestReverse
--- PASS: TestReverse (0.00s)
=== RUN    TestLongRun
--- SKIP: TestLongRun (0.00s)
        utils_test.go:91: Skipping test in short mode
=== RUN    ExampleReverse
--- PASS: ExampleReverse (0.00s)
=== RUN    ExampleSwapCase
--- PASS: ExampleSwapCase (0.00s)
```

Putting Tests in Separate Packages

Unit tests are usually put into the same package as the one being tested. The _test.go files are excluded from regular package builds, but are included when the go test command is run. In my opinion, it is better to move your test files into a separate package, which allows you to separate unit tests from the application code that improves the separation of concerns. (In previous examples, the application code and test files were written in the same package: stringutils.)

Let's move the utils_test.go file into a new package directory named stringutils_test and import the stringutils package so the functions to be tested can be accessed.

Figure 10-3 illustrates the directory structure of the application.

Figure 10-3. *Directory structure of the stringutils and stringutils_test packages*

The `utils.go` file is put into the `stringutils` package directory, and the test suite file `utils_test.go` is put into the `stringutils_test` package directory.

Listing 10-7 provides the combined source version of the `utils_test.go` file used in previous examples.

Listing 10-7. Source of Test Suite File utils_test.go

```go
package stringutils_test

import (
    "fmt"
    "testing"
    "time"

    . "github.com/shijuvar/go-web/chapter-10/stringutils"
)

// Test case for the SwapCase function to execute in parallel
func TestSwapCaseInParallel(t *testing.T) {
    t.Parallel()
    // Delaying 1 second for the sake of demonstration
    time.Sleep(1 * time.Second)
    input, expected := "Hello, World", "hELLO, wORLD"
    result := SwapCase(input)

    if result != expected {

        t.Errorf("SwapCase(%q) == %q, expected %q", input, result, expected)
    }
}

// Test case for the Reverse function to execute in parallel
func TestReverseInParallel(t *testing.T) {
    t.Parallel()
    // Delaying 2 seconds for the sake of demonstration
    time.Sleep(2 * time.Second)
    input, expected := "Hello, World", "dlroW ,olleH"
    result := Reverse(input)

    if result != expected {

        t.Errorf("Reverse(%q) == %q, expected %q", input, result, expected)
    }

}
```

```go
// Test case for the SwapCase function
func TestSwapCase(t *testing.T) {
    input, expected := "Hello, World", "hELLO, wORLD"
    result := SwapCase(input)

    if result != expected {

        t.Errorf("SwapCase(%q) == %q, expected %q", input, result, expected)
    }

}

// Test case for the Reverse function
func TestReverse(t *testing.T) {
    input, expected := "Hello, World", "dlroW ,olleH"
    result := Reverse(input)

    if result != expected {

        t.Errorf("Reverse(%q) == %q, expected %q", input, result, expected)
    }

}

//Benchmark for SwapCase function
func BenchmarkSwapCase(b *testing.B) {
    for i := 0; i < b.N; i++ {
        SwapCase("Hello, World")
    }
}

//Benchmark for Reverse function
func BenchmarkReverse(b *testing.B) {
    for i := 0; i < b.N; i++ {
        Reverse("Hello, World")
    }
}

//Example code for Reverse function
func ExampleReverse() {
    fmt.Println(Reverse("Hello, World"))
    // Output: dlroW ,olleH
}

//Example code for Reverse function
func ExampleSwapCase() {
    fmt.Println(SwapCase("Hello, World"))
    // Output: hELLO, wORLD
}
```

```
func TestLongRun(t *testing.T) {
    // Checks whether the short flag is provided
    if testing.Short() {
        t.Skip("Skipping test in short mode")
    }
    // Long running implementation goes here
    time.Sleep(5 * time.Second)
}
```

In the imports package, the stringutils package is imported:

. **"github.com/shijuvar/go-web/chapter-10/stringutils"**

When importing the stringutils package, use dot (.) import, which allows you to call exported identifiers without referring to the package name:

result := SwapCase(input)

Let's run the unit tests using the go test command:

```
go test -v -cover -short -parallel 2
```

You should see the output something like this:

```
=== RUN   TestSwapCaseInParallel
=== RUN   TestReverseInParallel
=== RUN   TestSwapCase
--- PASS: TestSwapCase (0.00s)
=== RUN   TestReverse
--- PASS: TestReverse (0.00s)
=== RUN   TestLongRun
--- SKIP: TestLongRun (0.00s)
        utils_test.go:93: Skipping test in short mode
--- PASS: TestSwapCaseInParallel (1.00s)
--- PASS: TestReverseInParallel (2.00s)
=== RUN   ExampleReverse
--- PASS: ExampleReverse (0.00s)
=== RUN   ExampleSwapCase
--- PASS: ExampleSwapCase (0.00s)
PASS
coverage: 0.0% of statements
ok      github.com/shijuvar/go-web/chapter-10/stringutils_test   2.573s
```

Although unit tests were run from a package separate from the one being tested, the go test command gave the proper output. Here, the only difference is that the test coverage is 0%:

```
coverage: 0.0% of statements
```

If you aren't concerned about the percentage of test coverage you get from the go test command, putting unit tests into separate packages is a recommended approach.

Testing Web Applications

The primary focus of this book is web development in Go, and this section takes a look at how to test web applications. The standard library package `net/http/httptest` provides the utilities for testing HTTP applications. The `httptest` package provides the following struct types that help test HTTP applications:

- `ResponseRecorder`
- `Server`

`ResponseRecorder` is an implementation of `http.ResponseWriter` that can be used for records returned HTTP response to inspect the response in unit tests. You can create the `ResponseRecorder` instance by calling the `NewRecorder` function of the `httptest` package. The `ResponseRecorder` object is passed when the HTTP request handlers are executed; the response can be inspected by testing the `ResponseRecorder` object that contains the returned response.

A `Server` is an HTTP server designed for testing HTTP applications with a test server. You can create a test HTTP server by calling the `NewServer` function of the `httptest` package by passing an instance of `http.Handler`, which starts an HTTP server by calling the `Serve` method of `http.Server`. By using `httptest.Server`, you can test your HTTP applications using a test server (HTTP server). Hence you can perform end-to-end HTTP tests by sending HTTP requests to the server from a HTTP client.

Testing with ResponseRecorder

Let's take a look at how to write unit tests to inspect HTTP responses by leveraging the `ResponseRecorder` type. First, we write an example HTTP API server with the endpoints shown in Table 10-1.

Table 10-1. *Example of HTTP API Server*

HTTP Verb	Path	Functionality
GET	/users	Lists all users in JSON format
POST	/users	Creates a user

Listing 10-8 provides an implementation of an example HTTP server.

Listing 10-8. Example HTTP API Server in main.go

```go
package main

import (
    "encoding/json"
    "errors"
    "net/http"

    "github.com/gorilla/mux"
)

type User struct {
    FirstName string `json:"firstname"`
    LastName  string `json:"lastname"`
    Email     string `json:email"`
}
```

```go
var userStore = []User{}

func getUsers(w http.ResponseWriter, r *http.Request) {
    users, err := json.Marshal(userStore)

    if err != nil {
        w.WriteHeader(http.StatusInternalServerError)
        return
    }
    w.Header().Set("Content-Type", "application/json")
    w.WriteHeader(http.StatusOK)
    w.Write(users)

}
func createUser(w http.ResponseWriter, r *http.Request) {

    var user User
    // Decode the incoming User json
    err := json.NewDecoder(r.Body).Decode(&user)
    if err != nil {
        w.WriteHeader(http.StatusInternalServerError)
        return
    }
    // Validate the User entity
    err = validate(user)
    if err != nil {
        w.WriteHeader(http.StatusBadRequest)
        return
    }
    // Insert User entity into User Store
    userStore = append(userStore, user)
    w.WriteHeader(http.StatusCreated)
}

// Validate User entity
func validate(user User) error {
    for _, u := range userStore {
        if u.Email == user.Email {
            return errors.New("The Email is already exists")
        }
    }
    return nil
}
func SetUserRoutes() *mux.Router {
    r := mux.NewRouter()
    r.HandleFunc("/users", createUser).Methods("POST")
    r.HandleFunc("/users", getUsers).Methods("GET")
    return r
}

func main() {
    http.ListenAndServe(":8080", SetUserRoutes())
}
```

Two HTTP endpoints are written: HTTP Post on "/users" and HTTP Get on "/users". Gorilla mux is used to configure the request multiplexer. When a new User entity is created, you validate whether the e-mail ID already exists. For the sake of the example demonstration, the User objects are persisted into a slice named userStore.

In TDD, a developer starts the development cycle by writing unit tests based on the requirements identified. Developers normally write user stories to write unit tests. Even though this book doesn't follow a test-first approach or the purest form of TDD, let's write user stories for writing unit tests:

1. Users should be able to view a list of User entities.

2. Users should be able to create a new User entity.

3. The e-mail ID of a User entity should be unique.

Listing 10-9 provides the unit tests for the HTTP server application (refer to Listing 10-8). The tests are based on the user stories defined previously.

Listing 10-9. Unit Tests for HTTP API Server using ResponseRecorder in main_test.go

```go
package main

import (
        "fmt"
        "net/http"
        "net/http/httptest"
        "strings"
        "testing"

        "github.com/gorilla/mux"
)

// User Story - Users should be able to view list of User entity
func TestGetUsers(t *testing.T) {
        r := mux.NewRouter()
        r.HandleFunc("/users", getUsers).Methods("GET")
        req, err := http.NewRequest("GET", "/users", nil)
        if err != nil {
                t.Error(err)
        }
        w := httptest.NewRecorder()

        r.ServeHTTP(w, req)
        if w.Code != 200 {
                t.Errorf("HTTP Status expected: 200, got: %d", w.Code)
        }
}

// User Story - Users should be able to create a User entity
func TestCreateUser(t *testing.T) {
        r := mux.NewRouter()
        r.HandleFunc("/users", createUser).Methods("POST")

        userJson := `{"firstname": "shiju", "lastname": "Varghese", "email":
        "shiju@xyz.com"}`
```

```go
        req, err := http.NewRequest(
                "POST",
                "/users",
                strings.NewReader(userJson),
        )
        if err != nil {
                t.Error(err)
        }

        w := httptest.NewRecorder()
        r.ServeHTTP(w, req)
        if w.Code != 201 {
                t.Errorf("HTTP Status expected: 201, got: %d", w.Code)
        }
}


//User Story - The Email Id of a User entity should be unique
func TestUniqueEmail(t *testing.T) {
        r := mux.NewRouter()
        r.HandleFunc("/users", createUser).Methods("POST")

        userJson := `{"firstname": "shiju", "lastname": "Varghese", "email":
        "shiju@xyz.com"}`

        req, err := http.NewRequest(
                "POST",
                "/users",
                strings.NewReader(userJson),
        )
        if err != nil {
                t.Error(err)
        }

        w := httptest.NewRecorder()
        r.ServeHTTP(w, req)
        if w.Code != 400 {
                t.Error("Bad Request expected, got: %d", w.Code)
        }
}
func TestGetUsersClient(t *testing.T) {
        r := mux.NewRouter()
        r.HandleFunc("/users", getUsers).Methods("GET")
        server := httptest.NewServer(r)
        defer server.Close()
        usersUrl := fmt.Sprintf("%s/users", server.URL)
        request, err := http.NewRequest("GET", usersUrl, nil)

        res, err := http.DefaultClient.Do(request)
```

```
        if err != nil {
                t.Error(err)
        }

        if res.StatusCode != 200 {
                t.Errorf("HTTP Status expected: 200, got: %d", res.StatusCode)
        }
}
func TestCreateUserClient(t *testing.T) {
        r := mux.NewRouter()
        r.HandleFunc("/users", createUser).Methods("POST")
        server := httptest.NewServer(r)
        defer server.Close()
        usersUrl := fmt.Sprintf("%s/users", server.URL)
        fmt.Println(usersUrl)
        userJson := `{"firstname": "Rosmi", "lastname": "Shiju", "email": "rose@xyz.com"}`
        request, err := http.NewRequest("POST", usersUrl, strings.NewReader(userJson))

        res, err := http.DefaultClient.Do(request)

        if err != nil {
                t.Error(err)
        }

        if res.StatusCode != 201 {
                t.Errorf("HTTP Status expected: 201, got: %d", res.StatusCode)
        }
}
```

Three test cases are written against the user stories. Follow these steps to write each test case:

1. Create a router instance using the Gorilla mux package and configure the multiplexer.

2. Create an HTTP request using the http.NewRequest function.

3. Create a ResponseRecorder object using the httptest.NewRecorder function.

4. Send the ResponseRecorder object and Request object to the multiplexer by calling the ServeHTTP method.

5. Inspect the ResponseRecorder object to inspect the returned HTTP response.

Let's explore the code of the test function TestGetUsers:
The multiplexer is configured to perform an HTTP Get request on "/users":

```
r := mux.NewRouter()
r.HandleFunc("/users", getUsers).Methods("GET")
```

The HTTP request object is created using http.NewRequest to send this object to the multiplexer:

```
req, err := http.NewRequest("GET", "/users", nil)
if err != nil {
        t.Error(err)
}
```

A ResponseRecorder object is created using the httptest.NewRecorder function to record the returned HTTP response:

```
w := httptest.NewRecorder()
```

The ServeHTTP method of the multiplexer is called by providing the ResponseRecorder and Request objects to invoke the HTTP Get request on "/users", which invokes the getUsers handler function:

```
r.ServeHTTP(w, req)
```

The ResponseRecorder object records the returned response so the behavior of the HTTP response can be verified. Here, the returned HTTP response of a status code of 200 is verified:

```
if w.Code != 200 {
    t.Errorf("HTTP Status expected: 200, got: %d", w.Code)
}
```

In the test function TestCreateUser, JSON data is provided to create a User entity. Here, the returned HTTP response of a status code of 201 is verified:

```
if w.Code != 201 {
    t.Errorf("HTTP Status expected: 201, got: %d", w.Code)
}
```

The test function TestUniqueEmail verifies that the behavior of the e-mail ID of a User entity is unique. To test this behavior, the same JSON data used for the TestCreateUser function is provided. Because test cases run sequentially, the TestUniqueEmail function is run after the TestCreateUser function is executed. Because a duplicate e-mail is provided, a status code of 400 should be received:

```
if w.Code != 400 {
    t.Error("Bad Request expected, got: %d", w.Code)
 }
```

Testing with Server

In the previous section, unit tests using the ResponseRecorder struct type were written, and this type is sufficient for testing HTTP responses. The httptest package also provides a Server struct type that allows you to create an HTTP server for performing end-to-end HTTP tests in which you can send HTTP requests to the server using an HTTP client. Listing 10-9 tested the behavior of HTTP responses without creating an HTTP server. Instead, an HTTP request and a ResponseRecorder object are sent into the multiplexer. With httptest.Server, an HTTP server can be created, and the behaviors can then be tested by sending requests from an HTTP client.

Let's write unit tests by using the httptest.Server type to test the example HTTP application written in Listing 10-8. In these example unit tests, test cases are written to verify the behavior of HTTP Get on "/users" and HTTP Post on "/users". The unit tests are written inside the main_test.go test suite file, in which unit tests using ResponseRecorder are already written.

Listing 10-10 provides the unit tests using httptest.Server.

Listing 10-10. Unit Tests for HTTP API Server using Server in main_test.go

```go
func TestGetUsersClient(t *testing.T) {
    r := mux.NewRouter()
    r.HandleFunc("/users", getUsers).Methods("GET")
    server := httptest.NewServer(r)
    defer server.Close()
    usersUrl := fmt.Sprintf("%s/users", server.URL)
    request, err := http.NewRequest("GET", usersUrl, nil)

    res, err := http.DefaultClient.Do(request)

    if err != nil {
        t.Error(err)
    }

    if res.StatusCode != 200 {
        t.Errorf("HTTP Status expected: 200, got: %d", res.StatusCode)
    }
}
func TestCreateUserClient(t *testing.T) {
    r := mux.NewRouter()
    r.HandleFunc("/users", createUser).Methods("POST")
    server := httptest.NewServer(r)
    defer server.Close()
    usersUrl := fmt.Sprintf("%s/users", server.URL)
    userJson := `{"firstname": "Rosmi", "lastname": "Shiju", "email": "rose@xyz.com"}`
    request, err := http.NewRequest("POST", usersUrl, strings.NewReader(userJson))

    res, err := http.DefaultClient.Do(request)

    if err != nil {
        t.Error(err)
    }

    if res.StatusCode != 201 {
        t.Errorf("HTTP Status expected: 201, got: %d", res.StatusCode)
    }
}
```

With httptest.Server, two test functions are written: TestGetUsersClient and TestCreateUserClient. In these test cases, an HTTP server is created, and behaviors are tested by sending HTTP requests to it from an HTTP client.

Follow these steps to write each test case:

1.   Create a router instance using the Gorilla mux package and configure the multiplexer.

2.   Create an HTTP server using the httptest.NewServer function.

3.   Create a Request object using the http.NewRequest function.

4.   Send an HTTP request to the server using the Do method of an http.Client object.

5.   Inspect the Response object to inspect the returned HTTP response.

Let's explore the test function TestGetUsersClient. First, the multiplexer is configured to perform an HTTP Get request on "/users":

```
r := mux.NewRouter()
r.HandleFunc("/users", getUsers).Methods("GET")
```

An HTTP server is created with the httptest.NewServer function. The NewServer function starts and returns a new HTTP server. The Close method of the Server object is added to the list of deferred functions:

```
server := httptest.NewServer(r)
defer server.Close()
```

An HTTP request is created with the http.NewRequest function and sends an HTTP request using the Do method of the http.Client object. An http.Client object is created with http.DefaultClient. The Do method is called, which sends an HTTP request and returns an HTTP response:

```
usersUrl := fmt.Sprintf("%s/users", server.URL)
request, err := http.NewRequest("GET", usersUrl, nil)
res, err := http.DefaultClient.Do(request)
```

Here, nil is provided as the request parameter to the NewRequest function because it is an HTTP Get request.

Finally, the behavior of the HTTP response return from the HTTP server is verified:

```
if res.StatusCode != 200 {
    t.Errorf("HTTP Status expected: 200, got: %d", res.StatusCode)
}
```

TestCreateUserClient is used to test HTTP Post on "/users". Because it is an HTTP Post request, data have to be sent to the server to create the User entity. When the http.NewRequest function is called to create an HTTP request, the JSON data is provided as the request parameter.

Here is the code block used to provide JSON data to the server for an HTTP Post request on "/users":

```
usersUrl := fmt.Sprintf("%s/users", server.URL)
    userJson := `{"firstname": "Rosmi", "lastname": "Shiju", "email": "rose@xyz.com"}`
request, err := http.NewRequest("POST", usersUrl, strings.NewReader(userJson))
```

If the request on "/users" is successful, the HTTP status code 201 should appear. The verification is shown here:

```
if res.StatusCode != 201 {
    t.Errorf("HTTP Status expected: 201, got: %d", res.StatusCode)
}
```

BDD Testing in Go

The Go testing and httptest standard library packages provide a great foundation for writing automated unit tests. The advantage of these packages is that they provide many extensibility points, so you can easily use these packages with other custom packages.

This section discusses two third-party packages: Ginkgo and Gomega. Ginkgo is a behavior-driven development (BDD) – based testing framework that lets you write expressive tests in Go to specify application behaviors. If you are practicing BDD for your software development process, Ginkgo is a great choice of package. Gomega is a matcher library that is best paired with the Ginkgo package. Although Gomega is a preferred matching library for Ginkgo, it is designed to be matcher-agnostic.

Behavior-Driven Development (BDD)

BDD is a software development process that evolved from TDD and other agile practices. BDD is designed to make an effective software development practice for agile software delivery. It is an evolved practice from many agile practices (mainly from TDD). The term *test* in TDD has created confusion in the developer community for those who practice TDD in their software development process.

Although TDD is a software development process and a design philosophy, many developers assumed that it was only about testing. But the idea of TDD was to design code by writing unit tests. It's all about designing and verifying the behavior of applications. BDD is an extension of TDD, with the emphasis on *behavior* instead of *test*. In BDD, you specify behaviors in automated tests and write code based on the behaviors.

Behavior-Driven Development with Ginkgo

You can easily adopt BDD-style testing if you have a basic understanding of automated tests. In BDD, the term *behavior* is used instead of *test*. Let's take a look at how to write BDD-style testing using Ginkgo and its preferred matcher library Gomega.

Refactoring the HTTP API

Let's write BDD-style testing for the example HTTP server written in Listing 10-8. When you write automated unit tests, you have to make the code testable by applying a loosely coupled design so that you can easily write tests. Let's refactor the HTTP server written in Listing 10-8.

Figure 10-4 illustrates the directory structure of the refactored application.

Figure 10-4. *Directory structure of the refactored application from Listing 10-8*

Listing 10-8 implemented everything in a single source file: main.go in the main package. In the refactored application, code is implemented in two packages: lib and main. The main package contains the main.go file that provides the entry point of the application, and all application logic is moved into the lib package.

The lib package contains the following source files:

- handlers.go contains the HTTP handlers and provides the implementation for setting up routes with Gorilla mux.

- repository.go contains the persistence logic and persistence store.

Other source files in the lib directory provide implementation for automated tests for BDD, but they are put in the lib_test package. (This topic is discussed later in the chapter.)

Listing 10-11 provides the handlers.go code in the lib package.

Listing 10-11. handlers.go in the lib Package

```go
package lib

import (
    "encoding/json"
    "net/http"

    "github.com/gorilla/mux"
)

func GetUsers(repo UserRepository) http.Handler {
    return http.HandlerFunc(func(w http.ResponseWriter, r *http.Request) {
        userStore := repo.GetAll()
        users, err := json.Marshal(userStore)

        if err != nil {
            w.WriteHeader(http.StatusInternalServerError)
            return
        }
        w.Header().Set("Content-Type", "application/json")
        w.WriteHeader(http.StatusOK)
        w.Write(users)
    })
}
```

```go
func CreateUser(repo UserRepository) http.Handler {
    return http.HandlerFunc(func(w http.ResponseWriter, r *http.Request) {
        var user User
        err := json.NewDecoder(r.Body).Decode(&user)
        if err != nil {
            w.WriteHeader(http.StatusInternalServerError)
            return
        }
        err = repo.Create(user)
        if err != nil {
            w.WriteHeader(http.StatusBadRequest)
            return
        }
        w.WriteHeader(http.StatusCreated)
    })
}
func SetUserRoutes() *mux.Router {
    userRepository := NewInMemoryUserRepo()
    r := mux.NewRouter()
    r.Handle("/users", CreateUser(userRepository)).Methods("POST")
    r.Handle("/users", GetUsers(userRepository)).Methods("GET")
    return r
}
```

The HTTP handler functions are refactored to obtain a parameter value that implements the persistence logic. The handler functions return an http.Handler by calling http.HandlerFunc. The handler functions have a parameter of UserRepository type, which is an interface defined in the repository.go file. Because it is an interface, you can provide any concrete implementation for this type. For example, you can provide implementations of the UserRepository type for application code and for automated tests separately, which provides better code testability. For application code, you can provide an implementation of the UserRepository interface to implement the persistence logic on a real database. But when you call handler functions from automated tests, you can provide a fake implementation of the UserRepository interface to mimic the functionality when you don't need to hit the real database. When you write tests, you may need to mock the interfaces in many places like this one.

Listing 10-12 provides the source code of repository.go in the lib package.

Listing 10-12. repository.go in the lib Package

```go
package lib

import (
    "errors"
)

type User struct {
    FirstName string `json:"firstname"`
    LastName  string `json:"lastname"`
    Email     string `json:email"`
}
```

```go
type UserRepository interface {
    GetAll() []User
    Create(User) error
    Validate(User) error
}
type InMemoryUserRepository struct {
    DataStore []User
}

func (repo *InMemoryUserRepository) GetAll() []User {
    return repo.DataStore
}
func (repo *InMemoryUserRepository) Create(user User) error {
    err := repo.Validate(user)
    if err != nil {
        return err
    }
    repo.DataStore = append(repo.DataStore, user)
    return nil
}
func (repo *InMemoryUserRepository) Validate(user User) error {
    for _, u := range repo.DataStore {
        if u.Email == user.Email {
            return errors.New("The Email is already exists")
        }
    }
    return nil
}
func NewInMemoryUserRepo() *InMemoryUserRepository {
    return &InMemoryUserRepository{DataStore: []User{}}
}
```

In the repository.go source file, an interface named UserRepository is written that provides the persistence logic for the model entity User. The Validate function validates whether the User entity has a duplicate e-mail ID and returns an error if the given e-mail ID exists:

```go
type UserRepository interface {
    GetAll() []User
    Create(User) error
    Validate(User) error
}
```

An implementation of UserRepository – InMemoryUserRepository is provided, which persists User objects into a slice. (A slice is used as the data store for the example demonstration; in a real-world implementation, it might be a database such as MongoDB.)

An HTTP server in main.go is started. Listing 10-13 provides the source code of main.go in the main package.

Listing 10-13. main.go in the main Package

```
package main
import (
    "net/http"

    "github.com/shijuvar/go-web/chapter-10/httptestbdd/lib"
)

func main() {
    routers := lib.SetUserRoutes()
    http.ListenAndServe(":8080", routers)
}
```

The main function in the main package starts the HTTP server.

Writing BDD-style Tests

The HTTP API application has been refactored to be more testable so that you can easily write automated tests. Now let's focus on writing tests based on BDD methodology. Like TDD, the user stories are defined and converted into test cases before the code is written. The primary objective of BDD is to define the behavior in more expressive way before the production code is written so that you can easily develop applications based on well-defined behavior. Because this book is not primarily focused on agile practices and BDD, the exact development process of BDD is not followed, but the focus is on how to write BDD-style tests using Go third-party libraries.

The Ginkgo package, paired with its preferred matcher library Gomega, is used to specify the behavior in test cases.

Installing Ginkgo and Gomega

To install Ginkgo and Gomega, run the following commands on the command-line window:

```
go get github.com/onsi/ginkgo/ginkgo
go get github.com/onsi/gomega
```

The Ginkgo package also provides an executable program named ginkgo, which can be used for bootstrapping test suite files and running tests. When the ginkgo package is installed, it also installs the ginkgo executable under $GOPATH/bin.

To work with Ginkgo and Gomega, you must add these packages to the import list:

```
import (

    "github.com/onsi/ginkgo"
    "github.com/onsi/gomega"
)
```

Bootstrapping a Suite

To write tests with Ginkgo for a package, you must first create a test suite file by running the following command on the command-line window:

```
ginkgo bootstrap
```

Let's navigate to the lib directory and then run the ginkgo bootstrap command. It generates a file named lib_suite_test.go that contains the code shown in Listing 10-14.

Listing 10-14. Test Suite File lib_suite_test.go in the lib_test Package

```
package lib_test

import (
    . "github.com/onsi/ginkgo"
    . "github.com/onsi/gomega"

    "testing"
)

func TestLib(t *testing.T) {
    RegisterFailHandler(Fail)
    RunSpecs(t, "Lib Suite")
}
```

The generated source file will be put into a package named lib_test, which isolates the tests from the application code sitting on the lib package. Go allows you to directly put the lib_test package inside the lib package directory. You can also change the package name to lib for the test suite file and tests.

The source of lib_suite_test.go shows that Ginkgo leverages the Go existing testing infrastructure. You can run the suite by running "go test" or "ginkgo" on the command-line window.

Let's explore the suite file:

- The ginkgo and gomega packages are imported with a dot (.) import, which allows you to call exported identifiers of ginkgo and gomega packages without using a qualifier.

- The RegisterFailHandler(Fail) statement connects Ginkgo and Gomega. Gomega is used as the matcher library for Ginkgo.

- The RunSpecs(t, "Lib Suite") statement tells Ginkgo to start the test suite. Ginkgo automatically fails the testing.T if any of the specs fail.

Adding Specs to the Suite

A test suite file named lib_suite_test.go is created, but to run the test suite, specs have to be added to the test suite by adding test files. Let's generate a test file using the ginkgo generate command on the command-line window:

```
ginkgo generate users
```

241

This command generates a test file named users_test.go that contains the code shown in Listing 10-15. As discussed earlier, tests are written in the lib_test packages under the lib directory, and Go allows you to do this. If you want to use the lib package for tests, you can also do so.

Listing 10-15. Test File users_test.go Generated by ginkgo

```
package lib_test

import (
    . "lib"

    . "github.com/onsi/ginkgo"
    . "github.com/onsi/gomega"
)

var _ = Describe("Users", func() {

})
```

The generated test file contains the code for importing ginkgo and gomega packages using the dot (.) import. Because test files are written in the lib_test package, the lib package has to be imported. Because the dot (.) import is used for packages, the exported identifiers of these packages can be called directly without needing a qualifier.

In BDD-style tests, specs are written to define code behavior. With Ginkgo, specs are written inside a top-level Describe container using the Ginkgo Describe function. Ginkgo uses the "var _ =" trick to evaluate the Describe function at the top level without requiring an init function.

Organizing Specs with Containers

Now a basic test file to write specs for the application code is created. Let's organize the specs using functions provided by the Ginkgo package.

Listing 10-16 provides the high-level structure of the Users spec.

Listing 10-16. High-level Structure of the Users Spec

```
var _ = Describe("Users", func() {

    BeforeEach(func() {

    })

    Describe("Get Users", func() {
      Context("Get all Users", func() {
        It("should get list of Users", func() {
          })
        })
      })
```

```
    Describe("Post a new User", func() {
      Context("Provide a valid User data", func() {
        It("should create a new User and get HTTP Status: 201", func() {
          })
      })
      Context("Provide a User data that contains duplicate email id", func() {
        It("should get HTTP Status: 400", func() {

          })
      })
  })
})
```

Describe blocks are used to describe a code's individual behaviors. Inside the Describe container, Context and It blocks are written. The Context block is used to specify different contexts under an individual behavior. You can write multiple Context blocks within a Describe block. You write individual specs inside an It block within a Describe or Context container.

The BeforeEach block, which runs before each It block, can be used for writing logic before running each spec.

Writing Specs in the Test File

High-level specs were specified in the previous section. In this section, the test file will be completed by writing concrete implementations in the It blocks. In the tests, HTTP handler functions are invoked by sending requests to the multiplexer.

Let's explore one of the HTTP handler functions that was written in Listing 10-11:

```go
func GetUsers(repo UserRepository) http.Handler {
    return http.HandlerFunc(func(w http.ResponseWriter, r *http.Request) {
        userStore := repo.GetAll()
        users, err := json.Marshal(userStore)

        if err != nil {
            w.WriteHeader(http.StatusInternalServerError)
            return
        }
        w.Header().Set("Content-Type", "application/json")
        w.WriteHeader(http.StatusOK)
        w.Write(users)
    })
}
```

The GetUsers function has a parameter of type UserRepository that is an interface:

```go
type UserRepository interface {
    GetAll() []User
    Create(User) error
    Validate(User) error
}
```

In the application code, a concrete implementation for the UserRepository interface is provided (InMemoryUserRepository), which provides persistence onto in-memory data of a collection. When you develop real-world applications, you might persist your application data onto a database. When you write tests, you may want to avoid persistence on to the database by providing a mocked implementation. Because the handler functions expect a concrete implementation of UserRepository as a parameter value, you can provide a separate version of UserRepository in the tests for invoking the handler functions.

Listing 10-17 provides a concrete implementation of the UserRepository interface for use in the tests.

Listing 10-17. Implementation of UserRepository in users_tests.go

```go
type FakeUserRepository struct {
    DataStore []User
}

func (repo *FakeUserRepository) GetAll() []User {

    return repo.DataStore
}
func (repo *FakeUserRepository) Create(user User) error {
    err := repo.Validate(user)
    if err != nil {
        return err
    }
    repo.DataStore = append(repo.DataStore, user)
    return nil
}
func (repo *FakeUserRepository) Validate(user User) error {
    for _, u := range repo.DataStore {
        if u.Email == user.Email {
            return errors.New("The Email is already exists")
        }
    }
    return nil
}
func NewFakeUserRepo() *FakeUserRepository {
    return &FakeUserRepository{
        DataStore: []User{
            User{"Shiju", "Varghese", "shiju@xyz.com"},
            User{"Rosmi", "Shiju", "rose@xyz.com"},
            User{"Irene", "Rose", "irene@xyz.com"},
        },
    }
}
```

FakeUserRepository provides an implementation of the UserRepository interface that is written for use with tests. You can create an instance of FakeUserRepository by calling the NewFakeUserRepo function, which also provides fake data for three User objects. The FakeUserRepository type is a kind of *test double*, a generic term used in unit testing for any circumstance in which a production object is replaced for testing purposes. Here, InMemoryUserRepository is replaced with FakeUserRepository for testing purposes.

Listing 10-18 provides the completed version of users_test.go, in which all the specs are implemented.

Listing 10-18. Completed Version of users_tests.go in the lib_test Package

```go
package lib_test

import (
    "encoding/json"
    "errors"
    "net/http"
    "net/http/httptest"
    "strings"

    "github.com/gorilla/mux"
    . "github.com/onsi/ginkgo"
    . "github.com/onsi/gomega"
    . "github.com/shijuvar/go-web/chapter-10/httptestbdd/lib"
)

var _ = Describe("Users", func() {
    userRepository := NewFakeUserRepo()
    var r *mux.Router
    var w *httptest.ResponseRecorder

    BeforeEach(func() {
        r = mux.NewRouter()
    })

    Describe("Get Users", func() {
        Context("Get all Users", func() {
            //providing mocked data of 3 users
            It("should get list of Users", func() {
                r.Handle("/users", GetUsers(userRepository)).Methods("GET")
                req, err := http.NewRequest("GET", "/users", nil)
                Expect(err).NotTo(HaveOccurred())
                w = httptest.NewRecorder()
                r.ServeHTTP(w, req)
                Expect(w.Code).To(Equal(200))
                var users []User
                json.Unmarshal(w.Body.Bytes(), &users)
                //Verifying mocked data of 3 users
                Expect(len(users)).To(Equal(3))
            })
        })
    })

    Describe("Post a new User", func() {
        Context("Provide a valid User data", func() {
            It("should create a new User and get HTTP Status: 201", func() {
                r.Handle("/users", CreateUser(userRepository)).Methods("POST")
                userJson := `{"firstname": "Alex", "lastname": "John", "email":
                "alex@xyz.com"}`
```

```go
                req, err := http.NewRequest(
                    "POST",
                    "/users",
                    strings.NewReader(userJson),
                )
                Expect(err).NotTo(HaveOccurred())
                w = httptest.NewRecorder()
                r.ServeHTTP(w, req)
                Expect(w.Code).To(Equal(201))
            })
        })
        Context("Provide a User data that contains duplicate email id", func() {
            It("should get HTTP Status: 400", func() {
                r.Handle("/users", CreateUser(userRepository)).Methods("POST")
                userJson := `{"firstname": "Alex", "lastname": "John", "email":
                "alex@xyz.com"}`

                req, err := http.NewRequest(
                    "POST",
                    "/users",
                    strings.NewReader(userJson),
                )
                Expect(err).NotTo(HaveOccurred())
                w = httptest.NewRecorder()
                r.ServeHTTP(w, req)
                Expect(w.Code).To(Equal(400))
            })
        })
    })
})

type FakeUserRepository struct {
    DataStore []User
}

func (repo *FakeUserRepository) GetAll() []User {

    return repo.DataStore
}
func (repo *FakeUserRepository) Create(user User) error {
    err := repo.Validate(user)
    if err != nil {
        return err
    }
    repo.DataStore = append(repo.DataStore, user)
    return nil
}
```

```go
func (repo *FakeUserRepository) Validate(user User) error {
    for _, u := range repo.DataStore {
        if u.Email == user.Email {
            return errors.New("The Email is already exists")
        }
    }
    return nil
}
func NewFakeUserRepo() *FakeUserRepository {
    return &FakeUserRepository{
        DataStore: []User{
            User{"Shiju", "Varghese", "shiju@xyz.com"},
            User{"Rosmi", "Shiju", "rose@xyz.com"},
            User{"Irene", "Rose", "irene@xyz.com"},
        },
    }
}
```

Let's explore the code in `users_test.go`:

- Individual behaviors are written in the `Describe` block. Here, behaviors for `"Get Users"` and `"Post a new User"` are defined on `"Users"`.

- Within the `Describe` block, the `Context` blocks are written to define circumstances under a behavior.

- Individual specs are written in the `It` block within the `Describe` and `Context` containers.

- Within the `"Get Users"` behavior, a `"Get all Users"` context is defined, which maps the functionality of HTTP Get on the `"/users"` endpoint. Within this context, an `It` block is defined as `"should get list of Users"`, which checks to see whether the returned HTTP response has the status code of 200. Dummy data of three Users are defined by creating an instance of `FakeUserRepository` so that the returned HTTP response shows having three Users.

- For the `"Post a new User"` behavior, two circumstances are defined: `"Provide a valid User data"` and `"Provide a User data that contains duplicate email id"`. This maps the functionality of HTTP Post on the `"/users"` endpoint. A new User should be able to be created if valid User data is provided. An error occurs if a User data with a duplicate e-mail ID is provided. These specs are specified in the `It` block.

- An instance of `FakeUserRepository`, which is an implementation of the `UserRepository` interface, is provided to the HTTP handler function as a parameter value.

- The Ginkgo preferred matcher library Gomega is used for assertion. Gomega provides a variety of functions for writing assertion statements. The `Expect` function is also used for assertion.

Running Specs

You can run the test suite using the go test or gingko commands.
Let's run the suite using the go test command:

```
go test -v
```

The go test command generates the output shown in Figure 10-5.

```
=== RUN   TestLib
Running Suite: Lib Suite
========================
Random Seed: 1447779361
Will run 3 of 3 specs

•••
Ran 3 of 3 Specs in 0.000 seconds
SUCCESS! -- 3 Passed | 0 Failed | 0 Pending | 0 Skipped --- PASS: TestLib (0.00s)
PASS
ok        github.com/shijuvar/go-web/chapter-10/httptestbdd/lib    0.025s
```

Figure 10-5. *Output of the specs run by the go test command*

Let's run the suite using the ginkgo command:

```
ginkgo -v
```

The ginkgo command generates the output shown in Figure 10-6.

```
Running Suite: Lib Suite
========================
Random Seed: 1447779467
Will run 3 of 3 specs

Users HTTP Get on '/users' Get collection of Users
  should get three Users
  /Users/shijuvar/go/src/github.com/shijuvar/go-web/chapter-10/httptestbdd/lib/users_test.go:37
•
------------------------------
Users HTTP Post '/user' Provide a valid data User data
  should create a new User and get HTTP Status: 201
  /Users/shijuvar/go/src/github.com/shijuvar/go-web/chapter-10/httptestbdd/lib/users_test.go:56
•
------------------------------
Users HTTP Post '/user' Provide a User data that contains duplicate email id
  should get HTTP Status: 400
  /Users/shijuvar/go/src/github.com/shijuvar/go-web/chapter-10/httptestbdd/lib/users_test.go:72
•
Ran 3 of 3 Specs in 0.001 seconds
SUCCESS! -- 3 Passed | 0 Failed | 0 Pending | 0 Skipped PASS

Ginkgo ran 1 suite in 1.434994294s
Test Suite Passed
Shijus-MacBook-Pro:lib shijuvar$ 
```

Figure 10-6. *Output of the specs run by the ginkgo command*

Summary

Automated testing is an important practice in software engineering that ensures application quality. Unit testing is a kind of automated testing process in which the smallest pieces of testable software in the application, called units, are individually and independently tested to determine whether they behave exactly as designed.

Test-driven development (TDD) is a software development process that follows a test-first development approach, in which unit tests are written before the production code. TDD is a design approach that encourages developers to think about their implementation before writing the code.

Go provides the core functionality to write automated unit tests through its testing standard library package. The testing package provides all the essential functionality required for writing automated tests with tooling support. It is intended to be used with the go test command. Besides the testing package, the Go standard library provides two more packages: httptest provides utilities for HTTP testing, and quick provides utility functions to help with black box testing.

The following naming conventions and patterns are used to write a test suite:

- Create a source file with a name ending in _test.go.

- Within the test suite (the source file ends in _test.go), write functions with the signature func TestXxx(*testing.T).

Test functions are run sequentially when tests using the go test command are run. In addition to providing support for code testing behavior, the testing package can also be used for benchmarking tests and testing example code.

You can test HTTP applications using the httptest package. When you test HTTP applications, you can use the ResponseRecorder and Server struct types provided by the httptest package. ResponseRecorder records the response of a returned HTTP response so it can be inspected. A Server is an HTTP server for testing to perform end-to-end HTTP tests.

This chapter showed you third-party packages Ginkgo and Gomega for testing. Ginkgo is a behavior-driven development (BDD) – style testing framework that lets you write expressive tests in Go to specify application. BDD is an extension of TDD, with an emphasis on *behavior* instead of *test*. In BDD, you specify behaviors in an expressive way in your automated tests, and you write code based on the behaviors.

CHAPTER 11

■ ■ ■

Building Go Web Applications on Google Cloud

Cloud computing is changing the way scalable applications are developed and run. Cloud computing allows you to fully focus on application engineering instead of managing the IT infrastructure. Developing Go applications on the Cloud infrastructure is a great choice because Go is the language designed for running on modern computer hardware and next-generation IT infrastructure platforms. Go is built to solve large-scale computing problems, and it is becoming the language of choice for building Cloud infrastructure technologies such as Docker and Kubernetes. This chapter shows you how to build Cloud native applications using Go by leveraging the Google Cloud platform.

Introduction to Cloud Computing

Cloud computing is gradually becoming a primary option for deploying applications. Instead of managing and maintaining on-premise computing resources, Cloud computing allows you to move the IT infrastructure and applications to a subscription-based computing model in which the software is accessed via the Internet. This allows a focus on application engineering instead of managing the IT infrastructure, so developers can build highly scalable applications with a greater level of agility.

Cloud computing is a "pay-as-you-go" computing model in which IT infrastructure and software development platforms are being offered in a service-based consumption model. The greatest advantage of Cloud computing is the operational agility you get while developing applications. The Cloud model enables on-demand scalability, which means that you can scale up computing resources whenever you require more and can use them for as long as you want, and then scale down computing resources when they are no longer needed. Most Cloud computing platforms provide autoscaling capabilities to their Cloud platform, which allows you to automatically scale up and scale down the number of computing resources based on configurations.

In Cloud computing, various options are available for hosting and running applications. These options provide different flexibility models to host, run, and scale your applications, which can be used for appropriate computing scenarios.

Here are the different options available in Cloud computing platforms to host and run applications:

- Infrastructure as a Service (IaaS)

- Platform as a Service (PaaS)

- Container as a Service (CaaS)

Infrastructure as a Service (IaaS)

The Infrastructure as a Service (IaaS) model provides virtualized computing resources as a service over the Internet. You can acquire virtual machines (VMs) from the Cloud platform for on-demand scalability. In this model, you have to set up everything on your end for hosting and running your applications. For example, if you want to run an HTTP server in Go, you have to manually set up the Go runtime environment and open up the HTTP ports to receive incoming web requests to the HTTP server. The most important thing about the IaaS model is that you have full control over the VMs acquired on the Cloud.

Platform as a Service (PaaS)

The Platform as a Service (PaaS) model provides a platform managed by the Cloud platform vendor to deploy and run applications. This model provides specialized language environments, tools, and software development kits (SDKs) to develop and run applications on the Cloud. The PaaS model provides more operational agility than the IaaS model because it is a managed service provided by the Cloud platform in which you can develop, test, deploy, and run applications by using SDKs and tools provided by the platform.

For example, if you want to leverage the PaaS platform provided by Google Cloud for developing Go applications, you can download the Google Cloud PaaS platform SDK for Go, which allows you to quickly build, test, and run your Go applications on the Google Cloud. Autoscaling can be easily achieved with this model of Cloud computing without requiring any manual intervention. You might only need to configure the parameters for KPIs to perform autoscaling. In this model, you don't have to manage and maintain your VMs, unlike the IaaS model. This model enables superior operational agility during the development process because developers are freed from many IT infrastructure management operations.

Container as a Service

Container as a Service (CaaS) is an evolutionary computing model from both IaaS and PaaS. It is a relatively new model that brings you the best of both IaaS and PaaS. This model allows you to run software containers on the Cloud platform by using popular container technologies such as Docker and Kubernetes. Application containers are gradually becoming a standard for deploying and running applications due to their benefits. When you run application containers on Cloud platforms, this model gives you many capabilities. Google Container Engine is a CaaS platform provided by Google Cloud.

Introduction to Google Cloud

Google Cloud is a public Cloud platform from Google that enables developers to build, test, deploy, and run applications on Google's highly scalable and reliable infrastructure. The Google Cloud platform provides a set of modular Cloud-based services that allow you to build a variety of applications, from web applications to larger Big Data solutions, with on-demand scalability and a greater level of operational agility.

Google Cloud provides three types of services for computing:

- Google App Engine (GAE) is a PaaS service.

- Google Compute Engine (GCE) is an IaaS service.

- Google Container Engine (GKE) is a CaaS service.

Figure 11-1 shows an infographic of the various services provided by the Google Cloud platform.

Figure 11-1. *Infographic of Google Cloud platform services*

This chapter primarily focuses on the Google App Engine, which is a PaaS in the Google Cloud platform.

Google App Engine (GAE)

Google App Engine is the PaaS offering from the Google Cloud platform that allows you to build highly scalable web applications and back-end APIs. App Engine applications are available for automatic scaling to scale up computing instances automatically when traffic picks up and scale down computing instances automatically when they are no longer needed. Unlike IaaS, you don't need to provision VMs and maintain them by leveraging an Ops (operations) team. With App Engine, you just upload source code using the tools provided by App Engine and run applications on the Cloud, which is available for load balancing and autoscaling. When compared with the IaaS model, App Engine provides lot of operational agility for developing and managing applications because you don't have to spend time managing the VMs for running your applications.

App Engine provides the support for following language environments:

- Python
- Java
- PHP
- Go

Cloud Services with App Engine

When you develop Go applications on App Engine, you can leverage various Cloud services provided by the Google Cloud platform. Google Cloud provides APIs for accessing these services from App Engine applications. Keep in mind that these services are not restricted to App Engine; you can also use them with Google Compute Engine and Google Container Engine.

The following sections describe some of the Cloud services that can be used for App Engine applications.

User Authentication

You can use User Authentication services to sign on users with a Google account or OpenID.

Cloud Datastore

Cloud Datastore is a schema-less NoSQL database that can be used for persisting data of your App Engine applications.

Cloud Bigtable

Cloud Bigtable is a fast, fully managed, massively scalable NoSQL database that is ideal for using the data store for large-scale web, mobile, Big Data, and IoT applications that deal with large volumes of data. If the App Engine application requires a massively scalable data store with high performance, Cloud Bigtable is a better choice than Cloud Datastore.

Google Cloud SQL

Google Cloud SQL is a MySQL-compatible, relational database in the Google Cloud platform available as a managed service. If an App Engine application requires a relational model for data persistence, you can use Google Cloud SQL.

Memcache

When you develop high-performance applications, caching your application data is an important strategy for improving application performance. Memcache is a distributed, in-memory data cache that can be used to cache application data to improve the performance of App Engine applications.

Search

The Search service allows you to perform Google-like searches over structured data such as plain text, HTML, atom, numbers, dates, and geographic locations.

Traffic Splitting

The Traffic Splitting service allows you to route incoming requests to different application versions, run A/B tests, and do incremental feature rollouts.

Logging

The Logging service allows App Engine applications to collect and store logs.

Task Queues

The Task Queues service enables App Engine applications to perform work outside of user requests by using small discrete tasks that are executed later.

Security Scanning

The Security Scanning service scans applications for security vulnerabilities such as XSS attacks.

Google App Engine for Go

App Engine provides a Go runtime environment to run natively compiled Go code on the Cloud that allows you to build highly scalable web applications on the Google Cloud infrastructure. With App Engine, Go applications run in a secured "sandbox" environment that allows the App Engine environment to distribute web requests across multiple servers and scaling servers for on-demand scalability. When you develop applications in the sandbox environment of App Engine, you don't need to provision servers or spend time managing infrastructure. App Engine provides a deployment tool that allows you to upload your Go applications into the Cloud.

Go Development Environment

You can develop, test, and deploy Go applications on App Engine using the App Engine SDK for Go, which provides the tools and APIs for developing, testing, and running applications on Google Cloud. The App Engine Go SDK includes a development web server that allows you to run an App Engine application on a local computer to test Go applications before uploading them into the Cloud.

The development web server simulates many Cloud services in the development environment so that you can test App Engine applications on your local computer. This is very useful because you don't need to deploy applications into the Cloud whenever you want to test an App Engine application during the development cycle. You can test your App Engine application locally, and whenever you want to deploy the application into the Cloud platform's production environment, you can do so by using the tools provided by App Engine. The development server application simulates the App Engine environment, including a local version of the Google Accounts data store, and gives the ability to fetch URLs and send e-mail directly from a local computer using the App Engine APIs.

The Go SDK uses a modified version of the development tools from the Python SDK and runs on Mac OS X, Linux, and Windows computers with Python 2.7. So you can download and install Python 2.7 for your platform from the Python web site. Most Mac OS X users already have Python 2.7 installed. To develop Go applications on App Engine, download and install the App Engine SDK for Go for your OS.

App Engine SDK for Go provides a command-line tool named goapp that provides the following commands:

- goapp serve: The command goapp serve runs Go applications on a local development server.

- goapp deploy: The command goapp deploy is used to upload a Go application into the App Engine production environment.

You can find the goapp tool in the go_appengine directory of the zip archive of App Engine SDK for Go. To invoke the goapp tool from a command line, add the go_appengine directory to the PATH environment variable. This command adds the go_appengine directory to the PATH environment variable:

```
export PATH=$HOME/go_appengine:$PATH
```

Building App Engine Applications

Once you have set up App Engine SDK for Go, you can start developing web applications on the App Engine platform. Although App Engine applications are very similar to stand-alone Go web applications, there are some fundamental differences between them. The main difference is that the Go App Engine runtime provides a special main package, so you shouldn't use the main package for your App Engine applications. Instead, you can put HTTP handler code in a package of your choice. The Go http standard library package has been slightly modified for the App Engine runtime environment for running App Engine applications in the sandbox environment.

Writing an HTTP Server

Let's write an example web application server to explore the App Engine platform for Go.

Listing 11-1 provides an HTTP server on the App Engine platform.

Listing 11-1. Web Application Server for App Engine

```
package task

import (
    "fmt"
    "html/template"
    "net/http"
)

type Task struct {
    Name        string
    Description string
}

const taskForm = `
<html>
  <body>
    <form action="/task" method="post">
      <p>Task Name: <input type="text" name="taskname" ></p>
      <p> Description: <input type="text" name="description" ></p>
      <p><input type="submit" value="Submit"></p>
    </form>
  </body>
</html>
`

const taskTemplateHTML = `
<html>
  <body>
    <p>New Task has been created:</p>
    <div>Task: {{.Name}}</div>
    <div>Description: {{.Description}}</div>
  </body>
</html>
`

var taskTemplate = template.Must(template.New("task").Parse(taskTemplateHTML))

func init() {
    http.HandleFunc("/", index)
    http.HandleFunc("/task", task)
}

func index(w http.ResponseWriter, r *http.Request) {
    fmt.Fprint(w, taskForm)
}
```

```go
func task(w http.ResponseWriter, r *http.Request) {
    task := Task{
        Name:        r.FormValue("taskname"),
        Description: r.FormValue("description"),
    }
    err := taskTemplate.Execute(w, task)
    if err != nil {
        http.Error(w, err.Error(), http.StatusInternalServerError)
    }
}
```

An example web application is written with several HTML pages. The HTTP handler code is written inside the init function of the task package because the App Engine runtime provides a special main package that you can't use in the application code.

Creating the Configuration File

To run App Engine applications, you have to write a configuration file named app.yaml, which specifies various kinds of information for running the application, including the application identifier, runtime, and URLs that should be handled by the Go web application.

Let's write a configuration file for the App Engine application (see Listing 11-2).

Listing 11-2. Configuration File for the App Engine in app.yaml

```yaml
application: gae-demo
version: 1
runtime: go
api_version: go1

handlers:
- url: /.*
  script: _go_app
```

The app.yaml configuration file says the following about the App Engine application:

- The application identifier is gae-demo. When you deploy an application into App Engine, you must specify a unique identifier as the application identifier. When you run the application in the development server, you can set any value as the application identifier. Here, it is set as gae-demo during the time the application runs on the development server.

- The version number of the application code is 1. If you properly update the versions before uploading a new application version of application into App Engine, you can roll back to a previous version of using the administrative console.

- This Go program runs in the Go runtime environment with the API version go1.

- Every request to a URL whose path matches the regular expression /.* (all URLs) should be handled by the Go program. The _go_app value is recognized by the development web server and ignored by the production App Engine servers.

Testing the Application in Development Server

In the previous steps, an App Engine application and a configuration file were created. Now the application is ready for running on the development web server provided by the App Engine SDK. The development web server allows you to test App Engine applications in a development environment.

Figure 11-2 illustrates the directory structure of the App Engine application.

Figure 11-2. Application directory structure

Let's run the example web application on the development web server by running the goapp tool:

```
goapp serve gae-server/
```

The development web server is run by providing a path to the gae-server directory. You can omit the application path if you are running the goapp tool from the application's directory:

```
goapp serve
```

Figure 11-3 shows that the web development server has been started and is listening for requests on port 8080 and requests for the admin server on port 8000.

```
Shijus-MacBook-Pro:gae-server shijuvar$ goapp serve
INFO     2015-09-19 02:36:14,600 devappserver2.py:763] Skipping SDK update check.
WARNING  2015-09-19 02:36:14,654 simple_search_stub.py:1126] Could not read search indexes from /var/folders/sh
ndexes
INFO     2015-09-19 02:36:14,659 api_server.py:205] Starting API server at: http://localhost:49225
INFO     2015-09-19 02:36:14,662 dispatcher.py:197] Starting module "default" running at: http://localhost:8080
INFO     2015-09-19 02:36:14,663 admin_server.py:118] Starting admin server at: http://localhost:8000
```

Figure 11-3. Running a development web server

Run and test the App Engine application by accessing the following URL in a web browser:
http://localhost:8080/.

Figure 11-4 shows that the application is running at http://localhost:8080/ under the development server.

Figure 11-4. *Development web server listening on port 8080*

■ **Note** You can get information about App Engine instances on the admin web server here: http://localhost:8000/.

Figure 11-5 shows that the admin web server is providing the information about App Engine instances running in the development web server.

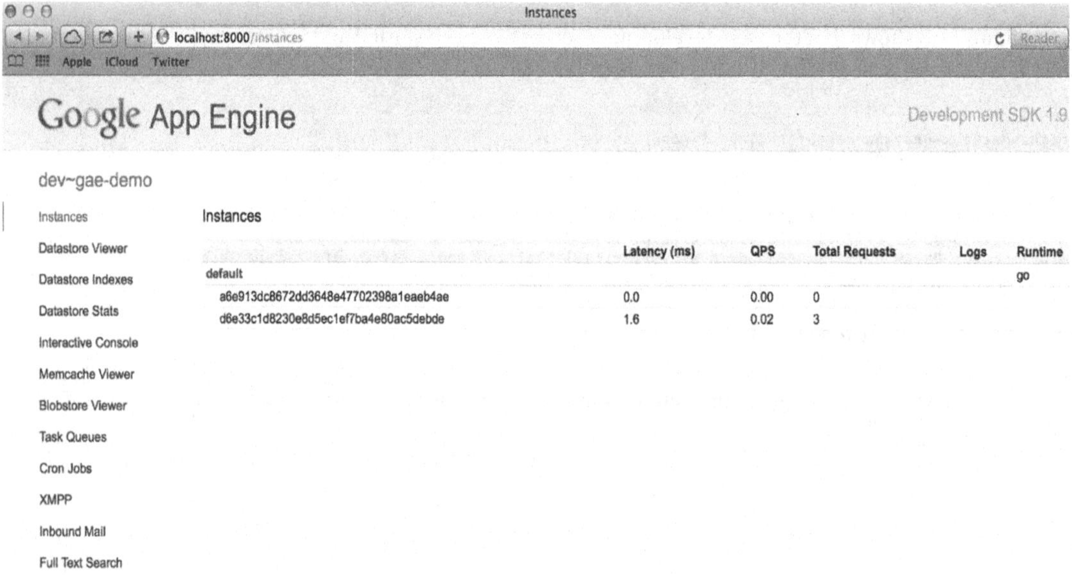

Figure 11-5. *Admin server listening on port 8000*

Deploying App Engine Applications into the Cloud

To deploy App Engine applications into the Cloud, you have to create a project in the Google Cloud platform for the App Engine instance. You also must provide a unique project ID, which will be used to deploy the application into the Cloud. Specify the application as `Project ID` in the `app.yaml` file.

You create and manage App Engine applications by using the Google Developers Console (see `https://console.developers.google.com/`). You can sign in to the Google Developers Console using your Google account (Google Cloud provides a free trial account for 60 days).

Let's create an App Engine project in the Google Developers Console. First, click the Create a Project button. You can then specify the project name, project ID, and App Engine location.

Figure 11-6 shows the New Project window that displays a new project in Google Developers Console.

New Project

Project name ⓘ

gae-demo

Your project ID will be gae-demo-1073 ⓘ Edit

Hide advanced options...

App Engine location ⓘ

us-central ▼

Create   Cancel

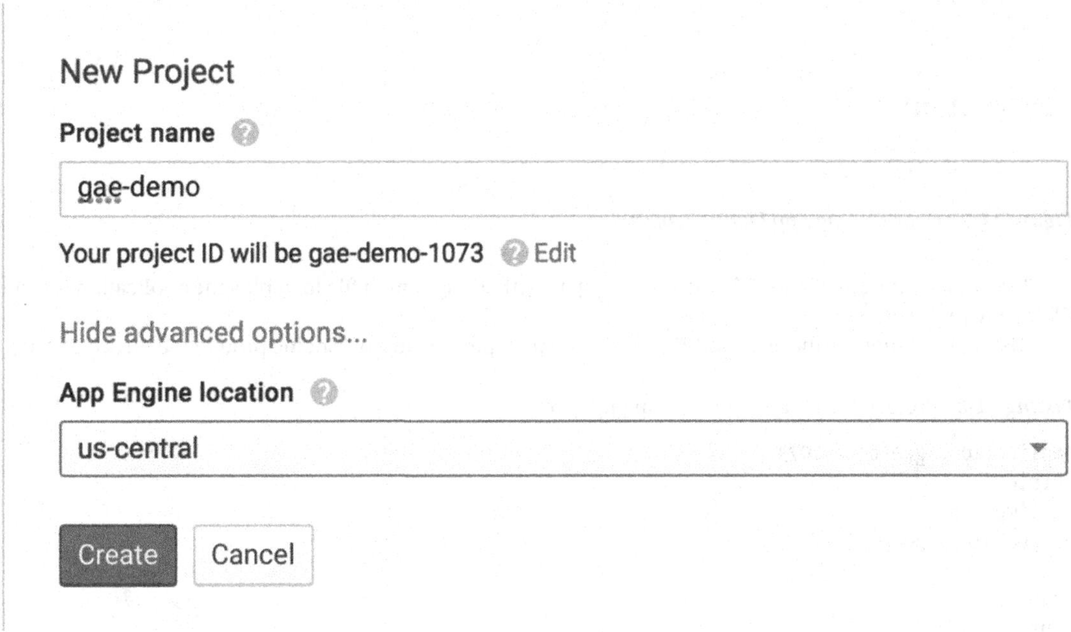

Figure 11-6. *Creating a new App Engine project*

You create an App Engine project with a unique project ID in the Google Developers Console (refer to Figure 11-6). The project ID is `gae-demo-1073`, which will be used to specify the application identifier in `app.yaml` before the application is deployed.

Figure 11-7 shows details about the newly created project from the Google Developers Console.

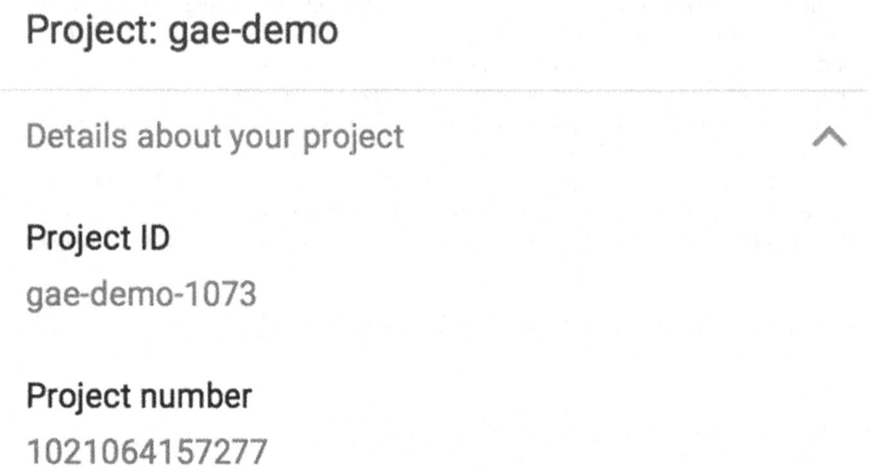

Project: gae-demo

Details about your project   ⌃

Project ID
gae-demo-1073

Project number
1021064157277

Figure 11-7. *Details of the App Engine project*

Let's modify the application identifier in the app.yaml configuration file to deploy the application into a Cloud environment.

Listing 11-3 provides the app.yaml file to be used to deploy on an App Engine production environment.

Listing 11-3. Project ID as the Application in app.yaml

```
application: gae-demo-1073
version: 1
runtime: go
api_version: go1

handlers:
- url: /.*
  script: _go_app
```

You can now deploy the App Engine application into the Google Cloud environment by running the goapp tool from the root directory of the application:

```
goapp deploy
```

The goapp deploy command deploys the App Engine application into the Google Cloud environment by taking the configuration from app.yaml. It takes the application identifier from app.yaml and uploads the compiled Go program to the associated App Engine project. When you deploy the application, you are asked to provide Google account credentials to access the App Engine application you created in the Google Developer Console. In the App Engine production environment, a URL is given with https://{project ID}.appspot.com. You receive the following URL for the App Engine application: https://gae-demo-1073.appspot.com/.

You can verify the application in the Cloud environment by visiting the URL for the production environment. Figures 11-8 and 11-9 show that the App Engine application is successfully running in the production environment of Google App Engine.

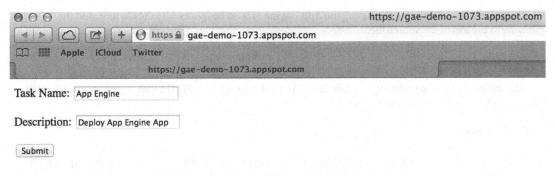

Figure 11-8. Task form in the App Engine app

New Task has been created:

Task: App Engine
Description: Deploy App Engine App

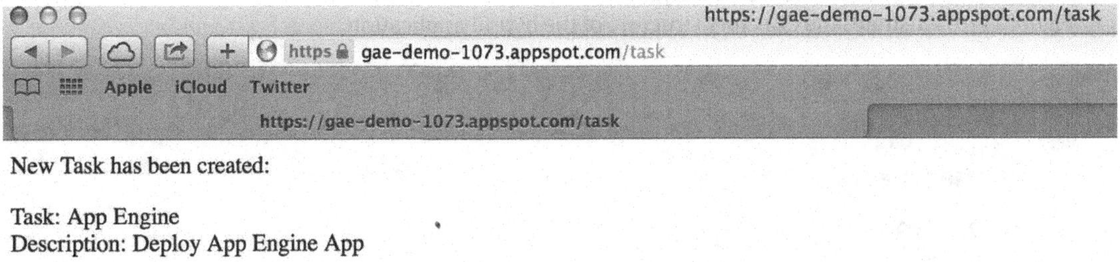

Figure 11-9. Response page of the Task form in the App Engine app

Creating Hybrid Stand-alone/App Engine applications

The fundamental differences between an App Engine application and a stand-alone application are very few. The App Engine environment provides a special main package, so you can't use it for App Engine applications. You can write handler logic in init functions of the Go package of your choice for App Engine applications. When you develop stand-alone applications, you need to write the main package.

It would be really helpful in some scenarios to write hybrid applications for both stand-alone and App Engine environments. Let's say you want to write a Go web application that tests and deploys on both on-premise servers and Google Cloud. Writing a hybrid application to be running in both environments would be really helpful for testing and deploying applications in multiple environments without modifying the source code before each deployment scenario. You can develop a hybrid application for both stand-alone and App Engine environments by using build constraints.

■ **Note** A *build constraint*, also known as a *build tag*, specifies conditions in which a file should be included in the package. A build constraint must appear near the top of the source files as a line comment that begins with // +build. Build constraints can appear in any kind of source file that is not restricted with Go source files.

The App Engine SDK provides a new build constraint, appengine, that can be used to differentiate the source code in stand-alone and App Engine environments when compiling the source code. Using the appengine build constraint, you can exclude some source files during the build process based on the build environment. For example, when you build the application source using the App Engine SDK, you can ignore the source code written in the main package.

If you want to build source files using the App Engine SDK to be ignored by the Go tool, add the following to the top of the source file:

```
// +build appengine
```

The following build constraint specifies that you want to build with the Go tool, so the source files will not be compiled in the App Engine SDK:

```
// +build !appengine
```

Let's rewrite the web application from Listing 11-1 to make it a hybrid application for both App Engine and stand-alone environments. In this hybrid implementation, you'll create separate source files for handling the HTTP handler logic using build constraints for both App Engine and stand-alone applications and putting common logic in a shared library.

Figure 11-10 illustrates the directory structure of the hybrid application.

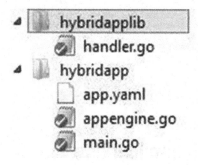

Figure 11-10. *Directory structure of the hybrid app*

`main.go` will be built with the Go tool, and `appengine.go` with the App Engine SDK. Common logic is put in a shared library named `hybridapplib`.

Listing 11-4 provides the implementation of `hybridapplib`, which is used for common logic.

Listing 11-4. Shared Logic in handler.go of hybridapplib

```
package hybridapplib

import (
    "fmt"
    "html/template"
    "net/http"
)

type Task struct {
    Name        string
    Description string
}
```

```go
const taskForm = `
<html>
  <body>
    <form action="/task" method="post">
      <p>Task Name: <input type="text" name="taskname" ></p>
      <p> Description: <input type="text" name="description" ></p>
      <p><input type="submit" value="Submit"></p>
    </form>
  </body>
</html>
`

const taskTemplateHTML = `
<html>
  <body>
    <p>New Task has been created:</p>
   <div>Task: {{.Name}}</div>
   <div>Description: {{.Description}}</div>
  </body>
</html>
`


var taskTemplate = template.Must(template.New("task").Parse(taskTemplateHTML))

func init() {
    http.HandleFunc("/", index)
    http.HandleFunc("/task", task)
}

func index(w http.ResponseWriter, r *http.Request) {
    fmt.Fprint(w, taskForm)
}

func task(w http.ResponseWriter, r *http.Request) {
    task := Task{
        Name:        r.FormValue("taskname"),
        Description: r.FormValue("description"),
    }
    err := taskTemplate.Execute(w, task)
    if err != nil {
        http.Error(w, err.Error(), http.StatusInternalServerError)
    }
}
```

HTTP handler logic is put in the init function of handler.go. The code in the handler.go source file is common for both stand-alone and App Engine applications.

Listing 11-5 provides the main.go source file of the main package that provides the main function. It is built with the Go tool.

Listing 11-5. main.go in the main Package

```
// +build !appengine

package main

import (
    "net/http"

    _ "github.com/shijuvar/go-web/chapter-11/hybridapplib"
)

func main() {
    http.ListenAndServe("localhost:8080", nil)
}
```

The build constraint !appengine is used in the main.go file to be included when the Go tool application is built. When the application is built with the Go tool, the main.go file is taken as part of the main package. In the main function, the ListenAndServe function of the http package is called to start the HTTP server on the on-premise server. The blank identifier (_) is used as the alias name for the hybridapplib package to invoke its init function without referring the package identifier in the programs.

When you run the application on the App Engine, you can't use the main package. Listing 11-6 provides the implementation to build the application in the App Engine environment in which the init function of the hybridapplib package is invoked.

Listing 11-6. appengine.go in the task Package

```
// +build appengine

package task

import (
    _ "github.com/shijuvar/go-web/chapter-11/hybridapplib"
)

func init() {
}
```

The build constraint appengine is used in the appengine.go file to be included when the application is built with the App Engine SDK. The appengine.go file is taken as part of the task package. Because the HTTP handler code was implemented in the hybridapplib package, this source file is kept without having any implementation.

When you build the application using the Go tool, the main.go source file is included for compiling Go packages, and the appengine.go source file is excluded from the compilation. When the application is built with the App Engine SDK, the HTTP server is run in the App Engine environment by taking the handler logic from the package init functions and is ignored by the main.go file.

This hybrid approach may not be useful when you develop App Engine applications with various Cloud services. For example, let's say you want to use the Cloud Datastore service for your App Engine application. You can test the application on a local computer as the App Engine web development server simulates Datastore, but you can't run this application in your on-premise environment.

Working with Cloud Native Databases

The App Engine, the platform as a service of the Google Cloud platform, allows you to build massively scalable web applications in which you don't have to worry about setting up an IT infrastructure. As discussed in previous sections, Go developers can develop, test, and deploy web applications on the App Engine by using the App Engine SDK for Go, and these applications are available for autoscaling. When you develop scalable applications, persisting data in a scalable storage mechanism is very important for achieving scalability and availability.

When you develop applications for the Google Cloud platform, you can use any kind of database. Chapters 8 and 9 discussed MongoDB, a NoSQL data store. You can set up a database like MongoDB, which can be used with web applications running on the Google Cloud platform. To use a database such as MongoDB on Google Cloud, you need to obtain a VM as a Google Compute Engine (GCE) service, which is an IaaS platform in the Google Cloud. Then you need to set up the database on the VM instance. It requires IaaS instances; managing and scaling these databases may require lot of manual interventions.

Google Cloud provides different data stores as managed services that can be used with web applications without worrying about setting up and managing IaaS instances. So you don't need Ops on your databases running on Cloud, giving you lots of operational agility for Google Cloud applications.

In Google Cloud Platform, you can use the following databases for persisting structured data:

- **Google Cloud SQL**: A MySQL-compatible relational database available for Cloud scale.

- **Google Cloud Datastore**: A NoSQL data store that provides scalable storage.

- **Google Cloud Bigtable**: A NoSQL database that can scale to billions of rows and thousands of columns, allowing petabytes of data. It is an ideal data store for Big Data solutions.

Google Cloud provides both NoSQL and relational databases. Google Cloud offers two options for NoSQL: Google Cloud Datastore and Google Cloud Bigtable. Both Datastore and Bigtable are designed to provide a massively scalable data store.

Even though both are designed to be massively scalable, Bigtable is a better choice when you deal with terabytes of data. Bigtable is designed for HBase compatibility and is accessible through extensions to the HBase 1.0 API, so it is compatible with the Big Data ecosystem. In Big Data solutions, you can store the massive volume of data in Bigtable and analyze it with analytics tools on the Hadoop ecosystem.

Cloud Datastore is built on the top of Bigtable. Datastore provides high availability with replication and data synchronization; Bigtable doesn't replicate data and runs in a single datacenter region. Datastore provides support for ACID transactions and SQL-like queries using GQL, which is a SQL-like language for retrieving entities from Datastore. Cloud Datastore is a great data store choice for App Engine web applications.

The following section describes how to use the Google Cloud Datastore with App Engine applications.

Introduction to Google Cloud Datastore

Google Cloud Datastore is a schema-less NoSQL data store that provides robust, scalable storage for applications. It has the following features:

- No planned downtime

- Atomic transactions

- High availability of reads and writes

- Strong consistency for reads and ancestor queries

- Eventual consistency for all other queries

The most important thing about Datastore is that it replicates data across multiple datacenter regions, providing a high level of availability for reads and writes. When you compare Datastore with Bigtable, note that Bigtable runs on a single datacenter.

Entities

The Cloud Datastore holds data objects known as *entities*. The values of the Go struct are persisted into entities, which hold one or more properties. The Go structs fields become the properties of the entity. The type of property values are taken from the structs fields.

Like many NoSQL databases, Cloud Datastore is schema-less database, which means that data objects of the same entity can have different properties, and properties with the same name can have different value types.

Cloud Datastore is an evolutionary NoSQL that has lot of advantages over traditional NoSQL databases. Cloud Datastore allows you to store hierarchically structured data using ancestor paths in a tree-like structure.

Ancestors and Descendants

When you create an entity in Datastore, you can optionally specify another entity as its *parent*. You can associate hierarchically structured data by specifying the parent entity. If you are not specifying any entity as a parent, it is designated as a root entity. An entity's parent, parent's parent, and so on recursively are its *ancestors*. An entity's children, children's children, and so on are its *descendants*. A root entity and all its descendants belong to the same *entity group*. Understanding the concept of entity groups can help you perform queries in an efficient way.

Working with Cloud Datastore

Google Cloud Datastore is a great data store choice when you develop highly scalable Cloud native applications on the Google Cloud platform using App Engine. Both App Engine and Cloud Datastore provide massive scalability to applications without developers having to manage infrastructure or work on Ops. When you use Datastore with your App Engine applications, you don't need to configure anything to work with it. You can simply use the Go package for Cloud Datastore and then persist and query data against the Datastore.

Let's create an example App Engine web application by using Cloud Datastore as the database. This example application works with a simple data model without using ancestors and descendants.

The following Go packages are used in the App Engine application:

- `google.golang.org/appengine`: The appengine package provides basic functionality for Google App Engine.

- `google.golang.org/appengine/datastore`: The datastore package provides a client for App Engine's datastore service.

You can install the packages using the goapp tool:

```
goapp get google.golang.org/appengine
goapp get google.golang.org/appengine/datastore
```

The example application provides the following functionalities:

- The home page of the application shows a list of tasks.

- Users can create a new task by choosing the Create task option, which displays a form for creating a new task.

Listing 11-7 provides an example App Engine application using Cloud Datastore.

Listing 11-7. App Engine Application with Cloud Datastore

```
package task

import (
    "fmt"
    "html/template"
    "net/http"
    "time"

    "google.golang.org/appengine"
    "google.golang.org/appengine/datastore"
)

type Task struct {
    Name        string
    Description string
    CreatedOn   time.Time
}

const taskForm = `
<html>
  <body>
    <form action="/save" method="post">
      <p>Task Name: <input type="text" name="taskname" ></p>
      <p> Description: <input type="text" name="description" ></p>
      <p><input type="submit" value="Submit"></p>
    </form>
  </body>
</html>
`

const taskListTmplHTML = `
<html>
<body>
<p>Task List</p>
{{range .}}
  <p>{{.Name}} - {{.Description}}</p>
{{end}}
<p><a href="/create">Create task</a> </p>
</body>
</html>
`
```

```go
var taskListTemplate = template.Must(template.New("taskList").Parse(taskListTmplHTML))

func init() {
    http.HandleFunc("/", index)
    http.HandleFunc("/create", create)
    http.HandleFunc("/save", save)
}

func index(w http.ResponseWriter, r *http.Request) {
    c := appengine.NewContext(r)
    q := datastore.NewQuery("tasks").
        Order("-CreatedOn")
    var tasks []Task
    _, err := q.GetAll(c, &tasks)
    if err != nil {
        http.Error(w, err.Error(), http.StatusInternalServerError)
    }
    if err := taskListTemplate.Execute(w, tasks); err != nil {
        http.Error(w, err.Error(), http.StatusInternalServerError)
    }
}
func create(w http.ResponseWriter, r *http.Request) {
    fmt.Fprint(w, taskForm)
}

func save(w http.ResponseWriter, r *http.Request) {
    task := Task{
        Name:        r.FormValue("taskname"),
        Description: r.FormValue("description"),
        CreatedOn:   time.Now(),
    }
    c := appengine.NewContext(r)
    _, err := datastore.Put(c, datastore.NewIncompleteKey(c, "tasks", nil), &task)
    if err != nil {
        http.Error(w, err.Error(), http.StatusInternalServerError)
        return
    }
    http.Redirect(w, r, "/", http.StatusMovedPermanently)
}
```

The following packages are imported to work with the App Engine application:

- google.golang.org/appengine
- google.golang.org/appengine/datastore

A Task struct is declared to persist values into Datastore entities.

Creating a New Entity

The Save application handler creates a new Task object and persists the values into Datastore with an entity named "tasks". The NewContext function of the appengine package is called, which returns a context for an in-flight HTTP request. You have to provide a context object to working with Datastore.

The datastore.Put function is used to create a new entity into Datastore by providing a struct instance and a key to the entity's key name. The Task struct type instance is provided to save it to Datastore.

There are multiple options for providing a key name. For example, the key name can be provided by passing a non-empty string ID to the datastore.NewKey function, as shown here:

```
c := appengine.NewContext(r)
key := datastore.NewKey(c, "tasks", "taskgae", 0, nil)
_, err := datastore.Put(c, key, &task)
```

You can also provide an empty key name or use the datastore.NewIncompleteKey function to pass a new incomplete key. The NewIncompleteKey function creates a new incomplete key. The Datastore automatically generates a unique numeric ID for the entity key.

In the example program, the incomplete key is used to insert records into the "tasks" entity:

```
c := appengine.NewContext(r)
key := datastore.NewIncompleteKey(c, "tasks", nil)
_, err := datastore.Put(c, key, &task)
```

The datastore.Put function returns a datastore.PendingKey that can be resolved into a datastore.Key value by using the return value from a successful transaction commit. If the key is an incomplete key, the returned PendingKey resolves to a unique key generated by the data store. PendingKey represents the key for a newly inserted entity. It can be resolved into datastore.Key by calling the Key method of Commit.

You can also use the datastore.Put function to update an existing entity. When you update an existing entity, modify the fields of the struct and then call the datastore.Put function to update the values. It overwrites the existing entity.

Querying the Datastore

The Go Datastore API provides Go idioms to query data against the Datastore. It provides a datastore.Query type for preparing and executing queries to retrieve entities from the App Engine Datastore. The NewQuery function prepares a query object:

```
q := datastore.NewQuery("tasks").
        Order("-CreatedOn")
```

A Datastore query includes the following:

- An entity (entity kind) to which the query applies

- Zero or more filters based on the entities' property values, keys, and ancestors

- Zero or more sort orders to sequence the results

In the preceding query, "tasks" was specified as the entity kind, but no filter conditions were specified. You can specify the filter condition using the Filter function:

```
q := datastore.NewQuery("tasks").
     Filter("Name =", "GAE").
     Order("-CreatedOn")
```

The Order condition is applied to get results sorted by descending order in the CreatedOn field. The - is used to sort in descending order.

The Query type instance prepares the query, so you need to call various Query type methods to execute the query and fill in the data for the Go object. The GetAll method executes the query and fills the data into a slice of Task type:

```
c := appengine.NewContext(r)
var tasks []Task
_, err := q.GetAll(c, &tasks)
```

Running the Application

Let's deploy the App Engine application into Google Cloud using the goapp tool and run the application.

Figure 11-11 shows the index page of the application. In this page, the App Engine application query against the "tasks" entity and displaying the data. The page shows the task list after inserting two tasks using the form for creating a new task.

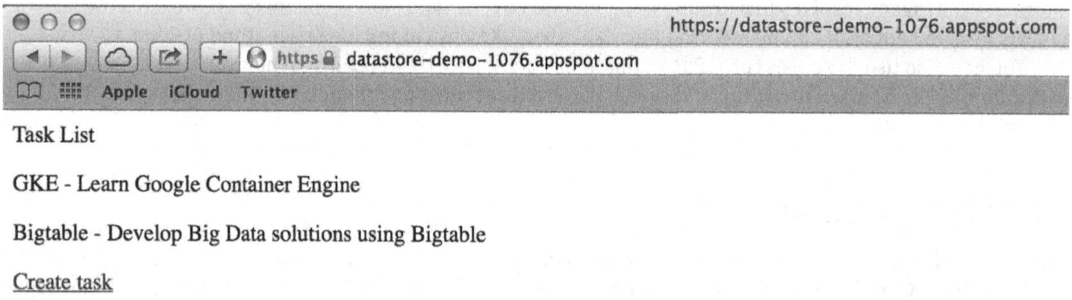

Figure 11-11. *Task List page*

When you select the Create task link, you see a page that allows you to create tasks (see Figure 11-12).

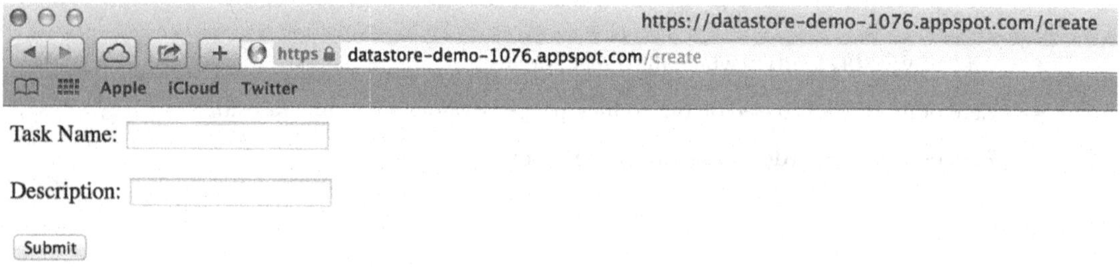

Figure 11-12. *Create task form*

You can query Datastore data from the web interface of the Google Developers Console. Figure 11-13 displays the data of the "tasks" entity from the Google Developers Console.

	Name/ID	CreatedOn	Description	Name
☐	id=5629499534213120	2015-09-23 00:06:10	Develop Big Data solutions using Bigtable	Bigtable
☐	id=5649391675244544	2015-09-23 00:07:16	Learn Google Container Engine	GKE

Figure 11-13. *Data from the Google Developers Console*

You can see that a unique ID is assigned as an entity key to be used when a data object is put into entities.

Building Back-end APIs with Cloud Endpoints

In Google Cloud, the App Engine platform lets Go developers build back-end APIs and web applications in the sandbox environment of App Engine, which is available for autoscaling. With App Engine, you can build massively scalable Cloud-native applications on Google's infrastructure using the tools and SDKs provided by the Google Cloud platform. Google Cloud Endpoints is an App Engine service that allows you to easily create back-end APIs for web clients and mobile clients.

Google Cloud Endpoints provides tools, libraries, and services to quickly generate APIs and client libraries from an App Engine application. Cloud Endpoints is an App Engine application that runs in the App Engine environment, but it provides extra capabilities for building API back ends and its client libraries improve developer productivity when building mobile back-end systems.

You can create back-end APIs on the App Engine platform without leveraging Cloud Endpoints. However, although you can create back-end APIs using a normal App Engine application, Cloud Endpoints makes the development process easier by providing extra capabilities. Cloud Endpoints allows you to generate native client libraries for iOS, Android, JavaScript, and Dart. Because natively generated libraries are available for various client applications, you can quickly build client applications on which you don't need to write native wrappers to communicate with the back-end API. For a back-end developer, it eliminates some complexities from the development process for developing RESTful APIs.

When you build an API with Cloud Endpoints, you don't have to write anything on HTTP Request and Response objects. You can write API methods like a normal Go function without leveraging these objects and can make them HTTP APIs by using the libraries provided by Cloud Endpoints.

Figure 11-14 illustrates the basic architecture of a Cloud Endpoints application.

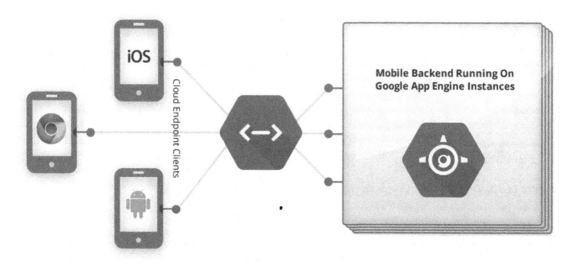

***Figure 11-14.** Basic architecture of a Cloud Endpoints application*

Figure 11-14 shows the back-end API running on App Engine instances that are powered as a back end for mobile clients and JavaScript web clients. The operations of back-end applications are made available to client applications through endpoints, which expose an API that clients can call using native libraries generated by Cloud Endpoints. Cloud Endpoints improves developer productivity to both back-end API developers and client application developers.

In Chapter 9, a RESTful API was developed as a back end for a client application. By using Cloud Endpoints, you can improve your developer productivity when you build RESTful APIs on the Google Cloud platform.

Cloud Endpoints for Go

With App Engine and its SDKs and Go tools, you can build Cloud Endpoints back-end APIs using Go. You create Cloud Endpoints back ends in Go using the endpoints package provided by the Google Cloud platform.

Installing the endpoints Package

To install the endpoints package, use the goapp tool provided by Google App Engine SDK for Go:

```
goapp get github.com/GoogleCloudPlatform/go-endpoints/endpoints
```

To use the endpoints package in Go programs, you must include the package in the import list:

```
import (
 "github.com/GoogleCloudPlatform/go-endpoints/endpoints"
)
```

By using the endpoints package, you can quickly write back-end APIs in Go.

Cloud Endpoints Back-end APIs in Go

In this section, you walk through an example that demonstrates how to write back-end APIs in Go by using Cloud Endpoints. Like a normal App Engine application, your Cloud Endpoints applications can also leverage the various Cloud services provided by Google Cloud. In this example application, Cloud Datastore is used as the persistence store.

Let's declare a struct to describe the data model for the application. Listing 11-8 provides a struct type to work as a Datastore entity.

Listing 11-8. Application Data Model

```
// Task is a datastore entity
type Task struct {
    Key         *datastore.Key `json:"id" datastore:"-"`
    Name        string         `json:"name" endpoints:"req"`
    Description string         `json:"description" datastore:",noindex" endpoints:"req"`
    CreatedOn   time.Time      `json:"createdon,omitempty"`
}
```

A struct type named Task is created to describe application data for the Cloud Endpoints application. The value of the Task struct is persisted into Datastore, and the necessary tags are provided to the fields of the Task struct to work with JSON encoding and the Datastore.

Two API methods are provided in the example application: the List method provides a list of Task data from the Datastore, and the Add method allows you to create a new Task entity into the Datastore. Let's write these methods through a struct type that can be registered with Endpoints later.

Listing 11-9 provides the Go source file that contains the struct type and API methods to be exposed as methods of the API provided by Cloud Endpoints.

Listing 11-9. TaskService Exposing Methods for the API

```
package cloudendpoint

import (
    "time"

    "golang.org/x/net/context"
    "google.golang.org/appengine/datastore"
)

// Task is a datastore entity
type Task struct {
    Key         *datastore.Key `json:"id" datastore:"-"`
    Name        string         `json:"name" endpoints:"req"`
    Description string         `json:"description" datastore:",noindex" endpoints:"req"`
    CreatedOn   time.Time      `json:"createdon,omitempty"`
}
```

```go
// Tasks is a response type of TaskService.List method
type Tasks struct {
    Tasks []Task `json:"tasks"`
}

// Struct is used to add API methods
type TaskService struct {
}

// List returns a list of all the existing tasks from Datastore.
func (ts *TaskService) List(c context.Context) (*Tasks, error) {
    tasks := []Task{}
    keys, err := datastore.NewQuery("tasks").Order("-CreatedOn").GetAll(c, &tasks)
    if err != nil {
        return nil, err
    }

    for i, k := range keys {
        tasks[i].Key = k
    }
    return &Tasks{tasks}, nil
}

// Add inserts a new Task into Datastore
func (ts *TaskService) Add(c context.Context, t *Task) error {
    t.CreatedOn = time.Now()
    key := datastore.NewIncompleteKey(c, "tasks", nil)
    _, err := datastore.Put(c, key, t)
    return err
}
```

A struct type named TaskService was written, and two methods were added: List and Add. These methods will be exposed later as the operations of a back-end API using the endpoints package. The HTTP Request and Response objects are not used in either method, despite being exposed as operations of an HTTP API.

The context package is used to carry the request-scoped values. The List method queries the data from the "tasks" Datastore entity. The GetAll method executes the query and returns all keys that match the query. The returned keys collection is used to assign the value of the Key field of the Task struct.

The Add method adds a new Task into the "tasks" Datastore entity. In normal HTTP API applications, incoming messages from the body of HTTP requests are read, and the JSON (or XML) values are decoded into struct types. In the Add method, a parameter of type Task is provided to get values into that parameter from the body of the HTTP request. Here, you don't write any logic or parse the incoming values into struct types; a parameter for binding the values from the HTTP request is provided. When you build back-end APIs using Cloud Endpoints, you can improve your developer productivity because Cloud Endpoints allows you to avoid writing the plumbing code required for writing RESTful APIs.

At this moment, the List and Add methods are normal functions. You need to make them operations of an HTTP API using Cloud Endpoints. Listing 11-10 provides the implementation for registering the methods of TaskService into Endpoints so that the methods can be exposed as operations of an HTTP API.

Listing 11-10. Registering TaskService to the HTTP Server

```go
package cloudendpoint

import (
    "log"

    "github.com/GoogleCloudPlatform/go-endpoints/endpoints"
)

// Register the API endpoints
func init() {
    taskService := &TaskService{}
    // Adds the TaskService to the server.
    api, err := endpoints.RegisterService(
        taskService,
        "tasks",
        "v1",
        "Tasks API",
        true,
    )
    if err != nil {
        log.Fatalf("Register service: %v", err)
    }

    // Get ServiceMethod's MethodInfo for List method
    info := api.MethodByName("List").Info()
    // Provide values to MethodInfo - name, HTTP method, and path.
    info.Name, info.HTTPMethod, info.Path = "listTasks", "GET", "tasks"

    // Get ServiceMethod's MethodInfo for Add method
    info = api.MethodByName("Add").Info()
    info.Name, info.HTTPMethod, info.Path = "addTask", "POST", "tasks"
    // Calls DefaultServer's HandleHttp method using default serve mux
    endpoints.HandleHTTP()
}
```

In the init function, TaskService methods are registered to the HTTP server using the
RegisterService function of the endpoints package. The RegisterService function adds a new service to
the server using DefaultServer, which is the default RPC server. "tasks" is furnished as the name, and "v1"
is the API version to the HTTP service:

```go
api, err := endpoints.RegisterService(
    taskService,
    "tasks",
    "v1",
    "Tasks API",
    true,
)
```

The information is provided to the methods of HTTP service. It is used to provide discovery documentation for the back-end APIs:

```
// Get ServiceMethod's MethodInfo for List method
    info := api.MethodByName("List").Info()
    // Provide values to MethodInfo - name, HTTP method, and path.
    info.Name, info.HTTPMethod, info.Path = "listTasks", "GET", "List Tasks"

    // Get ServiceMethod's MethodInfo for Add method
    info = api.MethodByName("Add").Info()
    info.Name, info.HTTPMethod, info.Path = "addTask", "POST", "Add a new Task"
```

Finally, the HandleHTTP function of the endpoints package is called, which calls the DefaultServer HandleHttp method using the default http.ServeMux:

```
// Calls DefaultServer's HandleHttp method using default serve mux
    endpoints.HandleHTTP()
```

Now the TaskService methods are made available as HTTP endpoints of a RESTful API, which can be used for building web and mobile client applications. Because the Cloud Endpoints application is an App Engine application, let's add an app.yaml file to be is used for the goapp tool and as the configuration for the App Engine application.

Listing 11-11 provides the app.yaml file for the App Engine application.

Listing 11-11. app.yaml file for the App Engine Application

```
application: go-endpoints
version: v1
threadsafe: true

runtime: go
api_version: go1

handlers:
- url: /.*
  script: _go_app

# Important! Even though there's a catch all routing above,
# without these two lines it's not going to work.
# Make sure you have this:
- url: /_ah/spi/.*
  script: _go_app
```

The Cloud Endpoints application is now ready for running on both a development web server and an App Engine production environment.

Running Cloud Endpoints Back-end API

The App Engine Cloud Endpoints application is complete. Let's run the application in a local development server using the goapp tool. Run the goapp tool from the root directory of the application:

```
goapp serve
```

The application runs in the local web development server. The discovery doc of the API is available at http://localhost:8080/_ah/api/discovery/v1/apis/tasks/v1/rest.

The APIs Explorer is available at http://localhost:8080/_ah/api/explorer.

Let's navigate to the APIs Explorer in the browser window. Figure 11-15 shows the APIs Explorer showing the API services.

Figure 11-15. *APIs Explorer running in the browser window*

When you click any available API service, you navigate to a window in which you can see the service's available operations. Figure 11-16 shows the tasks API operations.

APIs Explorer

	Services	tasks.addTask
	All Versions	tasks.listTasks
	Request History	

Figure 11-16. *Operations of the tasks API*

When you click any operation, you navigate to a window on which you can test the API operation by providing request data in an input window and clicking the Execute button.

Figure 11-17 shows the input window for testing the addTask operation.

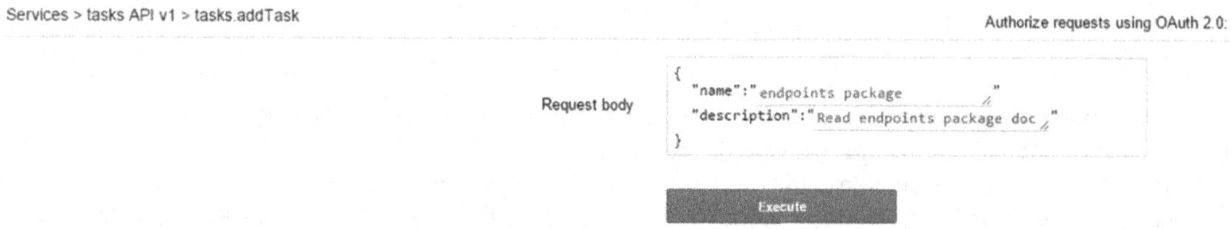

Services > tasks API v1 > tasks.addTask   Authorize requests using OAuth 2.0:

Figure 11-17. *Input window for the addTask operation*

Figure 11-18 shows the HTTP Request and Response for the addTask operation.

Figure 11-18. *HTTP Request and Response from the addTask operation*

The addTask operation is an HTTP Post request to the URI endpoint: http://localhost:8080/_ah/api/tasks/v1/tasks.

Figure 11-19 shows the HTTP Request and Response for the listTasks operation. The listTasks operation is executed after the addTask operation is executed three times so that you can see three records.

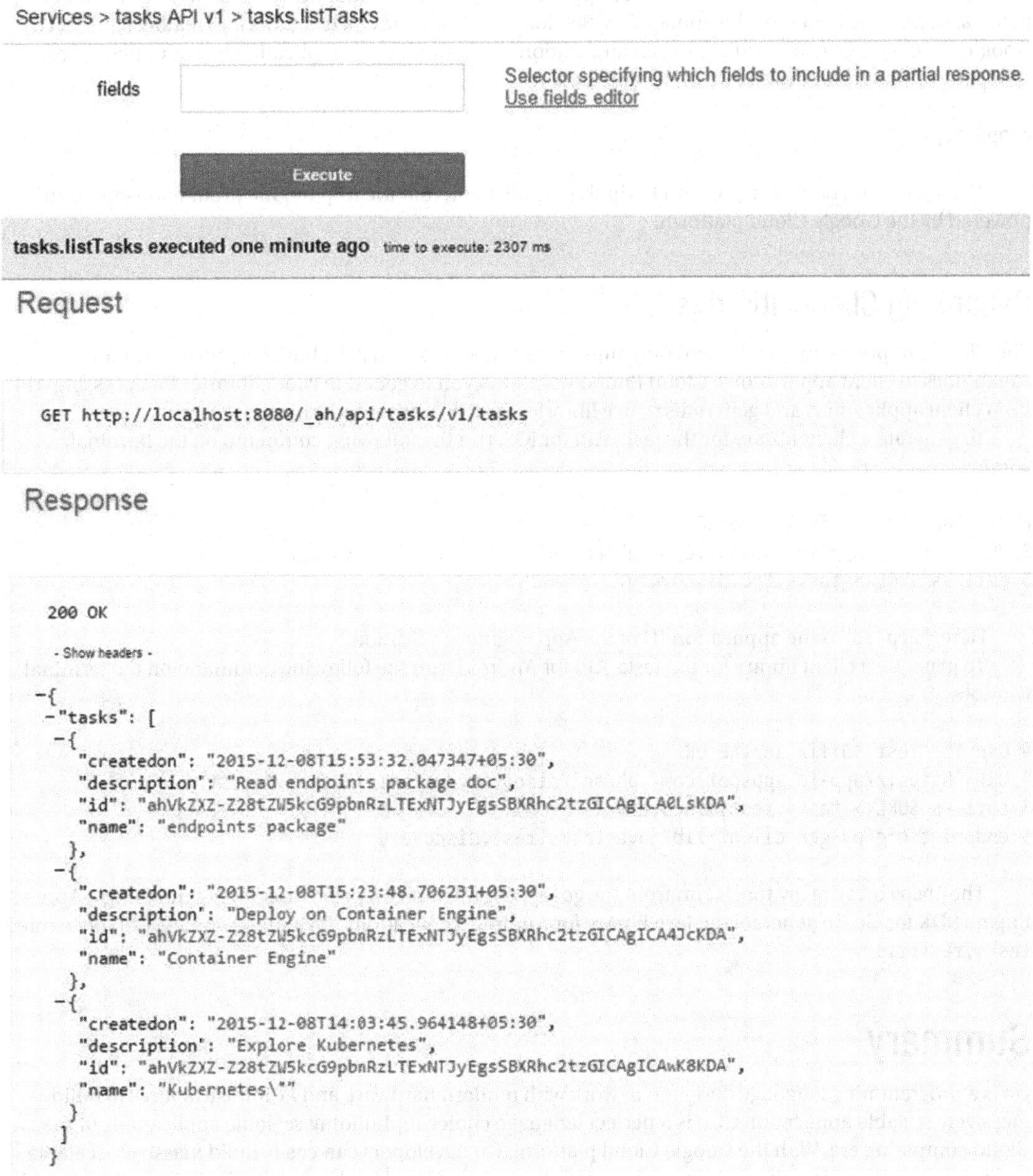

Services > tasks API v1 > tasks.listTasks

| fields | | Selector specifying which fields to include in a partial response. Use fields editor |

Execute

tasks.listTasks executed one minute ago time to execute: 2307 ms

Request

GET http://localhost:8080/_ah/api/tasks/v1/tasks

Response

200 OK

- Show headers -

```
-{
 -"tasks": [
  -{
    "createdon": "2015-12-08T15:53:32.047347+05:30",
    "description": "Read endpoints package doc",
    "id": "ahVkZXZ-Z28tZW5kcG9pbnRzLTExNTJyEgsSBXRhc2tzGICAgICA9LsKDA",
    "name": "endpoints package"
  },
  -{
    "createdon": "2015-12-08T15:23:48.706231+05:30",
    "description": "Deploy on Container Engine",
    "id": "ahVkZXZ-Z28tZW5kcG9pbnRzLTExNTJyEgsSBXRhc2tzGICAgICA4JcKDA",
    "name": "Container Engine"
  },
  -{
    "createdon": "2015-12-08T14:03:45.964148+05:30",
    "description": "Explore Kubernetes",
    "id": "ahVkZXZ-Z28tZW5kcG9pbnRzLTExNTJyEgsSBXRhc2tzGICAgICAwK8KDA",
    "name": "Kubernetes\""
  }
 ]
}
```

Figure 11-19. *HTTP Request and Response for the listTasks operation*

The listTasks operation is an HTTP Get request to the URI endpoint: http://localhost:8080/_ah/api/tasks/v1/tasks.

The application has been tested in the local web development server provided by Google App Engine SDK for Go. You can deploy the Cloud Endpoints application into the production environment of App Engine using the goapp tool. Deploying a Cloud Endpoints application into a production environment is exactly the same process as that of a normal App Engine application. You must provide the application ID in the app.yaml file to deploy the application. Section 11.4.4 provides instructions for creating a project in Google Developer Console and getting an application ID. To deploy the application into production, run the goapp tool from the root directory of the application:

```
goapp deploy
```

This command deploys the Cloud Endpoints application into the App Engine production environment, powered by the Google Cloud platform.

Generating Client Libraries

The Cloud Endpoints application not only supports writing back-end APIs but also provides useful capabilities to client applications. Cloud Endpoints allows you to generate client libraries for accessing APIs from client applications and generates native libraries for iOS, Android, Dart, and JavaScript.

To generate a client library for the tasks API for iOS, run the following command on the terminal window:

```
# Use the rpc suffix in the URL:
$ URL='https://app-id.appspot.com/_ah/api/discovery/v1/apis/tasks/v1/rpc'
$ curl -s $URL > tasks.rpc.discovery
```

Here, "app-id" is the application ID of the App Engine application.

To generate a client library for the tasks API for Android, run the following command on the terminal window:

```
# Use the rest suffix in the URL
$ URL='https://app-id.appspot.com/_ah/api/discovery/v1/apis/tasks/v1/rest'
$ curl -s $URL > tasks.rest.discovery
$ endpointscfg.py gen_client_lib java tasks.rest.discovery
```

The endpointscfg.py tool is run from the go_appengine directory (the directory of the Google App Engine SDK for Go) to generate the Java library for Android applications. It should generate a zip file named tasks.rest.zip.

Summary

Go is a programming language designed to work with modern hardware and IT infrastructures to build massively scalable applications. Go is a perfect language choice for building scalable applications in the Cloud computing era. With the Google Cloud platform, Go developers can easily build massively scalable applications on the Cloud by leveraging the tools and APIs provided by the Google Cloud platform.

Google Cloud provides App Engine, a Platform as a Service (PaaS) offering that lets Go developers build highly scalable and reliable web applications using the App Engine SDK for Go and Go APIs to various Cloud services. When you build App Engine applications, you don't need to spend time managing the IT infrastructure. Instead, you can fully focus on building your application, which is available for automatic scaling whenever there is a need to increase computing resources. With App Engine, developers are freed from system administration, load balancing, scaling, and server maintenance.

App Engine SDK for Go provides the goapp tool that allows you to test the App Engine application in a development web server. The goapp tool can also be used for deploying App Engine web applications into the Google Cloud production environment that runs on the App Engine sandbox environment.

The App Engine environment provides a `main` package, so you can't use a package called `main`. Instead, you can write HTTP handler logic in the package of your choice. App Engine applications easily access many Cloud services provided by the Google Cloud platform. When you leverage many of Cloud services from your App Engine application, you don't need to configure these services to be used with App Engine because you can directly access them from your application by using the corresponding Go API.

The Google Cloud platform provides various managed services for persisting structured data, including Google Cloud SQL, Google Cloud Datastore, and Google Bigtable. When you build App Engine applications with large volumes of data, the Google Cloud Datastore is the best database choice. You can build massively scalable web applications using App Engine and Cloud Datastore without spending time managing the IT infrastructure.

Google Cloud Endpoints is an App Engine service that builds back-end APIs for mobile client applications and web client applications. It provides tools, libraries, and capabilities for quickly building back-end APIs and generating native client libraries from App Engine applications. Although you can create back-end APIs using a normal App Engine application, Cloud Endpoints makes the development process easier by providing extra capabilities. Cloud Endpoints allows you to generate native client libraries for iOS, Android, JavaScript, and Dart, so client application developers are freed from writing wrappers to access back-end APIs.

References

https://github.com/GoogleCloudPlatform/gcloud-golang

https://cloud.google.com

Google Cloud Services infographic: https://cloud.google.com/

Endpoints architecture diagram: https://cloud.google.com/appengine/docs/python/endpoints/

Index

Get the eBook for only $5!

Why limit yourself?

Now you can take the weightless companion with you wherever you go and access your content on your PC, phone, tablet, or reader.

Since you've purchased this print book, we're happy to offer you the eBook in all 3 formats for just $5.

Convenient and fully searchable, the PDF version enables you to easily find and copy code—or perform examples by quickly toggling between instructions and applications. The MOBI format is ideal for your Kindle, while the ePUB can be utilized on a variety of mobile devices.

To learn more, go to www.apress.com/companion or contact support@apress.com.